1984

THE OCCULT IN AMERICA

The Occult in America:
New Historical Perspectives

EDITED BY
HOWARD KERR
AND CHARLES L. CROW

UNIVERSITY OF ILLINOIS PRESS
URBANA AND CHICAGO

© 1983 BY THE BOARD OF TRUSTEES OF THE UNIVERSITY OF ILLINOIS
MANUFACTURED IN THE UNITED STATES OF AMERICA

This book is printed on acid-free paper.

LIBRARY OF CONGRESS CATALOGING IN PUBLICATION DATA

Main entry under title:

The Occult in America.

Includes bibliographical references and index.
1. Occult sciences—United States—History.
2. Spiritualism—United States—History. I. Kerr,
Howard. II. Crow, Charles L.
BF1434.U6033   1983   133'.0973   82-24770
ISBN 0-252-00983-5

Contents

Introduction   HOWARD KERR AND CHARLES L. CROW   1

1. *Explaining Modern Occultism*   ROBERT GALBREATH   11

2. *Andover Witchcraft and the Causes of the Salem Witchcraft Trials*   CHADWICK HANSEN   38

3. *The Dark Ages of American Occultism, 1760–1848*
   JON BUTLER   58

4. *The Fox Sisters and American Spiritualism*
   ERNEST ISAACS   79

5. *The American Theosophical Synthesis*
   ROBERT S. ELLWOOD, JR.   111

6. *The Occult Connection? Mormonism, Christian Science, and Spiritualism*   R. LAURENCE MOORE   135

7. *Vivekananda and American Occultism*
   STEVEN F. WALKER   162

8. *Women in Occult America*
   MARY FARRELL BEDNAROWSKI   177

9. *Paranormal Memorates in the American Vernacular*
   LARRY DANIELSON   196

10. *UFOs and the Search for Scientific Legitimacy*
    DAVID M. JACOBS   218

    Note on the Contributors   233

    Index   235

Introduction

THE TEN CHAPTERS of this volume explore one of the least understood elements in American history. The authors, who come from several scholarly disciplines, assess almost three hundred years of occult activity in America. Defining "the occult" has proved a thorny problem for occultists and scholars alike, but in this book as in general modern usage the term inclusively denotes esoteric belief systems such as those based on Hermetic or Eastern lore; practices such as astrology, "dowsing," and magical healing; and supernatural and paranormal "phenomena" such as ghosts, ESP, and UFOs. As the reader will observe, these categories are often intertwined in historical configuration.

However defined, the occult has been difficult to ignore since its eruption into popular culture during the last fifteen years, an efflorescence sometimes called an "occult revival," even an "explosion."[1] Neo-pagan witchcraft and Satanism, ritual magic and flying saucer cults, university investigations of psi and survival phenomena, predictions by psychics and claims by spiritualists for messages from "the other side," renewed interest in Oriental mysteries, Tarot and I Ching, poltergeist disturbances in Amityville—all have drawn wide attention from the mass media. Movies and novels dealing with the supernatural have found eager audiences. Serious occult books have proliferated too, as indicated by crowded bookstore shelves. Equally serious admonitions against trafficking with the occult have come from churchmen, some of whom see the "revival" as demonic, from social commentators who view it as a lapse into subjectivity, and from scientists who think it a frustrating resurgence of superstition.[2]

While many of these examples can be dismissed as creatures of the hour caught in the media spotlight, the widespread contemporary interest in the occult may seem puzzling, the emergence of an unexpected dimension in the American experience that leads to questions about the past. Is the occult only sporadically evident in our history? Or has it been a constant presence? With notable exceptions, until recently scholars have scanted such questions. Major works of American social and religious history ignored the occult or gave it short shrift, leaving interested readers to the uncritical recitals of believers, the polemics of skeptics, and the sensational anecdotes and data-free generalizations of popular chroniclers of the "bizarre." The title of a 1973 review-essay complained, "Wanted: Serious Historians of the Occult."[3]

In fact, such scholars had already begun to answer the call. From the 1960s on, excellent studies of particular movements or themes have appeared in ever-growing number. These works, some of them by contributors to this volume, have established the occult as a significant field of American historical inquiry.[4] As yet, however, there has been no serious presentation of the occult presence throughout the nation's past. Thus *The Occult in America*. While this book does not pretend to discuss every relevant topic, its chapters chart major episodes, movements, and motifs—from trepidation over witchcraft in seventeenth-century Massachusetts to fascination with UFOs today. The editors make no claim whatever for the intrinsic value of apparitions, astrology, or arcane wisdom. Rather, they suggest that the continuous interest in such matters forms a distinct pattern in American history.

The most obvious feature in this pattern is the historical ubiquity of the occult. The early colonists brought with them not only their well-known fear of witchcraft but also Renaissance esotericism and such practices as astrology, palmistry, and magical healing—arts that have persisted ever since at the popular level. Occult religion took root among black slaves during the eighteenth century, as did Illuminist and Swedenborgian thought among some white elites. Amidst the conflicting triumphs of evangelical Protestantism and positivistic science, the nineteenth century also saw the rise of successive occult movements. Mesmerism arrived in the 1830s with its universal "magnetic" fluid, which allowed the mesmerist to control the minds of others, to elicit clairvoyant visions, and to prescribe for internal ailments. Spiritualism, ignited in 1848 by an outbreak of "mysterious phenomena"—the spirit rappings of the Fox sisters—claimed the curiosity of millions and the belief of not a few Americans with its demonstrations of intelligible communication from the dead and thus "proof" of personal immortality. Theosophy, born in 1875, reinvigorated and enlarged the scope of

Western esoteric tradition by turning toward India and Tibet. In the last decades of the century psychical research initiated the "scientific" investigation of psi and survival phenomena. Spiritualism, Theosophy and its progeny of "wisdom" religions, and psychical research (now called "parapsychology") remain important segments in the occult spectrum today, alongside and sometimes overlapping a multitude of other activities ranging from "white" witchcraft through ever-flourishing modes of divination like astrology to occult interpretations of UFOs. The contemporary revival is thus a simultaneous restaging of impulses that have never been quiescent on the American scene.

This brief sketch rightly suggests that such impulses have been marked by diversity. There are large differences between the esoteric search for "ancient" wisdom and belief in ghosts, between laboratory experiments with ESP and the casting of horoscopes. Yet as the case of spiritualism illustrates, striking continuities run beneath the surface of differences. At its height in the 1850s the movement was often attacked as a recrudescence either of the demonism that had led to witchcraft at Salem or of the superstitious credulity that had led to the witchcraft trials. Quite willing to accept the connection, the spiritualists replied that "the history of Salem Witchcraft is but an account of spiritual manifestations, and of man's incapacity to understand them."[5] The accused witches had simply been mediums before their time. Similarly, the allegedly spontaneous spirit rappings that kept the Fox family and (as the "rapping mania" spread) other households awake nights were explained as benevolent versions of the troublesome poltergeist disturbances of popular supernatural lore. The process by which mediums elicited messages from the departed at seances was adapted from the "magnetic" theory of mesmerism. And the eschatology of spiritualism—its revelation of an afterlife of personal identity and evolutionary progression through the spheres—owed a debt to Swedenborgian thought as interpreted by the mesmeric prophets who quickly became the philosophers of the new movement.

Equally strong are the continuities leading away from spiritualism. Colonel Henry S. Olcott's address to the first meeting of the Theosophical Society in 1875 may have announced the group's purpose as the study of "the primeval source of all religions, the books of Hermes and the Vedas," while denouncing spiritualism for its "imposture, tricky mediums, lying spirits, and revolting social theories."[6] But until recently Olcott himself had eagerly attended seances, and Helena P. Blavatsky, his guide and companion on the path to Theosophical wisdom, had off and on for years been a medium in command of the usual repertoire of

seance phenomena. Nor did her mediumistic feats cease with the formation of the society.

In a different direction spiritualism also led toward modern parapsychology. Having long sought and sometimes won scientific creden-
tials, parapsychologists might object to this linkage. Yet the spiritualists
had been scientistic too, sharing the popular empiricism of the time and
drawing on electrical and evolutionary theory to explain their replicated
demonstrations of immortality. In its early years as "psychical research" parapsychology carried forward the spiritualistic quest, searching for evidence to support the "hypothesis" of survival. Although they
rejected the methodological vagaries and social milieu of the professional medium's seance, hopeful psychical researchers were sometimes
difficult to distinguish from their spiritualistic predecessors. All three of
these movements—spiritualism, Theosophy, and psychical research—
were responses to the growing apprehension that science and skepticism
threatened to make religion untenable.

What we have, then, is a historical hourglass in which the sands of
witchcraft, popular ghostlore, mesmerism, Swedenborgianism, and scientism pour through the channel of spiritualism, then to disperse into
Theosophy and parapsychology. If the emphasis were shifted to esotericism, Theosophy would become the central passage, synthesizing
and redisseminating various elements of Hermetic, Gnostic, Swedenborgian, and Eastern thought. A similar figure would illustrate the relationship of American to foreign occultism. Many of the components
in the nineteenth-century pattern came from elsewhere, mixed here in
the crucible of nonnormative pluralism, and then returned abroad in
new guise—as in the "invasion" of England by American mediums in
the 1850s or the passage to India of Blavatsky, Olcott, and Theosophy
in 1879.

The more visible forms of the occult have shared a continuing relationship of tension with the values and institutions of the cultural
mainstream. For normative religion—whether colonial Puritanism,
nineteenth-century evangelicism, or the modern Judaic-Protestant-
Catholic triad—popular interest in the occult has often been troublesome. The Puritan fear of witchcraft led to the emphatic suppression
of the alleged practitioners at Salem, and although with the passing of
a generation most educated people looked upon witchcraft and the
fright it had caused as superstition, Cotton Mather was vexed well into
the eighteenth century by colonists who persisted in resorting to devil-
ish folk cures for illness. In 1853 Harriet Beecher Stowe's brother
Charles Beecher reported to the Congregational Association of New

York and Brooklyn that demonic agency was responsible for medium-istic spiritual manifestations. There is nothing new, then, in such books as *Out! in the Name of Jesus* (1972) or *My Name Is Legion* (1972).

Nor is organized religion's concern with the occult an idle one. The existence of "alternative altars" and the pursuit of "forbidden myster-ies" pose at the very least a leavening threat to institutional and doc-trinal authority. Oliver Wendell Holmes cheerfully described the solvent impact of spiritualism on orthodox ideas of immortality: "You cannot have people of cultivation, of pure character, sensible enough in com-mon things . . . professing to be in communication with the spiritual world and keeping up constant intercourse with it, without its gradually reacting on the whole conception of that other life."[7] Many spiritualists, of course, saw their movement as strengthening rather than weakening Christianity. But other occultists may directly repudiate or seek to transcend established faiths. Theosophists and other esotericists delib-erately attempted to develop a more cosmic religious synthesis by turn-ing to the "ancient" East, and today's "white" witchcraft has created its own explicitly neopagan tradition.

That some contemporary witches add a strong feminist emphasis to their worship of "the goddess" is not surprising. Occult movements have often been linked with secular countercultures. Spiritualism was attacked almost as much for the affiliation of some spiritualists with reform and radical causes—abolition, women's rights, free love, so-cialism—as for its religious heterodoxy. The occult "explosion" of the 1960s and 1970s was in part the arcane phase of the radical counter-culture of the time, announcing the "new consciousness" that would mark the astrologically designated Age of Aquarius. That activism can lead to occultism may strike some proponents of change as a self-indulgent diversion of energy. Yet such alternative altars, as Mircea Eliade has noted, often constitute a rejection of conventional social as well as religious constructions of reality.[8]

They also articulate a dissatisfaction with the modern scientific world view. Through the Renaissance occultism went hand in hand with sci-ence, but the intellectual revolution of the seventeenth century sep-arated alchemy and chemistry, astrology and astronomy, numerology and mathematics, magic and medicine.[9] Ever since, scientists and skep-tics of every stripe have dismissed the occult as a compound of fraud and delusion—an explanation which, however accurate in the given instance, is of little aid to historical understanding. Without discounting the achievements of science, occultists have argued that what they see as the positivist deification of quantity and objectivity ignores metaphysical realities which, rightly approached, are ultimately knowable. Their revalorization of the spiritual realm, they maintain, provides a hope for reconciling science and religion that is not to be found in normative faiths. Thus the ambitious subtitle of Helena Blavatsky's *Isis Unveiled: A Master-Key to the Mysteries of Ancient and Modern Science and Theology* (1877).

Poll research suggests, in fact, that at the popular level there is little correlation between occult beliefs and antagonism toward science.[10] For many Americans, it must be emphasized, the occult has not always seemed a counterculture, a mutually exclusive alternative to accepted religious, social, or scientific values.[11] Not all spiritualists saw a conflict a century ago between attending conventional worship services and receiving messages from departed loved ones at seances, nor do they today. Secularists and church members alike scan newspaper horoscopes, follow the predictions of psychics in the *National Enquirer,* and may consult magic healers when all else fails. If Freemasons or Odd Fellows, they take part in secret rites that were occultist in their beginnings, however much the original impulse has faded. Chiropractic, now covered by medical insurance and federal income tax deductions, grew out of the same nineteenth-century "occult-metaphysical tradition" that fostered transcendentalism, mesmerism, spiritualism, Theosophy, Christian Science, and New Thought.[12] Self-help mentalist movements like dianetics and est are typically marked by traces of occultist influence. The dissemination of Jungian thought in America has occult as well as clinical bearings. And people go on "believing" in ghosts and paranormal human powers—or refusing to disbelieve—generation after generation. Whatever the opposition between discrete movements and the cultural mainstream, the popular diffusion of occult attitudes in American life may perhaps be better described in terms of amorphous pluralism or cognitive dissonance than in terms of "normative/non-normative" polarities.

Although their common concern is the occult in America, the studies in this collection approach the subject from a variety of historical and methodological perspectives. In the first contribution, "Explaining Modern Occultism," Robert Galbreath ranges through the scholarly literature to isolate four major "problem-clusters" that have made a community of discourse on the subject difficult: inadequate definitions of "the occult" and imprecise historical hypotheses, based on "revival," "crisis," and "irrationalism" models, for periodic surges in occult activity. Offering suggestions for further work, Galbreath challenges scholars to "map the cultural location of the occult more precisely." The rest of the essays are just such attempts.

The most notorious occult episode in American history is the Salem witchcraft trials of 1692. Chadwick Hansen, whose *Witchcraft at Salem* (1969) is a standard work on the subject, re-examines this episode in "Andover Witchcraft and the Causes of the Salem Witchcraft Trials." Sifting through the records, Hansen finds that the supposedly stable town of Andover, which was under the jurisdiction of the court at Salem, yielded more accusations of witchcraft than did any other community, including strife-torn Salem itself. Going on to assess the causes of the accusations and trials in light of recent interpretations, Hansen cautions us that no single-cause theory can provide an adequate explanation of these complex events.

Interest in the occult was long thought to have lapsed during the eighteenth and early nineteenth centuries. But Jon Butler shows in "The Dark Ages of American Occultism, 1760–1848" that it never disappeared. A provocative argument that occult or even more normative forms of collective religious practice did not take root among black slaves until the mid-1700s, Butler's essay also charts the persistence of occult practices in the white working class and the reception among white elites of counter-Enlightenment Illuminist, Swedenborgian, and mesmeric thought—importations from Europe that helped prepare the way for spiritualism in the 1850s. This threefold social layering of occult activity, he notes, reflected the stratification of American culture.

In "The Fox Sisters and American Spiritualism," Ernest Isaacs traces the troubled lives of Margaret, Kate, and Leah Fox, the most famous of nineteenth-century mediums. For Margaret and Kate spiritualism brought little in the way of happiness. Never understanding their mediumistic talents and rejecting the reformist philosophy articulated by more reflective spiritualists, they were the subjects of a long series of exposés and investigations that reached a climax in 1888 with Margaret's confession that she and Kate had produced the spirit rappings by snapping their toe joints. The paradox of their careers, Isaacs shows, lay in their self-deception and in their unsought status as the originators of an important religious and social movement.

Theosophy is best known as an esoteric adaptation of Oriental lore and as an international movement headquartered in India. It began, however, in New York City in 1875, and by the time Helena Blavatsky and Colonel Olcott took it abroad in 1878 it had already absorbed many strands of European and American occult thought and style, including Neoplatonic and Gnostic tradition, Swedenborgianism, transcendentalism, spiritualism, and Native American shamanism. In "The American Theosophical Synthesis," Robert S. Ellwood, Jr., who has previously examined the meaning of Theosophy's eastward pilgrimage in *Alternative Altars* (1979), delineates the movement's expansive syncretism during its formative years in this country.

One measure of the appeal of occultism is its impact on religions that are not ordinarily considered occult. R. Laurence Moore's "The Occult Connection? Mormonism, Christian Science, and Spiritualism" traces the permeation of magical and esoteric ideas not only into spiritualism but also into two other emergent nineteenth-century faiths that today are regarded as socially normative if not theologically orthodox. Observing that all three were attacked by outsiders and by one another as occult, Moore identifies the features of these religions that led to the application of the label, and the role such features played in forging each group's sense of identity.

The World Parliament of Religions at the Columbian Exposition of 1893 witnessed the first appearance in America of authentic representatives of major Oriental religions. Swami Vivekananda, the founder of the Vedantist movement in this country, spoke at the exposition and went on to lecture widely here during the next few years. The occult faddists he encountered in his travels struck him as engaged in sincere but trivial and essentially materialistic endeavors. Often amusing, these encounters as described by Steven F. Walker in "Vivekananda and American Occultism" provide a crosscultural perspective on *fin de siècle* occultism.

Like other unconventional spiritual groups, American occult movements have often addressed the interests of women and offered them leadership roles not available in conventional faiths. In "Women in Occult America," Mary Farrell Bednarowski examines the increasingly militant concern for women's rights in three such movements—mid-nineteenth-century spiritualism, Theosophy, and the feminist witchcraft of our own day. In light of current demands from women for a stronger role in traditional religious establishments, Bednarowski's findings confirm the wisdom of regarding even the occult "fringe" as an organic and sometimes predictive component of American culture.

Beneath and outside of organized forms of occult activity lies a substratum of popular belief in ghosts and other "mysterious phenomena." That such attitudes can fuel occult movements is clear in the case of spiritualism, and even the search for esoteric wisdom can begin in curiosity about the supernatural. "True" stories of ghostly encounters told by ordinary people are the subject of Larry Danielson's "Paranormal

Memorates in the American Vernacular." Analyzing a host of such personal experience narratives taken from contemporary folklore and popular print sources, Danielson argues that storytelling conventions inevitably work to shape and traditionalize these accounts. This process, he suggests, has been ignored by parapsychologists who look to such narratives for evidence of survival.

The mysterious phenomenon of greatest popular interest since World War II is the UFO. As David M. Jacobs shows in "UFOs and the Search for Scientific Legitimacy," "ufologists" sought unsuccessfully for years to establish scientific proof that UFOs are "extraterrestrial"—from outer space. In the late 1960s, however, UFO research began to take on an occult character, giving credence to claims that UFOs can materialize out of invisibility and that their occupants can communicate telepathically with human "contactees," and to use regression hypnosis to elicit the experiences of the contactees. The resulting shift toward hypotheses of an "ultraterrestrial" or "alternate reality," says Jacobs, has left the UFO research community confused, divided, and as far as ever from gaining scientific credibility.

Whatever the fate of the ufologists' quest, the occult in America will probably continue in the fashion noted here—marginal but persistent in the esoteric search for "The Master-Key to the Mysteries of Ancient and Modern Science and Theology," and widely diffused in popular consciousness. Neither the millennia proclaimed by enthusiasts nor the chaos feared by critics is likely to come to pass; such predictions are themselves a recurrent part of the historical pattern. What is clear from that pattern is that the occult, whether seen as a shadow-self, an alter ego, in the American identity, or as a characteristically American expression of pluralism, has played a continuing role in the national experience. This volume is offered toward a fuller understanding of that role.

NOTES

1. "The Occult Explosion," *McCall's,* Mar., 1970; "The Occult Revival," *Time,* June 19, 1972; Nat Freedland, *The Occult Explosion* (New York: Putnam's, 1972).

2. Edward A. Tiryakian, *On the Margin of the Visible: Sociology, the Esoteric, and the Occult* (New York: John Wiley, 1974), p. 12, n. 2; Marvin Harris, *Cows, Pigs, Wars & Witches* (New York: Random House, 1974), pp. 243–66; Barry Singer and Victor A. Benassi, "Occult Beliefs," *American Scientist,* 69 (1981): 49–55.

3. Robert A. Lindner, "Wanted: Serious Historians of the Occult," *Fides et Historia,* 7 (1973): 60.

4. Among the more important of these historical studies are Jon Butler, "Magic, Astrology, and the Early American Religious Heritage, 1600–1760," *American Historical Review*, 84 (1979): 317–46; Bruce F. Campbell, *Ancient Wisdom Revived: A History of the Theosophical Movement* (Berkeley and Los Angeles: University of California Press, 1980); Mircea Eliade, *Occultism, Witchcraft, and Cultural Fashions: Essays in Comparative Religions* (Chicago: University of Chicago Press, 1976); Robert S. Ellwood, Jr., *Alternative Altars: Unconventional and Eastern Spirituality in America* (Chicago: University of Chicago Press, 1979); Ellwood, *Religious and Spiritual Groups in Modern America* (Englewood Cliffs, N.J.: Prentice-Hall, 1973); Chadwick Hansen, *Witchcraft at Salem* (New York: George Braziller, 1969); J. Stillson Judah, *The History and Philosophy of the Metaphysical Movements in America* (Philadelphia: Westminster Press, 1967); Howard Kerr, *Mediums, and Spirit-Rappers, and Roaring Radicals: Spiritualism in American Literature, 1850–1900* (Urbana: University of Illinois Press, 1972); Herbert Leventhal, *In the Shadow of the Enlightenment: Occultism and Renaissance Science in Eighteenth-Century America* (New York: New York University Press, 1976); Seymour Mauskopf and Michael McVaugh, *The Elusive Science: Origins of Experimental Psychical Research* (Baltimore: Johns Hopkins University Press, 1980); and R. Laurence Moore, *In Search of White Crows: Spiritualism, Parapsychology, and American Culture* (New York: Oxford University Press, 1977). Of the many sociological studies of contemporary occultism, two are especially well informed by historical perspective: William Simms Bainbridge, *Satan's Power: Ethnography of a Deviant Psychotherapy Group* (Berkeley and Los Angeles: University of California Press, 1978), and Tiryakian, *On the Margin of the Visible*. For fuller bibliographies see the notes to the essays in this collection and Robert Galbreath, "Occult and the Supernatural," in M. Thomas Inge, ed., *Handbook of American Popular Culture* (Westport, Conn.: Greenwood Press, 1980), 2:213–36.

5. John Worth Edmonds and George T. Dexter, *Spiritualism* (New York: Partridge and Brittan, 1853), 1: 44.

6. Olcott, "Inaugural Address," quoted in Campbell, *Ancient Wisdom Revived*, p. 29.

7. Holmes, "The Professor at the Breakfast Table," *Atlantic Monthly*, 3 (1859): 90.

8. Eliade, *Occultism, Witchcraft, and Cultural Fashions*, pp. 52–53.

9. Keith Thomas, *Religion and the Decline of Magic* (New York: Scribner's, 1971).

10. Singer and Benassi, "Occult Beliefs," p. 55.

11. For the compatibility of occult beliefs with middle-class social values, see Martin Marty, "The Occult Establishment," *Social Research*, 37 (1970): 212–30.

12. For this observation about chiropractic we are indebted to Catherine L. Albanese, "Religious Freedom, Pluralism, and Nineteenth-Century American Religion" (position paper delivered at the Religion Workshop of the Conference on Religious Freedom in America, Center for Study of the American Experience, University of Southern California, Apr. 28, 1981).

1

Explaining Modern Occultism

ROBERT GALBREATH

KEITH THOMAS prefaces his influential and justly esteemed *Religion and the Decline of Magic* with the remark that

> this book began as an attempt to make sense of some of the systems of belief which were current in sixteenth- and seventeenth-century England, but which no longer enjoy much recognition today. Astrology, witchcraft, magical healing, divination, ancient prophecies, ghosts and fairies, are now all rightly disdained by intelligent persons. But they were taken seriously by equally intelligent persons in the past, and it is the historian's business to explain why this was so.[1]

Thomas's formulation of the task confronting the historian who wishes to explain early modern occultism is not in question. But the clear implication of his statement is that the historian of nineteenth- and twentieth-century occultism faces no comparable task. Occult belief systems, we are told, "no longer enjoy much recognition today" and are "rightly disdained by intelligent persons." As it happens, this is not Thomas's final word on the matter,[2] but it comes at the beginning of a widely read work of scholarship where it cannot be overlooked, and it is taken here to represent a not uncommon attitude that the occult in the modern world is of little or no historical significance. There is nothing to explain.

This viewpoint is obviously not shared by the literary and cultural critic George Steiner, who claims that "in terms of money and of time spent, of the number of men and women involved to a greater or lesser degree, in terms of the literature produced and of institutional ramifications, ours is the psychological and the social climate most infected by superstition, by irrationalism, of any since the decline of the Middle Ages and, perhaps, even since the time of the crisis in the Hellenistic world."[3] For Steiner the present situation is extraordinary, nearly unique. The irrational, in the form of the occult, is rampant. He divides his examples into three broad categories: "the astral or galactic" (astrology, UFOs, ancient astronauts), "the occult" (psi phenomena, divination) and "Orientalism" (Eastern traditions, meditation). He explains contemporary irrationalism as a further manifestation of the "nostalgia for the absolute" that has arisen from the decay of religion and has found more serious expression, in his judgment, in the "post-religious" systems of Marx, Freud, and Lévi-Strauss. Occult beliefs and practices are, to Steiner, ludicrous, aberrant, and often fraudulent, but their prevalence is symptomatic, he fears, of the Western crisis of confidence.

Theodore Roszak, who is both a historian and a cultural critic, provides yet a third perspective on the problem of explaining modern occultism. He shares Steiner's sense of the momentousness of what is happening, but his interpretation differs sharply. Writing in 1975, he declares that

> within the last few years, I have found myself more and more in the company of people like my former student: bright, widely read, well-educated people whose style it has become to endorse and accept all things occultly marvelous. In such circles, skepticism is a dead language, intellectual caution an outdated fashion. That Edgar Cayce could diagnose the illnesses of distant patients and predict earthquakes by psychic readings . . . that the pyramids were built by ancient astronauts . . . that orgone boxes can trap the life energy of the universe . . . that the continents of the Earth were settled by migrations from lost Lemuria . . . one does not question these reports, but, calmly letting the boundary between fact and fairy tale blur, one *uses* them—uses them to stretch one's powers of amazement. One listens *through* them to hear still another intimation of astounding possibilities, a shared conviction which allows one to say, "Yes, you feel it too, don't you? That we are at the turning point, the *kairos,* where the orders of reality shift and the impossible happens as naturally as the changing of the seasons."[4]

Roszak and Thomas seem to move in different groups of intelligent persons. Unlike Steiner, Roszak sees behind these occult currents not a new age of superstition and irrationalism, although to be sure he warns against the dangers of "intellectual permissiveness," but an evolutionary shift of consciousness no less profound, he asserts, than the acquisition of speech and the ability to fashion tools.[5]

Explanatory hypotheses and analytical strategies are unavoidably affected by the presuppositions of their authors. When the presuppositions differ as radically as do those of Thomas, Steiner, and Roszak, the task of achieving historical understanding becomes confused and unfocused. Despite overlapping examples, the three authors do not establish a community of discourse. Their apparent subject in common, modern occultism, mutates from text to text, shifting from a nonexistent problem for which no explanation is necessary to a cultural symptomatology verging on the metahistorical for which no explanation seems possible. Their unspoken assumptions about the nature, status, and significance of the occult in the contemporary world lead to other puzzles as well. How can it be that the occult no longer enjoys much recognition today, yet in sheer numbers attracts more people than at any time since the end of the Middle Ages? How is it that occult systems of belief are disdained by intelligent persons, yet are openly accepted by well-educated people? Are these apparent paradoxes outright contradictions or misstatements of fact? Or are there specifiable senses in which they might be reconcilable? How can we decide, if Steiner gives us no comparative statistics and Thomas does not indicate what he means by recognition?

The passages I have quoted are taken from relatively informal sources—a preface, a radio talk, a popular book—and they should not be made to carry burdens for which they were not designed. They are not fully developed historical arguments. Yet we cannot ignore the fact that all three state or imply historical generalizations that are both superficial and excessive. Moreover, in their lack of specificity and conceptual clarity, they are unfortunately representative of the general understanding, both academic and popular, of modern occultism. Especially with the increased public attention given to the occult in America since approximately 1966–68, efforts to make historical sense of modern occultism have produced a melange of other, often equally impressionistic generalizations about social crisis, secularization, the return of the sacred, and new religions; metaphors of underground streams, countercultures, and occult explosions; and analogies to the late Hellenistic world and to Weimar Germany. They all tend to exhibit common failings. They often rest on unexamined or ambiguous assumptions, they are vulnerable to counterexamples, and they ordinarily fail to take note of significant variations in historical development, cultural stratification, and types of occult belief systems and practices. Their lack of specificity on these points, among others, supports excessive claims and fears. It also lends itself to the practice of drawing false dichotomies (rational/irrational, approved/disapproved, establishment/underground, mainstream/marginal), which place the occult in an exclusively adversarial or deviant relationship with society as a whole.[6]

For the purposes of this essay, I have selected four problem-clusters that illustrate with particular clarity many of the difficulties posed by a lack of specificity in explaining modern occultism. These problem-clusters concern definition of the occult and explanatory hypotheses in terms of occult revivals, the occult as a manifestation of historical crisis, and the occult as a form of irrationalism. It appears to be widely assumed that definition can be ignored and that occultism of the nineteenth and twentieth centuries is adequately explained by linking it to revivals, crises, and the irrational. Yet in an area so little understood as modern occultism, an unwillingness to engage in historical definition in order to identify problems condemns explanation to impressionism. To refer the occult generally to revivals, crises, and irrationalism is to explain one unknown in terms of another. Each problem-cluster in turn encompasses interlocking considerations that need to be sorted out in treating the occult within the context of modern intellectual, religious, and social history.

These four problem-clusters do not, of course, exhaust the questions that efforts to explain modern occultism may encounter. They are, however, basic. The problem of definition is fundamental to the issues of clarity and specificity, the three explanatory hypotheses are among the most commonly cited in popular and historical literature, none of the four has been adequately treated in existing surveys of scholarship,[7] and all of them point toward similar conclusions regarding future research needs. In raising criticisms, counterexamples, and alternative possibilities, my purpose is neither to condemn these explanatory hypotheses as invariably mistaken nor to formulate new hypotheses in their place. My concern is rather to indicate their problematic nature as general explanations, to suggest modifications and further considerations, and to argue for greater definitional clarity and historical specificity.

In the following discussion "explanation" is used to mean only "to make sense of," "to understand," "to account for"; it does not strictly denote causation. Historical data and examples are taken primarily from the American context, but the general points raised are applicable, in my judgment, to modern Europe as well, and some non-American and pre-modern examples are included for illustrative and comparative purposes. Readers who are familiar with the sources cited in the notes will recognize my indebtedness to recent debates in the study of early modern European popular culture, religion, and occultism. I am indebted to them not only for the issues they raise but also for their example as scholarly debates. The growth of historical understanding is materially aided by the ongoing discussion of scholars who, in the process of weighing factors and raising objections, establish a shared vocabulary of problems, methods, and hypotheses—in short, a community of discourse. To date there has been nothing in the historical study of modern occultism comparable to the social process of evaluating, for example, the work of Frances Yates on Hermeticism and Neoplatonism in the Renaissance and the Scientific Revolution, Keith Thomas's anthropological approach to magic in preindustrial England, or the philosophical and anthropological issues involved in applying Western standards of rationality to the presumptively irrational magic and religion of nonliterate peoples. There are now some indications that the situation may be changing, as increasing recognition is given to problems such as the ones discussed here.[8]

DEFINITION

Few studies of modern occultism attempt definitions of the occult. A list of examples, usually astrology, magic, and witchcraft, is thought to suffice. Yet historical explanation is not possible without clarity about what it is that is to be explained. The basic meaning of "occult," from its Latin root *occulere* (to cover over, hide, conceal), is "hidden," "concealed," "secret," no longer in the general sense of anything hidden from sight but, rather, denoting particular practices, belief systems, and phenomena that are considered to be in some sense mysterious to ordinary understanding. This definition, adapted from the *OED*, does not indicate the qualities, whether universal or specific, by virtue of which a thing is classified as occultly hidden or mysterious. A definition of modern occultism must be able to specify both the criteria for inclusion in the occult and the characteristics of its modernity. Thus neither James Webb's identification of the occult with rejected knowledge nor Marcello Truzzi's with anomalies is satisfactory as a general definition.[9] Neither one is applicable to any time before the modern period. At least until the end of the seventeenth century, occult belief systems were commonly accepted at all levels of society; the occult in general was neither rejected nor anomalous, although it may well be both for substantial segments of the educated public today.

An inclusive definition of the occult cannot be simple if it is to do justice to the broad array of phenomena, states of consciousness, beliefs, teachings, practices, behavior, and organizations that are today loosely called occult, psychic, esoteric, paranormal, supernatural, magical, or mystical. As a generic term, "occult" is preferable for the modern period, despite pejorative connotations that cause some occultists to reject it for themselves and their beliefs. "Magic" seems to have once served as an inclusive term—the evidence is not clear—but since approximately the end of the seventeenth century it has become increasingly identified with a particular occult discipline (and with stage illusion).[10] "Mystical" is properly limited to experiences, teachings, and consciousness of the state of oneness with ultimate reality; "psychic" is used broadly, but it still retains its primary referent of psi phenomena (ESP, PK, mediumistic and survival phenomena). "Supernatural" is rejected by modern occultists of all types for whom the point of the occult is its ability to provide empirical, experiential, natural proofs of matters heretofore accepted on faith. "Paranormal" avoids the suggestions of irrationality and nonsense that taint "occult," but it has the disadvantage, shared by "supernatural," of prejudging the ontological status of its phenomena. It is doubtful in any case if the claim of being beyond the normal conveys any useful information.[11] "Esoteric" still retains perfectly good non-occult meanings of "abstruse" and "recondite."

Terminological confusion has complicated the task of establishing a generic definition of occultism. It has also given rise to misleading interpretations or explanations. Two examples are provided by the work of J. Stillson Judah and Edward A. Tiryakian. Judah seeks to establish a difference between "metaphysics" and "occultism," Tiryakian attempts to separate "occult" from "esoteric." In his study of metaphysical movements in America (principally spiritualism, New Thought, Theosophy, and their offshoots), Judah adopts the New Thought term "metaphysics" as a generic label for movements that teach an optimistic, highly pragmatic philosophy of salvation through the discovery of a higher ("metaphysical") reality and the utilization of its laws. In discussing the origins of the metaphysical outlook, Judah cites occultism (especially nineteenth-century French ideas) as a formative influence, thereby creating the impression that metaphysics and occultism are significantly different belief systems.[12] As others have recognized,

this is a distinction without a difference.[13] "Metaphysics" and "occultism" are virtually interchangeable in the modern occult. Spiritualism,
New Thought, and Theosophy are regularly cited as three of the most
influential occult movements of the nineteenth century.

Rather than drawing a false distinction between metaphysics and
occultism, Judah would be on safer ground identifying a particular
metaphysical thrust in occultism and tracing its development in America.[14] As it is, his insistence on metaphysics as a generic category mis-
leads him into ascribing a peculiarly American quality to metaphysical
movements. America is undoubtedly hospitable to such movements
(although whether it is more so than, for example, Britain or Germany
remains to be proven), but it has no monopoly on them. Despite being
organized in New York in 1875, the Theosophical Society soon established its main centers in England and India, where its impact was much
greater. Many groups of Asian and European origin also share the
metaphysical outlook. In Bryan Wilson's classification of sects by response to the world, metaphysical movements correspond to the Manipulationist category, in which he places Christian Science, New Thought,
Theosophy, Anthroposophy, Subud, transcendental meditation, Vedanta, the Aetherius Society, Scientology, and The Process, several of
which are not primarily American in origin or popularity. The Manipulationist response to the problem of evil in the world is, according to
Wilson, to bring the objective world into harmony with a new perception of it and its laws, thus allowing for manipulation that will produce
health, wealth, longevity, success.[15]

Tiryakian's influential paper "Toward the Sociology of Esoteric Culture," differentiates "esoterism" from "occultism" in arguing for the
importance of esoteric ideas in the development of both modernism and
modernization.[16] He likens the distinction to that between theoretical
and applied knowledge. The occult he defines as "intentional practices,
techniques, or procedures" which "draw upon hidden or concealed
forces in nature or the cosmos that cannot be measured or recognized
by the instruments of modern science" and which have "empirical results" as their goal, "such as either obtaining knowledge of the empirical
course of events or altering them from what they would have been
without this intervention." "Esoterism" refers to the "religiophilosophic
belief systems which underlie occult techniques and practices," the epis-
temology and ontology of the occult. This distinction is as misleading in
its arbitrariness as Judah's. "Occultists" and "esotericists" may take
various stands on the merits of engaging in magic rather than meditation, for example, but the notion of a purely abstract knowledge di-

vorced from personal development and personal participation is alien to them. It is a nonexistent distinction. I suspect it is the lack of a distinction between abstract and personal that partly accounts for the appeal of the occult to the avant-garde artists and intellectuals with whom Tiryakian is especially concerned. Moreover, Tiryakian subsequently confuses his own distinction by commenting that esoteric knowledge is in fact participatory rather than detached.

Tiryakian's distinction is unconvincing on other grounds as well. He deliberately omits psychical phenomena from his classification because "these are harder to integrate within a sociological scheme." There is no obvious reason why this should be so. A comprehensive understanding of modern occultism requires their inclusion. Tiryakian's approach, which also excludes pertinent altered states of consciousness (e.g. mystical, visionary, and trance experiences), moves resolutely away from the possibility of generic definition. It also creates confusion when Tiryakian states that both occultism and esoterism concern the nonempirical, yet claims that the occult has empirical goals. His emphasis on secrecy in esoteric knowledge (as opposed to the occult) causes him to overlook a distinctive feature of modern organized occultism: the purpose of engaging in the public dissemination of occult knowledge on the model of scientific societies. Occult knowledge, as a matter of fact, is not secret in Rosicrucianism, spiritualism, Theosophy, and Anthroposophy in the sense of being withheld from the public, although ritual magic orders tend to be secretive in this way; rather, it is acquired through "hidden" cognitive processes awakened through special training.[17]

These examples are sufficient to indicate that a generic definition of modern occultism must avoid misleading or nonexistent distinctions, retain the traditional meaning of "hidden," specify the defining characteristics of occult hiddenness, and locate the changed historical position (or perception) of the occult in the modern world. A tentative, rather unwieldy formulation can be suggested. Modern occultism pertains to matters that are "hidden" or "secret" in one or more of the following senses: (1) extraordinary matters that by virtue of their intrusion into the mundane world are thought to possess special significance (e.g. omens, portents, apparitions, prophetic dreams); (2) matters such as the teachings of the so-called mystery schools that are kept hidden from the uninitiated and the unworthy; and (3) matters that are intrinsically hidden from ordinary cognition and understanding but are nonetheless knowable through the awakening of hidden, latent faculties of appropriate sensitivity. In the modern context occult matters thus characterized are also anomalous (although not all anomalies are occult); that is, they are widely regarded, often by critics and adherents alike, as not fitting into, and perhaps also directly critical of, the prevailing interpretations of science, historical scholarship, and "common sense."

With this definition, or set of characteristics, it should be possible to indicate the occult or hidden qualities of any particular type of occultism: the phenomena or experiences themselves, the means of cognizing them, the interpretations or teachings concerning them, or combinations of these factors. Whether the several senses of "hidden" can be further reduced to a single defining characteristic is unclear. Identification of a least common denominator would presumably simplify the task of distinguishing occultism from closely related cultural phenomena, e.g. millennialism, apocalypticism, healing and charismatic movements, religious revivalism, and a variety of self-help and self-realization techniques. That the dividing lines are difficult to map indicates further areas for research; it also suggests that the occult may best be defined ultimately as an attitude toward the world rather than as a classification of phenomena, practices, and beliefs. The fact that the occult is most easily confused with cultural movements that are also commonly called marginal is undoubtedly of some social significance, but marginality per se does not define occultism, and its applicability as a social category is strictly limited.

Before leaving the problem of definition, an alternative approach needs to be mentioned briefly. Instead of generic definitions, this approach focuses on context-dependent definitions intrinsic to the self-conceptions of particular occult movements. It is often important to such groups that they divorce themselves from undesirable connotations of the word "occult" or that they differentiate their positions from those with which they might be confused in the public mind. Mystics emphatically deny any association with the occult, early Theosophy was sharply critical of spiritualism, and Rudolf Steiner, the founder of Anthroposophy, went to considerable length to separate his "spiritual science" from magic, mysticism, and mediumship. In the study of American history this approach has been followed with considerable success by R. Laurence Moore in dealing with the spiritualists' rejection of "occultism" and by Hal Bridges in formulating a definition of mysticism, adapted from Stace, Underhill, and Jones, that permits him to distinguish twentieth-century American mysticism from magic, psychical phenomena, visions, spiritualism, and occultism.[18] This approach is appropriate to studies of particular problems and tendencies, and it is needed if we are to understand the self-image and goals of specific groups, but it should not be mistaken for generic definition.

OCCULT REVIVALS

There may be no consensus on a definition of modern occultism, but there is a widely shared view that we are currently in the midst of an occult revival.[19] By the quantitative indices of books published and organizations founded, there can be little doubt that public interest in the occult has grown rapidly in America since the mid-1960s, a situation fully exploited by entertainment, commerce, and the mass media. The most recent occult bibliography of value annotates 1,856 original and reprinted English-language books published in just five years, 1971–75, a figure that confirms earlier statistics of a publishing boom in the occult.[20] Statistics compiled by J. Gordon Melton on American religious bodies indicate that the three classifications (or "families," in Melton's terminology) which most closely correspond to the occult— the New Thought, Psychical, and Magical families—increased as a group in the number of new organizations from 1920 to 1935, fell off during World War II, and then dramatically increased from 1950 through his cut-off date of 1970. Based on figures for five-year periods, the Psychical family ranks first in new organizations founded as of 1950 (16), 1955 (21), 1960 (28), and 1965 (39), and third in 1970 (23); the Magical family ranked first in 1970 (30).[21]

These figures must be interpreted cautiously. They point to a growth in public and commercial activity but do not indicate depth of commitment or extent of membership. They do not justify the fears of George Steiner or the Committee for the Scientific Investigation of Claims of the Paranormal that we are witnessing a massive and perhaps critical rebirth of irrationalism and obscurantism. Even the concept of a "rebirth" or "revival" is rather more ambiguous than it may seem at first glance, and it is not the only conclusion that can be deduced from the evidence.

What is the implied relationship between a revival of the occult and the past? A revival denotes a revitalization or renewal of something that is (or is perceived as) dormant, decadent, dead, or otherwise deficient. The concept of an occult revival presupposes a preceding period in which the occult was moribund, minor, or even nonexistent. The relationship is identical to that encountered in certain discussions of secularization which presuppose a mythical age of faith from which a subsequent falling away from religion can be charted. Can we identify periods in the nineteenth and twentieth centuries when the occult was in decline and thereby determine the propriety of speaking of later occult revivals? This question has not yet been confronted. Profiles of peaks and valleys in publishing and organizational activity do not prove that the occult disappears at certain times, only that public attention has turned elsewhere. The noncontinuation of the occult is a conclusion no more warranted than the disappearance of religion between great awakenings or politics between elections.

A further misconception is that the present popularity of the occult is unique in modern times. Whether or not they should properly be called revivals, there have been a number of peaks in popular interest in the occult during the past two hundred years. Principal examples include the impact of Swedenborgianism, mesmerism, secret societies, and phrenology in Western Europe in the late eighteenth and early nineteenth centuries; the rapid rise of spiritualism in America beginning in 1848 and its equally rapid conquest of England and the Continent; the popularity of Theosophy and psychical research by the mid-1880s, of Asian religions, especially Vedanta, following the World Parliament of Religions in 1893, of ritual magic, divination, and other occult practices that led the British occult writer G. R. S. Mead to speak eloquently in 1912 of a "rising psychic tide";[22] the international prominence after World War I of Krishnamurti, Rudolf Steiner, and G. I. Gurdjieff; the growth of cults and newspaper astrology in the 1930s. Since the end of World War II in America alone there has been a steady interest in occult and Oriental subjects—flying saucers, *The Search for Bridey Murphy* (1956), Zen Buddhism—culminating in 1966–68 with the convergence of several popular currents, media events, and entertainments that brought the occult home to a vast audience: psychedelics, Hermann Hesse's novels, *Rosemary's Baby,* the Maharishi, *The Sleeping Prophet* (the bestselling biography of Edgar Cayce), the counterculture, *2001: A Space Odyssey,* and much more. Comparative studies of these peaks of public interest are needed in order to judge their social contexts, relative numbers, and cultural impact, but they are sufficient as examples to refute the notion of the uniqueness of contemporary popular occultism.

Uniqueness, however, is not the principal difficulty with the concept of an occult revival. The problem is, in fact, just the opposite: recurrence. Here too there are both conceptual and empirical difficulties, not least of all with the ambiguous metaphors commonly applied to occult revivals. "Psychic tides," "occult waves," "underground streams" —all carry misleading connotations, if they are to be taken seriously, of pattern and relationship for which no empirical data are forthcoming. A psychic tide, like an occult wave, implies a rhythm, a regularity of ebb and flow reminiscent of Arnold's "Dover Beach," but ineffective as historical explanation. An underground stream suggests an always active, if normally hidden, current surfacing occasionally, perhaps to flow into the mainstream as a tributary or to act as a countercurrent. What these images may mean in relation to the actual history of occult movements and ideas in modern times has not yet been worked out in any detail.[23] Any explanation of modern occultism, moreover, obviously depends on the image that is adopted. Very different problems of explanation arise from seeing in modern occultism a unique revival, a cyclical pattern, or an occasional, sudden manifestation of the otherwise hidden, latent, or marginal.

Different as they otherwise are, these approaches share the assumption that the occult has declined since the end of the seventeenth century, when the process Max Weber called "the disenchantment of the world" was largely completed for the literate elite of Western Europe and would be extended in the course of the next century to the cultural periphery of America and Southern and Eastern Europe. Evidence is accumulating, however, that the "decline of magic," in Thomas's phrase, was a variable process, taking place—if at all—at different rates in popular and elite cultures. Thomas interprets the decline of magic as a twofold process by which religion, especially Catholicism, abandoned claims to physical efficacy and the prestige (and perhaps the practice) of magic diminished. The decline is attributed to a transformation of collective attitudes resulting in a "new faith in the potentialities of human initiative." Thomas admits that the source of the new faith is obscure, but it is part of the growing separation of the educated elite from traditional popular culture.[24]

The emergence of two cultures in early modern European society is being subjected to increasing historical analysis. Peter Burke has written of the "withdrawal" of the literate elite from traditional popular culture at this time. As examples, he points to the increase in published attacks on popular "errors" and charlatanry in medicine, skepticism about witchcraft accusations and nonbiblical prophecies, and efforts, such as those by Newton and Joseph Mede, to put biblical prophecy on firmer intellectual foundations.[25] French almanacs of the eighteenth century show less concern with the supernatural than do those of the preceding century, and in general during the eighteenth century, in both America and Europe, a conceptual distinction between the occult and the scientific is drawn with greater firmness.[26]

While the occult declined as an article of belief among the educated elite, it survived in popular culture. The extent and nature of the survival are still a matter of conjecture. Thomas cites evidence of survivals in his book and has since come to think that survival may have been more extensive than he first realized, but he is not prepared to abandon his thesis of overall decline. E. P. Thompson, by contrast, has argued that the occult not only survived, but flourished in eighteenth-century English rural society. J. F. C. Harrison and Eugen Weber have provided brief accounts of occult survivals in nineteenth-century England and France respectively. To take a specific example, credence in Mother Shipton's prophecies, especially a faked one predicting the end of the world in 1881, sparked panic in parts of rural England that year, as Jacqueline Simpson has demonstrated. In America astrology and witchcraft continued into the eighteenth century, although both were in decline and no longer held universal recognition. American spiritualism presumably drew on North American Indian shamanism, e.g. the Spirit Lodge. Folklorists have often documented the survival of traditional superstitions among American college students.[27]

These examples and many others need sorting, further investigation, and evaluation. But they are noteworthy because they demonstrate, first, that the consideration of occult revivals necessarily entails the further questions of the decline, survival, and persistence of the occult; second, that these are essentially problems in cultural stratification; and third, that the argument that the occult declined either rapidly or completely is far from self-evident.

THE OCCULT AND HISTORICAL CRISIS

The most familiar explanation of modern occultism sees it as a manifestation of historical crisis. In this interpretation crisis is presented in social and economic terms, but it may also be religious, cultural, intellectual, or psychological. It is generally viewed as the consequence of rapid social and technological change, which leads to the dislocation of values, uncertainty about traditional authorities and roles, alienation, anxiety, deprivation, tension, and anomie. In this context the occult may be seen as further evidence of fragmentation and experimentalism, as a means of coping with uncertainty and finding relief from tension and anxiety, or as a dangerous symptom, perhaps even an exacerbating factor, leading toward the impending breakdown of Western science and rationalism. Thus G. K. Nelson sees American spiritualism arising from the "chaos of social change," "a series of rapid changes unparalleled in history" that stimulated new cults, sects, and movements "whose latent function was the relief of tension."[28] To James Webb nineteenth-century occultism is part of a "crisis of consciousness," a "flight from reason" into the irrational, while Robert N. Bellah associates "the new religious consciousness" of America in the 1960s and 1970s with a "crisis in meaning."[29] C. G. Jung's analysis of "The Spiritual Problem of Modern Man" links the upheaval in the world with the upheaval in consciousness, in which everything becomes relative and uncertain. The powerful interest in psychology, the unconscious, and the occult reflects a condition in which psychic energy can no longer find appropriate expression through obsolete forms of religion.[30] At the opposite ideological pole Theodor Adorno connects the occult to the decay of late capitalism in the third of his "Theses against Occultism" and his analysis of Carroll Righter's astrology columns in the *Los Angeles Times*.[31] Gustav Jahoda sees superstition becoming prominent in periods of acute distress and uncertainty, either as a regression to infantile thinking or as an attempt to gain some illusory sense of control.[32]

Other "marginalities," such as millennialism, apocalypticism, utopianism, heresy, charismatic religion, radical politics, fascism, the romance, and science fiction, have all been interpreted in similar terms. The interpretation admittedly has a certain common-sense quality. Much of what is taught or depicted by these visionary currents takes the form of radical discontinuities with the world as it is or as we know it. This distancing effect can be interpreted as an attitude of criticism, rejection, or disaffection, and it is then plausible to regard the prevalence of such attitudes as an expression of social malaise. Certainly there are examples to support this view, not least of all the American counterculture. But the correlation is not exact. Robert Wuthnow, for example, discovered in his sociological survey of the San Francisco Bay Area in 1973 that although there is a "positive relation between countercultural involvement and attraction to astrology," the greatest appeal of astrology was nonetheless to the more traditionally marginal groups, "the poorly educated, the unemployed, nonwhites, females, the unmarried, the overweight, the ill, and the lonely."[33]

There are further considerations, some of them bearing on the general nature of historical crisis itself, which need to be taken into account before concluding that the occult is sufficiently explained by reference to social crisis. It is not legitimate, for example, to infer social crisis from critical attitudes and the desire to modify existing conditions. Criticism does not necessarily entail an attitude of total rejection. In Bryan Wilson's classification of religious sects, only two of his eight categories propose total rejection of the world. The Revolutionist (millennialism, Seventh Day Adventists, Jehovah's Witnesses) aims at the destruction of the world or the social order through divine intervention, and the Introversionist (Rappites, Amish Mennonites, Doukhobors, Hutterians) aims at a total withdrawal from an evil world. Neither of the two categories that correspond to the occult is extremist in this sense. The Manipulationist (Christian Science, Theosophy, Anthroposophy, etc.), mentioned earlier, seeks to transform the perception of the world and through the harmonious understanding so achieved to manipulate its laws to serve individual needs. The Thaumaturgist (spiritualism, healers, organized magic) seeks magical salvation from immediate personal ills and emphasizes healing, miracles, oracles, and consolation, with little or no regard for general applicability.[34] Unless one defines the occult in such a way that any desired change constitutes radical criticism of society, it cannot be equated with a sense of crisis.

Scholarly studies have demonstrated that phrenology, for example, had an important impact on reform movements in both America and mid-Victorian England. Now regarded as a pseudoscience and an occult system of character divination, phrenology helped mold liberal and positivist social philosophy and contributed to the popularization of Enlightenment and naturalistic ideas among British artisans and workers.[35] Ameliorative activity does not support the hypothesis that the occult depends on historical crisis. A more conservative example that reinforces this conclusion is Martin Marty's 1970 report on "The Occult Establishment" in America. Based on a rather random sample of astrology journals, *Fate, Beyond,* and other popular occult periodicals, his report depicts an "aboveground," "middle America" form of the occult at odds with the more highly publicized underground, countercultural form. Its social values are politically conservative, suspicious of the new morality and youth culture, and noticeably focused on the enhancement of personal life through occult practices.[36]

In addition to these considerations, there is the more general question of the nature of a crisis. What is it? How may it be recognized? Some commentators see all of modern history as a continuous crisis; others do not perceive crisis at all. The latter view is represented by Alice Felt Tyler's classic *Freedom's Ferment.* Tyler places spiritualism, millennialism, utopianism, the Mormons, and transcendentalism of the pre–Civil War period in a social context of democratic experimentation, along with the humanitarian crusades for the reform of education and prisons, the establishment of women's rights, temperance, and the abolition of slavery and war. But for Tyler all this is evidence not of crisis but of the vitality of America, its tolerance, exuberance, and optimism.[37]

If there can be disagreement about the existence of a crisis, then the explanatory value of the concept becomes uncertain. How does the existence of a crisis explain why some people turn to the occult and others do not, or why some forms of the occult prove more popular or lasting than others? G. K. Nelson confesses that "little is known at present about which factors are responsible for determining that a religious rather than any other reaction takes place at any time," and the same may be said of the heuristic value of tension, anxiety, stress, and other psychosocial factors.[38] This is not to say that crisis and related factors are irrelevant in explaining modern occultism, but simply that they are not universally valid. Their relevance must be demonstrated in particular contexts and the nature of the crisis specified in convincing fashion. Occult belief systems do not always develop in periods of social crisis. The major Gnostic systems of radical world rejection constructed by Valentinus, Basilides, and others appeared during the prosperous Antonine peace of the second century.[39] It may also be that crisis periods do not necessarily stimulate the occult. To cite an example from the related field of apocalyptic, the outbreak of the calamitous Black Death in the 1340s surprisingly had, according to Bernard McGinn, "at best a minor effect upon the history of apocalypticism, at least in comparison with other less troubled times."[40] We need to consider the possibility of modern counterparts to these examples; in the meantime these and the other considerations adduced here should render the hypothesis of a causal relationship between crisis and the occult as not proven.

THE OCCULT AND IRRATIONALISM

Equating the occult with irrationalism presents a final cluster of problems for discussion. As an explanation of modern occultism, the equation is more often asserted than demonstrated. James Webb identifies the occult revival of the nineteenth century (he speaks of a single, continuous process rather than successive revivals) with a widespread "flight from reason" into the "Age of the Irrational." Yet we are given no understanding by Webb of what irrationalism may be, other than a rejection of eighteenth-century rationalism, or in what sense it is sig-

the term, but it is not necessarily irrational in the sense of being \
unreasonable, incoherent, emotional, or in favor of abandoning scie\
and reason, although depending on context this may be true of some \
the occult some of the time.

Implicit in these objections to the uncritical identification of the
occult with an undefined irrationalism is another concern. The indis-
criminate use of irrationalism as a label has a prejudicial effect on historical understanding. The pejorative connotations make it all too easy
to dismiss whatever the term is attached to as undeserving of serious examination. There is also the danger that the overhasty identification of
occultism with an undefined irrationalism will obscure precisely those
aspects of the occult which claim to be rational or which elude ready
categorization into rational/irrational. The initial manifesto of the
Committee for the Scientific Investigation of Claims of the Paranormal
illustrates the point. Under the sponsorship of the American Humanist
Association, the committee was organized in 1976 by Paul Kurtz, editor of the *Humanist,* out of a long-felt concern about the uncritical
acceptance of paranormal claims by the public and the mass media.
The publicity generated by publication of "Objections to Astrology,"
a statement signed by 186 astronomers and other scientists, in the
September-October, 1975, issue of the *Humanist,* was the immediate
stimulus to the formation of the committee. The manifesto's penulti-
mate paragraph states, quite properly, "We wish to make it clear that
the purpose of the committee is not to reject on a priori grounds, an-
tecedent to inquiry, any or all such claims, but rather to examine
them openly, completely, objectively, and carefully." The possibility of
achieving this laudable goal is flatly contradicted, however, by the
manifesto's second paragraph. Its emotionally loaded language precludes objectivity in scientific investigation or historical understanding:

> Many individuals now believe that there is considerable need to
> organize some strategy of refutation. Perhaps we ought not to as-
> sume that the scientific enlightenment will continue indefinitely;
> for all we know, like the Hellenic civilization, it may be over-
> whelmed by irrationalism, subjectivism, and obscurantism. Per-
> haps antiscientific and pseudoscientific irrationalism is only a pass-
> ing fashion; yet one of the best ways to deal with it is for the
> scientific and educational community to respond—in a responsible
> manner—to its alarming growth.[43]

The assumption is clearly that claims to the paranormal represent the
worst sort of irrationalism and constitute a threat to what is stated as a
rather nineteenth-century attitude of scientific progressivism.

nificantly related to the occult. Instead he follows Gustav Jahod
in claiming that superstition flourishes in conditions conducive
ings of anxiety, uncertainty, and the fear of freedom, and in spec
that superstition may mark a regression to infantile attitudes
attempt to gain a sense of control over a difficult situation. He
moreover, that the new irrationalism progressed from initial su
in the first half of the century to a position in the 1890s of "per
hysteria."[41]

There is much to dispute in this reading of nineteenth-century
ism and intellectual history, but I am more concerned by the
implications of Webb's approach. For a variety of reasons, the
not ipso facto evidence of irrationalism. Defining occultism in t
irrationalism, as Webb does in associating it with superstition, i
regression, and hysteria, yields a tautological historical expla
the occult is irrational, therefore it must appear during periods
tionalism. Both occultism and irrationalism are in any case to
form for a simple identification. Furthermore, there are obviou
terexamples of the occult in periods dominated, at the elite
least, by rationalist currents of thought, e.g. the Enlightenment
mid-nineteenth-century period of positivism, materialism, reali
scientism. Whether these discrepancies are apparent or real,
they can be resolved through recourse to analyses of cultural
cation, hypotheses of social marginality, or evidence of mate
scientific, or rationalistic varieties of occultism, they pose p
for the explanatory hypothesis that modern occultism is a
irrationalism.

I have assumed from Webb's usage that he intends irration
mean the willful abandonment of reason or direct attacks
tionality. As historical labels go, however, irrationalism is m
biguous than most. In applying it to the late nineteenth and t
centuries, intellectual historians characteristically use it to
much broader range of attitudes and ideas whose least com
nominator is the belief that human reason is not sufficient in
grasp the whole of reality. This belief may be expressed in a
ways: that reality itself is not rational, that human reason is
tool, that human thought and behavior are decisively affected
rational factors, that excessive rationality prevents full awa
reality. In turn these views may be offered in either descr
normative modes, how things actually are or how they ough
Which of the many varieties of irrationalism is meant when it
with occultism? The occult is surely irrational in one or more

Historical analysis, by contrast, cannot simply apply presentist or Western scientific criteria to other times, cultures, and beliefs with the expectation that they will prove universally valid. Beliefs are not rational or irrational by only one set of standards. To their adherents, beliefs—statements about what is true—are plausible, coherent, even commonsensical, not irrational. Modern occult beliefs and belief systems are no different. They need to be studied as coherent statements, as symbol systems, as myths, grammars, and responses to the world, according to their own context-dependent criteria of rationality and meaningfulness.[44] In the debate between Hildred Geertz and Keith Thomas over the latter's analysis of magic, Geertz is, I believe, on firmer ground in arguing that magic is more nearly an "ontology" than a collection of ad hoc, apparently random practices; it is, or it implies, an attitude toward the world, a perspective on reality, to which the key is its plausibility to its adherents.[45] That plausibility or coherence is a factor even in rather minor occult groups and practices has been shown by Festinger and his colleagues in their analysis of the belief system of a millennialistic flying saucer group and by Vogt in his publications on the folklore and value structure of dowsing (water witching).[46]

Internal and context-dependent analyses of occult beliefs provide not only the possibility of understanding the occult in its own terms but also of mapping it in its larger social and intellectual milieu, of placing it, for example, in relation to science. Attitudes toward science will have a bearing on the question of the irrationalism of modern occultism. Is modern occultism antiscientific? Or does it claim to be scientific itself or otherwise to demonstrate adaptation to science? Or does it ignore science altogether? The multiform nature of modern occultism precludes any single answer. Wuthnow found in his sociological survey of the Bay Area no correlation between belief in astrology and rejection of science. There was, in fact, a nearly equal representation of strongly positive and strongly negative attitudes toward science among those who believe in astrology or who are strongly interested in it.[47] On the other hand, among urban dowsers Barrett and Vogt uncovered considerable mistrust of the scientific community owing to its reluctance to accept the validity of dowsing and its failure or unwillingness to produce an explanation of how dowsing works.[48]

Although criticism of what is perceived as narrow-mindedness among professional scientists is widespread in modern occultism, much of the occult also expresses itself in scientific or quasi-scientific terminology and addresses itself to those who have been at least somewhat influenced by the modern emphasis on scientific analysis. Urban dowsers make use of professional organizations and journals, a written rather than an oral tradition of instruction and results, and a technical vocabulary that excludes both rural and occult usages ("dowsing," "divination," or "radiesthesia," rather than "doodlebugging" or "witching").[49] One of the most characteristic forms of modern occultism is the intellectualized, systematic synthesis aimed at the educated reader and intended to adapt occult practices and knowledge, Eastern and Western, to the needs of urban, industrial society. Andrew Jackson Davis, Éliphas Lévi, Mme. Blavatsky, Mary Baker Eddy, Papus, Annie Besant, Aleister Crowley, Charles Leadbeater, Rudolf Steiner, Alice A. Bailey, and others published massive treatises and systematic investigations on the occult, most of them containing evidence for the reality of occult claims and methods for personally verifying them. In this connection, one source of appeal of these teachings to the educated reader was their claim that they overcame the split between science and religion. The claim was not a repudiation of science, but it was a rejection of the opinion that science provided the only legitimate access to reality. By offering what they alleged was empirical, replicable evidence for matters that formerly had to be taken on faith in religion or through deductive reasoning in philosophy—afterlife, the existence of the soul, the purpose of human existence, and others—these highly rationalized forms of the occult asserted their function as a bridge between science and religion. Some pioneers of psychical research were similarly attracted by the possibility of obtaining incontrovertible evidence in favor of formerly held religious convictions through the study of mediumistic phenomena.

Although intellectualized versions of the occult frequently adopt the language of science and parallel science's appeal to verifiable evidence even while rejecting its philosophical limitations, it is easy to surmise that much popular occultism simply does not find science relevant to its reality. Jacob Burckhardt is reputed to have characterized nineteenth-century religion as "rationalism for the few and magic for the many."[50] William James pointed out in his essay on "What Psychical Research Has Accomplished" that the dominant view of life outside scientific circles is "personal" and "romantic." Personal experience lies at its foundation—experiences of premonitions, apparitions, omens, visions, dreams, answers to prayers, miracles, and much else that is taken to signify that "events may happen for the sake of their personal significance." James goes on to say that "thousands of sensitive organizations in the United States today live as steadily in the light of these experiences, and are as indifferent to modern science, as if they lived in Bohemia in the twelfth century. They are indifferent to science, because science is so callously indifferent to their experiences." Psychical research, James believed, had attempted to bridge the gulf between impersonal science and personal reality.[51]

There is not much comfort for science to derive from occult attitudes toward itself, but however disagreeable they may seem to conventional science, they do not constitute, from occult perspectives, either a rejection of science or a denial of reason. Popular occultism, like most popular thought, seems to ignore the matter, as James stated in the 1890s. The more intellectualized versions of occultism seek to go beyond science by placing it in a higher synthesis in which metaphysical questions are joined with personal experience and systematic investigation. It is likely that it is the self-proclaimed incompetence of science to handle metaphysical questions which provides the chief justification for the intellectualized syntheses of modern occultism.[52]

CONCLUSION

The four problem-clusters of definition, revivals, historical crisis, and irrationalism illustrate the difficulties of explaining modern occultism without due regard for historical precision. They also indicate areas for further research. We have seen explanations in terms of revivals, crisis, and irrationalism repeatedly founder on the questions of decline, marginality, and cultural stratification. Future explanations of modern occultism will need to map the cultural location of the occult more precisely. It is fair to say that during the late seventeenth and early eighteenth centuries occult belief systems were displaced from a position of general acceptance by the educated elite, but this is not to say that the occult did not survive. We need to know more about how the occult has survived in popular culture, whether its status there has diminished or flourished, whether and to what extent it has adapted itself to the indifference, skepticism, and scientific rationalism prevalent in elite culture. In view of the not inconsiderable interest in the occult by various intellectuals, scholars, artists, and literary figures during the past two hundred years, we need to know more about the function of the occult in elite culture as well. These are problems in cultural stratification, the differentiation of and relationship between popular and elite cultures. More detailed cultural mapping may locate a variety of other strata, as well as subcultures and countercultures, that have a bearing on the existence of occultism in modern society. Is the marginality of the occult primarily a function of social labeling and cultural perception or is there also a substantial sociological basis?[53] Is the occult marginal because there is little of it, because it is associated with popular culture, or because from the perspective of scientific enlightenment it appears to be a throwback to an earlier, darker age? These are some of the questions to be answered. We can be certain that no satisfactory answers will be forthcoming if history concentrates on the "mainstream" and dismisses the occult as "irrational." "My own conviction," E. R. Dodds has written in *The Greeks and the Irrational,* "is that our chance of understanding the historical process depends very largely on removing this quite arbitrary restriction upon our notion of it."[54]

NOTES

1. Keith Thomas, *Religion and the Decline of Magic* (New York: Scribner's, 1971), p. ix.

2. In his concluding pages Thomas contradicts his earlier statement, noting that the incidence of a magical world view today, while smaller than that for the seventeenth century, "is not a trivial one." "Indeed," he goes on to say, "the role of magic in modern society may be more extensive than we yet appreciate. . . . If magical acts are ineffective rituals employed as an alternative to sheer helplessness in the face of events, then how are we to classify the status of 'scientific' remedies, in which we place faith, but which are subsequently exposed as useless?" His primary example is medicine. See *Religion and the Decline of Magic,* pp. 666–67; cf. his article "An Anthropology of Religion and Magic, II," *Journal of Interdisciplinary History,* 6 (1975): 95, where he admits that his characterization of magic as an ineffective technique was introduced "half-frivolously."

3. George Steiner, *Nostalgia for the Absolute* (CBC Massey Lectures, 1974; Toronto: Canadian Broadcasting Company, 1974), p. 38.

4. Theodore Roszak, *Unfinished Animal: The Aquarian Frontier and the Evolution of Consciousness* (New York: Harper and Row, 1975), pp. 2–3.

5. Ibid., p. 3.

6. See the remarks of Natalie Zemon Davis, "Some Tasks and Themes in the Study of Popular Religion," in Charles Trinkaus and Heiko A. Oberman, eds., *The Pursuit of Holiness in Late Medieval and Renaissance Religion* (Leiden: E. J. Brill, 1974), pp. 308–9, 311–12. See also J. Huizinga, *The Waning of the Middle Ages* (1924; Garden City, N.Y.: Doubleday Anchor Books, 1954), chs. xiii–xiv, for a classic account of the complexity of religious attitudes and positions during the fourteenth and fifteenth centuries.

7. See Margot Adler, *Drawing Down the Moon: Witches, Druids, Goddess-Worshippers and Other Pagans in America Today* (New York:

Viking, 1979), ch. 12, a brief discussion of theories concerning the contemporary growth of the occult, classified as favorable, unfavorable, and those which fit neither category; Robert S. Ellwood, Jr., "Emergent Religion in America: An Historical Perspective," in Jacob Needleman and George Baker, eds., *Understanding the New Religions* (New York: Seabury, 1978), pp. 267–84, essentially concerned with social science theories about the new religions; Lennart Ejerfeldt, "Sociology of Religion and the Occult Revival," in Haralds Biezais, ed., *New Religions* (*Scripta Instituti Donneriani Aboensis,* vol. 7; Stockholm: Almqvist and Wiksell, 1975), pp. 202–14; Robert Galbreath, "The History of Modern Occultism: A Bibliographical Survey," *Journal of Popular Culture,* 5 (1971):726–54, reprinted in Galbreath, ed., *The Occult: Studies and Evaluations* (Bowling Green, Ohio: Bowling Green University Popular Press, 1972), pp. 98–126; and Robert Galbreath, "Occult and the Supernatural," in M. Thomas Inge, ed., *Handbook of American Popular Culture* (Westport, Conn.: Greenwood Press, 1980), 2: 213–36.

8. I have in mind especially the reception given to R. Laurence Moore's *In Search of White Crows: Spiritualism, Parapsychology, and American Culture* (New York: Oxford University Press, 1977). See Brian Mackenzie, "Parapsychology and the History of Science," *Journal of Parapsychology,* 42 (1978): 194–209; and the reviews by Michael McVaugh in *Parapsychology Review,* 9 (Mar.-Apr. 1978): 14–16, and by Edward Ayers in *Reviews in American History,* 6 (1978): 306–12. J. G. Pratt's review essay, "Obituary for Parapsychology?" *Journal of the American Society for Psychical Research,* 72 (1978): 257–66, seeks to defend parapsychology from what Pratt sees as Moore's intentional effort to topple it; despite this, a number of historical points and errors of interest are raised.

9. James Webb, *The Occult Underground* (La Salle, Ill.: Open Court, 1974), pp. 191–93; Marcello Truzzi, "Definition and Dimensions of the Occult: Toward a Sociological Perspective," *Journal of Popular Culture,* 5 (1971): 635–46, reprinted in Galbreath, ed., *The Occult: Studies and Evaluations,* pp. 7–18.

10. Lynn Thorndike, *A History of Magic and Experimental Science,* 8 vols. (New York: Columbia University Press, 1923–58), 1:4, states that in classical and medieval times the term "magic" was "applied not merely to an operative art, but also to a mass of ideas or doctrine, and that it represented a way of looking at the world." However, Thomas, "Anthropology of Religion and Magic, II," pp. 94–95, claims that only in the sixteenth century did "magic" become a comprehensive term for "enchantment," "sorcery," "necromancy," and "conjuration." As he notes, much work needs to be done on the semantic history of the term.

11. Stan Gooch, *The Paranormal* (1978; New York: Harper Colophon, 1980), p. 298, defines "paranormal" as "that which lies outside or beyond the normal objective universe of cause and effect and outside normal time," a remarkably fuzzy definition.

12. J. Stillson Judah, *The History and Philosophy of the Metaphysical Movements in America* (Philadelphia: Westminster Press, 1967), pp. 12–18 (fifteen characteristics of metaphysical movements), 45–49 (occultism).

13. Martin Marty, "The Occult Establishment," *Social Research,* 37 (1970): 212–13; Harriet Whitehead, "Reasonably Fantastic: Some Per-

spectives on Scientology, Science Fiction, and Occultism," in Irving I. Zaretsky and Mark P. Leone, eds., *Religious Movements in Contemporary America* (Princeton, N.J.: Princeton University Press, 1974), p. 558.

14.   J. Gordon Melton, *The Encyclopedia of American Religions*, 2 vols. (Wilmington, N.C.: McGrath, 1978), 2:51–81, places New Thought groups in the "Metaphysical Family" of American religions. Melton, like Judah, follows the New Thought terminology; unlike Judah, however, he does not extend the term to spiritualism and Theosophy, which he places instead in the "Psychic/New Age Family." I have used "metaphysical" as a designation for those occult groups, such as Theosophy, Anthroposophy, Rosicrucianism, Gnosticism, that emphasize the acquisition of personal empirical knowledge of metaphysical truths by means of occult modes of cognition awakened through specific disciplines and exercises. But my use of the term is drawn from philosophical metaphysics, not from New Thought. See Galbreath, "Occult and the Supernatural," *Handbook of American Popular Culture*, 2:214.

15.   Bryan R. Wilson, *Religious Sects: A Sociological Study* (New York: McGraw-Hill, 1970), pp. 141–66, and *Magic and the Millennium* (London: Heinemann, 1973), p. 24.

16.   Edward A. Tiryakian, "Toward the Sociology of Esoteric Culture" (1972), reprinted in his *On the Margin of the Visible: Sociology, the Esoteric, and the Occult* (New York: John Wiley, 1974), pp. 265–66.

17.   Mircea Eliade, "The Occult and the Modern World," in his *Occultism, Witchcraft, and Cultural Fashions: Essays in Comparative Religions* (Chicago: University of Chicago Press, 1976), pp. 65–67, offers another basis for distinguishing between occultism and esoterism: the work of René Guénon, in which Western occultism is rejected as fraudulent and true esoterism can be found only in Oriental traditions.

18.   Moore, *In Search of White Crows*, pp. 231–36; Hal Bridges, *American Mysticism: From William James to Zen* (New York: Harper and Row, 1970), pp. 2–8.

19.   See, for example, Marcello Truzzi, "The Occult Revival as Popular Culture: Some Random Observations on the Old and Nouveau Witch," *Sociological Quarterly*, 13 (1972): 16–36; Eliade, "The Occult and the Modern World," pp. 58–63; Tiryakian, "Toward the Sociology of Esoteric Culture," pp. 257–63; Richard Woods, *The Occult Revolution: A Christian Meditation* (New York: Herder and Herder, 1971); and, more popularly, Nat Freedland, *The Occult Explosion* (New York: Putnam's, 1972); and the issues of *McCall's*, Mar., 1970, on "The Occult Explosion" and *Time*, June 19, 1972, on "The Occult Revival."

20.   Thomas C. Clarie, *Occult Bibliography: An Annotated List of Books Published in English, 1971 through 1975* (Metuchen, N.J.: Scarecrow Press, 1978).

21.   J. Gordon Melton, with James V. Geisendorfer, *A Dictionary of Religious Bodies in the United States* (New York: Garland, 1977), pp. 7–15. Another family, the Non-Christian, also impinges on the occult (although it is a grab-bag category, including Judaism as well as Asian religions), and ranks second or third in every five-year period since 1915 except 1935, and was second in both 1965 (27) and 1970 (27). According to Mel-

ton's figures, the Psychical family has been active throughout the present
century; the New Thought family only modestly active during 1920–35 and
minor since 1950; the Magical family appeared once in 1915, then not again
until 1955. See also Melton's *Encyclopedia of American Religions*, 2:51–
308, for a more detailed discussion (but without the statistics cited in his
Dictionary) of these three families, which he now renames Metaphysical
(formerly New Thought), Psychic and New Age, and Magick. The latter
spelling is adopted, he notes (2:514, n. 1), to avoid confusion with sleight-
of-hand and stage illusions. For his use of "metaphysical" in a New Thought
sense, see 2:52.

22. G. R. S. Mead, "The Rising Psychic Tide" (1912), in his *Quests Old
and New* (London: G. Bell, 1913), pp. 226–47.

23. Nathan Adler, *The Underground Stream: New Life Styles and the
Antinomian Personality* (New York: Harper Torchbooks, 1972), is superficial as a historical work.

24. Thomas, *Religion and the Decline of Magic*, pp. 661, 663, 666.

25. Peter Burke, *Popular Culture in Early Modern Europe* (New York:
Harper Torchbooks, 1978), pp. 270–81. On Mede, see James West David-
son, *The Logic of Millennial Thought: Eighteenth-Century New England*
(New Haven, Conn.: Yale University Press, 1977), pp. 43–48.

26. Burke, *Popular Culture in Early Modern Europe*, pp. 258–59; Herbert Leventhal, *In the Shadow of the Enlightenment: Occultism and Renaissance Science in Eighteenth-Century America* (New York: New York University Press, 1976), p. 10.

27. Thomas, *Religion and the Decline of Magic*, pp. 664–67; Thomas,
"Anthropology of Religion and Magic, II," pp. 98, 101; E. P. Thompson,
"Anthropology and the Discipline of Historical Context," *Midland History*,
1 (1972): 53–54; J. F. C. Harrison, *The Second Coming: Popular Mil-
lenarianism, 1780–1850* (New Brunswick, N.J.: Rutgers University Press,
1979), ch. 3; Eugen Weber, *Peasants into Frenchmen: The Modernization
of Rural France 1870–1914* (Stanford, Calif.: Stanford University Press,
1976), ch. 2 (I am indebted to Roland Stromberg for this reference); Jacqueline Simpson, "The World Upside Down Shall Be: A Note on the Folklore of Doomsday," *Journal of American Folklore*, 91 (1978): 559–67;
Leventhal, *In the Shadow of the Enlightenment*, pp. 262–64; Jan Harold
Brunvand, *The Study of American Folklore: An Introduction*, 2d ed. (New
York: Norton, 1978), pp. 222–43; Ake Hultkrantz, "Spirit Lodge, a North
American Shamanistic Seance," in Carl-Martin Edsman, ed., *Studies in
Shamanism* (*Scripta Instituti Donneriani Aboensis*, vol. 1; Stockholm:
Almqvist and Wiksell, 1967), pp. 32–68, esp. p. 47 and n. 6.

28. G. K. Nelson, *Spiritualism and Society* (New York: Schocken,
1969), p. 78. Linda K. Pritchard's "Religious Change in Nineteenth-
Century America," in Charles Y. Glock and Robert N. Bellah, eds., *The
New Religious Consciousness* (Berkeley and Los Angeles: University of
California Press, 1976), pp. 297–330, offers a detailed analysis of the "Sec-
ond Great Awakening" of 1820–60 in the context of social change and re-
ligious crisis. William G. McLoughlin's *Revivals, Awakenings, and Reform:
An Essay on Religion and Social Change in America, 1607–1977* (Chicago:
University of Chicago Press, 1978) provides a more sophisticated under-

standing of religious revivals, but it does not specifically discuss nineteenth-century occult movements in this connection; see, however, pp. 199–211 for brief references to the occult and related phenomena during the "Fourth Great Awakening" beginning in the 1960s.

29. Webb, *Occult Underground*, pp. 5–13; Robert N. Bellah, "New Religious Consciousness and the Crisis in Modernity," in Glock and Bellah, eds., *New Religious Consciousness*, p. 339.

30. C. G. Jung, "The Spiritual Problem of Modern Man" (1931), in *Civilization in Transition*, trans. R. F. C. Hull, 2d ed. (*Collected Works*, vol. 10; Princeton, N.J.: Princeton University Press, 1970), pp. 74–94.

31. Theodor W. Adorno, "Theses against Occultism" (translation of an article first published in German in 1951), *Telos*, no. 19 (1974): 8, and in the same issue, "The Stars down to Earth: The Los Angeles Times Astrology Column" (1957), p. 90.

32. Gustav Jahoda, *The Psychology of Superstition* (1969; Baltimore: Penguin, 1970), p. 146, but his point is that superstition is not odd and abnormal but, rather, ubiquitous.

33. Robert Wuthnow, *Experimentation in American Religion: The New Mysticisms and Their Implications for the Churches* (Berkeley and Los Angeles: University of California Press, 1978), p. 60.

34. Wilson, *Religious Sects*, pp. 141–77; *Magic and the Millennium*, pp. 24–25.

35. See the assessment of recent scholarship on phrenology by R. J. Cooter, "Phrenology: The Provocation of Progress," *History of Science*, 14 (1976): 211–34.

36. Marty, "Occult Establishment," pp. 212–30.

37. Alice Felt Tyler, *Freedom's Ferment: Phases of American Social History from the Colonial Period to the Outbreak of the Civil War* (1944; New York: Harper Torchbooks, 1962), pp. 1–2, 548.

38. Nelson, *Spiritualism and Society*, p. 76; Thomas, "Anthropology of Religion and Magic, II," p. 99 and n. 21; Jahoda, *Psychology of Superstition*, pp. 89–90.

39. E. R. Dodds, *Pagan and Christian in an Age of Anxiety* (1965; New York: Norton, 1970), p. 4; cf. pp. 3, 100.

40. Bernard McGinn, *Visions of the End: Apocalyptic Traditions in the Middle Ages* (New York: Columbia University Press, 1979), p. 31; see also pp. 28–36 for a discussion of the often conservative functions of medieval apocalyptic thought and a criticism of "crisis" explanations.

41. Webb, *Occult Underground*, pp. 6, 10–11, and *The Occult Establishment* (La Salle, Ill.: Open Court, 1976), pp. 8–9.

42. Patrick Gardiner, "Irrationalism," in *The Encyclopedia of Philosophy*, ed. Paul Edwards (New York: Macmillan/Free Press, 1967), 4:213–19, provides a useful overview of the subject.

43. Paul Kurtz, "Committee to Scientifically Investigate Claims of Paranormal and Other Phenomena," *Humanist*, 36 (1976): 28. For the criticism of astrology, see "Objections to Astrology: A Statement by 186 Leading Scientists," *Humanist*, 35 (1975): 4–6, and two accompanying articles in the same issue: Bart J. Bok, "A Critical Look at Astrology," pp. 6–9, and Lawrence E. Jerome, "Astrology: Magic or Science?" pp. 10–16.

44. The concept of context criteria of rationality was developed by Steven Lukes, "Some Problems about Rationality" (1967), in Bryan R. Wilson, ed., *Rationality* (1970; New York: Harper Torchbooks, 1971), pp. 194–213; cf. the criticisms offered by Martin Hollis, "The Limits of Irrationality" (1967), on pp. 214–20.

45. Hildred Geertz, "An Anthropology of Religion and Magic, I," *Journal of Interdisciplinary History,* 6 (1975): 83–87; Thompson, "Anthropology and the Discipline of Historical Context," pp. 51–53. See also Tiryakian, *On the Margin of the Visible,* pp. 9–10, on the role of a "grammar of symbols" in magic, religion, science.

46. Leon Festinger, Henry W. Riecken, and Stanley Schachter, *When Prophecy Fails* (1956; New York: Harper Torchbooks, 1964), ch. 2; Evon Z. Vogt and Peggy Golde, "Some Aspects of the Folklore of Water Witching in the United States," *Journal of American Folklore,* 71 (1958):519–31; Evon Z. Vogt and Ray Hyman, *Water Witching U.S.A.* (Chicago: University of Chicago Press, 1959).

47. Wuthnow, *Experimentation in American Religion,* pp. 55–56, 60.

48. Linda K. Barrett and Evon Z. Vogt, "The Urban American Dowser," *Journal of American Folklore,* 82 (1969):195–213.

49. Ibid., pp. 198–99.

50. Quoted by E. R. Dodds, *The Greeks and the Irrational* (Berkeley and Los Angeles: University of California Press, 1951), p. 192.

51. William James, "What Psychical Research Has Accomplished" (1897 version), in *William James on Psychical Research,* ed. Gardner Murphy and Robert O. Ballou (New York: Viking Compass, 1969), pp. 44–45, 46–47.

52. On the relationship of modern occultism to science and to the theme of the reconciliation of science and religion, see Mary Farrell Bednarowski, "Nineteenth Century American Spiritualism: An Attempt at a Scientific Religion" (Ph.D. dissertation, University of Minnesota, 1973); Robert Galbreath, "Spiritual Science in an Age of Materialism: Rudolf Steiner and Occultism" (Ph.D. dissertation, University of Michigan, 1970); Moore, *In Search of White Crows,* esp. pp. 221–43; and Frank M. Turner, *Between Science and Religion* (New Haven, Conn.: Yale University Press, 1974).

53. See Moore, *In Search of White Crows,* pp. xii–xiii, on "mainstream" as a social label and labeling as a political act.

54. Dodds, *The Greeks and the Irrational,* p. 269, n. 108.

2

Andover Witchcraft and the Causes of the Salem Witchcraft Trials

CHADWICK HANSEN

I

OVER THE PAST THIRTEEN YEARS American scholars have offered an extraordinary number of explanations of that most grotesque episode in our colonial history, the Salem witchcraft trials. John Demos has suggested that generational hostility was the "underlying" cause. Richard Slotkin has suggested that it was racial hostility: demonic possession in his view becomes merely a neurotic parody of the experience of Indian captivity. Paul Boyer and Stephen Nissenbaum have suggested factional hostility. Linnda R. Caporeal has suggested that ergotism, a kind of food poisoning occasioned by a fungus infestation of the rye from which bread was made, was responsible for the seizures, hallucinations, and other symptoms of the "afflicted" persons. David Thomas Konig has seen malefic witchcraft as one of several means by which "opponents of law" might take the law into their own hands, and has suggested that servants constitute a class to which such extralegal power might seem particularly attractive. Lyle Koehler has suggested sexual hostility and the resulting anxieties as the cause of much feminine hysteria, including the hysterical seizures at Salem. And Cedric B. Cowing has suggested hostilities between persons with origins in the southeast of England and those from the northwest as "the roots" of Salem witchcraft.[1]

There is considerable merit in some of these explanations. Konig's view of witchcraft as one of several extralegal avenues to power is particularly illuminating. If Cowing's regional characterizations are valid, his statistics are impressive. Certainly there was abundant factional hos-

tility in Salem Village. And sexual hostility, or at least conjugal hostility, is very clearly present in many of the more important cases. Bridget
Bishop was alleged to have bewitched her first husband to death. Edward Bishop accused his wife Sarah of being "familiar with the Devil."
Martha Corey's, Sarah Good's, and Sarah Osburn's husbands testified
against them at their hearings. "Indeed," said Sarah Good's husband,
in one of the more memorable lines in the legal testimony, "I may say
with tears that she is an enemy to all good." John Procter was alleged
to have contemplated suicide because of his wife's quarreling with him,
and he left her out of the will that he made in prison. George Burroughs
was alleged to have been cruel to his wives, and John Willard to have
beaten his wife.[2]

   With any single explanation, however, there is always the temptation
to see it as comprehensive and sufficient in itself. Witchcraft is so alien
to the experience of twentieth-century American scholars, so medieval,
so primitive a matter, that it is tempting to dismiss all the evidence of
folk belief and folk behavior at Salem and to account for the events
there in terms that are modern, and thus comfortable and familiar, to
say, for example, "Oh, so that's all it was—just something they ate."
Boyer and Nissenbaum, among others, yield temporarily to this temptation. Having described the two main Salem Village factions as allied to
the mercantile-capitalist economy of Salem Town on the one hand and
to the agrarian economy of Salem Village on the other, they announce
that "a superhuman force" was loose in Essex County and conclude,
"We have chosen to construe this force as emergent mercantile capitalism. Mather, and Salem Village, called it witchcraft."[3]

   The purpose of this essay, however, is less to review the recent scholarship than to return to the documents in the light of it, to see whether
there is anything more that they can tell us about the causes of the
Salem trials. Such a return has been made more convenient by Boyer
and Nissenbaum, chiefly by their publication of *The Salem Witchcraft
Papers*,[4] which is a much more comprehensive collection of the basic
legal documents than Woodward's nineteenth-century collection, but
also by their various lists and maps, which make it easier to find one's
way around in the documents. Here their "List of All Persons Accused
of Witchcraft in 1692"[5] will be particularly useful. It gives the names of
the accused, the town in which they were living at the time of the trials,
and the date of the complaint against them or the warrant for their
arrest. It is not complete, but of course no modern list could be. And it
does contain a number of inaccuracies.[6] But it is complete enough, and
accurate enough, for the present purposes.

There are 141 names on the list. One each come from Amesbury, Boston, Chelmsford, Marblehead, Rumney Marsh, Salisbury, Wells (Maine), and Wenham. Two each come from Billerica, Charlestown, Ipswich, Malden, Manchester, and Piscataqua (Maine). Three come from Woburn and four from Beverly. Five each come from Haverhill, Lynn, and Reading. Six each come from Gloucester, Rowley, and Topsfield. Nineteen come from Salem Town (now Salem). Twenty come from Salem Village (now Danvers). Forty-three come from Andover.

One's first reaction to this simple analysis of the list of the accused is that we have been remiss in talking about the Salem witchcraft. If we want to be geographically comprehensive, we ought to call it the Essex County, Middlesex County, Suffolk County, and Maine witchcraft. Or if we want to name it after the town where it was at its worst, we ought to call it the Andover witchcraft, relegating to a subtitle or a footnote the information that it began in Salem Village and that the trials were held in Salem Town, the Essex County seat.

These statistics are all the more surprising because recent studies of seventeenth-century New England communities have portrayed Salem Town and Salem Village as subject to extraordinary social stress of one kind or another, and thus as thoroughly unstable,[7] while Andover has been seen as virtually devoid of stress. Richard P. Gildrie, the author of a recent community study of Salem (both Town and Village), contrasted Dedham and Andover to his own stress-torn subject as "Puritan utopia[s]," "organic and stable agricultural commune[s]."[8] Philip J. Greven, Jr., the author of the groundbreaking demographic study of Andover, said of that community in the second half of the seventeenth century that "during this period, the evidence reveals that people were extraordinarily healthy, lives were unusually long, and women were exceedingly fecund. . . . What the basic demographic characteristics of life in seventeenth-century Andover imply . . . seems clear enough: stability and health. . . . [T]he small rural agricultural towns like Andover probably proved to be excellent places in which to realize the [Puritan] goals of order, hierarchy, and the closely-knit community." He adds that "in no significant sense were the lives of the first and second generations in disorder, once their permanent roots had been firmly established in early Andover."[9] Yet Andover, at the height of its second generation, produced 30 percent of the accused persons during the witchcraft trials, more than Salem Village (14 percent) and Salem Town (13 percent) put together. What had gone wrong in this orderly agricultural utopia?

II

It is more difficult to tell what happened at Andover than what happened at Salem Village and Salem Town. In part this is because so
many of the accused persons from Andover confessed. When the magistrates had obtained a confession, they seem to have stopped looking
for further evidence. As a consequence it is generally impossible to tell,
with confessors, what brought them under suspicion in the first place.
With most of them one has only the confession (or the report of it) and
the names of some of the accusers. Another difficulty is that many of
the Andover accused were first examined in Andover by Dudley Bradstreet, the local magistrate. The accounts of these examinations are
much more sketchy than the accounts of examinations at the county
seat in Salem.[10] Andover is poorly documented in the contemporary
narratives as well as in the surviving legal evidence. Nevertheless, it is
possible to sketch at least a broad outline of what took place there.

The witchcraft proceedings began with the issuing of warrants for
three Salem Village women on February 29, 1692. It was not until almost three months later, on May 28, when matters were well under-
way and dozens of persons had been arrested, that the first warrant was
issued for a resident of Andover. It was for Martha Carrier. Her accusers were several of the afflicted girls of Salem Village, and at her
examination they went into convulsive seizures and began hallucinating, complaining that her "specter" was biting, pinching, pricking, and
choking them, and accusing her of looking "upon the black man."
When the examining magistrate (presumably John Hathorne) asked
her, "What black man did you see?" her reply was, "I saw no black man
but your own presence." Twentieth-century readers are bound to ap-
plaud such words, but they may have struck seventeenth-century hear-
ers as impudent or even malicious. Shortly afterward she said to
Hathorne one of the most sensible things, from a twentieth-century
point of view, that he was to hear during the entire proceedings: "It is
a shameful thing that you should mind these folks that are out of their
wits." Her defiance evoked even more violent seizures from the afflicted
girls. According to the anonymous court reporter, "The tortures of the
afflicted was so great that there was no enduring of it, so that she was
ordered away and to be bound hand and foot with all expedition, the
afflicted in the meanwhile almost killed, to the great trouble of all spec-
tators, magistrates, and others." "Note," he added, "As soon as she was
well bound they all had strange and sudden ease."[11]

By the time of her trial in August there were other kinds of testimony against her, and some of it, from her former neighbors, suggests why she first came under suspicion. John Roger of Billerica testified, "That about seven years since, Martha Carrier, being a nigh neighbor unto this deponent, and there happening some difference betwixt us she gave forth several threatening words, as she often used to do." Shortly afterward Roger missed two of his sows. One he never found. The other he found "dead, nigh the said Carrier's house, with both ears cut off." During the same summer one of his cows for no apparent reason suddenly stopped giving milk in the mornings for about a month's time. Roger concluded by saying, "I did in my conscience believe, then in the day of it, and have so done ever since, and do yet believe, that Martha Carrier was the occasion of those ill accidents by means of witchcraft, she being a very malicious woman."[12]

The importance of the dead sow with the ears cut off is that taking a part of the body, or a body product, and subjecting it to occult manipulation was one of the commonest means of working either white or black magic on a person or an animal. With a person you took some of their hair, or their nail parings, or their urine or feces. The hair and nail parings and urine were most commonly boiled; the urine and feces might also be stopped up tight in a container. With an animal it was most common to cut off one or both ears, and boil or burn them. (For a proposal to cut a piece off of a sick mare and burn it, as white magic, see the hilarious affair of the mare's fart.)[13]

There were others of her neighbors who thought that Martha Carrier was a witch. Samuel Preston testified that "about two years since I had some difference with Martha Carrier, which also had happened several times before, and soon after I lost a cow [i.e., it died] in a strange manner. . . . Within about a month after this the said Martha and I had some difference again, at which time she told me I had lost a cow lately, and it would not or should not be long before I should lose another, which accordingly came to pass."

The implication here, of course, is that Martha Carrier predicted the death of the cow because she intended to kill it with a charm or a spell. A similar implication is present in the threats she made against human beings. Benjamin Abbott testified that a little over a year before, when the town of Andover had granted him some land next to Goodman Carrier's,

> Goodwife Carrier was very angry, and said that she would stick as close to Benjamin Abbott as the bark stuck to the tree, and that I

should repent of it afore seven years came to an end, and that Doctor Prescott could never cure me. . . . Presently after I was taken with a swelling in my foot, and then was taken with a pain in my side, exceedingly tormented, which bred to a sore which was lanced by Dr. Prescott, and several gallons of corruption did run out, as was judged, and so continued about six weeks very bad. And then one other sore did breed in my groin which was lanced by Doctor Prescott also and continued very bad a while. And then one other sore bred in my groin which was also cut, and put me to very great misery, so that it brought me almost to death's door, and continued until Goodwife Carrier was taken and carried away by the constable. And that very day I began to grow better. My sores grew well and I grew better every day, and so have been well ever since, and have great cause to think that the said Carrier had a great hand in my sickness and misery.

It should be kept in mind that Goodwife Carrier's threat would have been understood as something more than an ill wish in the seventeenth century. Such words were a curse. In and of themselves they were believed to be a dangerous weapon. One would not utter them lightly. It is most unlikely, of course, that they had anything to do with Benjamin Abbott's actual physical condition. But that is not the point. Benjamin Abbott believed they did, and the chances are that so did Martha Carrier.

Martha Carrier's own nephew, Allen Toothaker, testified that he had been a witness to her cursing of Benjamin Abbott. She had once cursed Toothaker as well: "I was wounded in the war. Martha Carrier told me I would never be cured. Afore she was apprehended I could thrust in my wound a knitting needle four inches deep, but since she have been taken I am thoroughly healed." He was so afraid of his aunt that once, during a fight with her son, Richard Carrier, he had suffered an attack of hysterical paralysis, followed by a hallucination: "I fell down flat upon my back to the ground, and had not power to stir hand nor foot. Then I told said Richard I would yield to him and own him the best man. And then I saw Martha Carrier go off from my breast, but when I was risen up I saw none of her." The sudden appearance and disappearance of his aunt's shape meant, of course, to Allen Toothaker, that it was her "specter" that had been restraining him. He concluded by saying that several of his animals had died after his aunt had threatened him. "And I know not of any natural causes of the death of the abovesaid creatures, but have always feared it hath been the effect of my Aunt Martha Carrier her malice."

Toothaker was not the only Andover resident whose fear of Martha

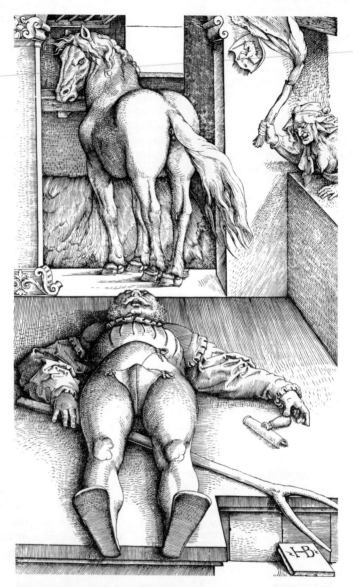

Hans Baldung Grien, *The Bewitched Groom* (woodcut).
National Gallery of Art, Washington, D.C. Gift of W. G.
Russell Allen. Like Allen Toothaker in seventeenth-century
Andover, Baldung Grien's sixteenth-century German be-
twitched groom has fallen flat on his back, without the
"power to stir hand nor foot."

Carrier produced psychogenic disorders. Phoebe Chandler, "aged about twelve years," testified that

> about a fortnight before Martha Carrier was sent for to Salem to be examined, upon the Sabbath Day when the psalm was singing, said Martha Carrier took me, said deponent, by the shoulder and shaked me, in the Meeting House, and asked me where I lived. But I made her no answer (not doubting but that she knew me, having lived some time the next door to my father's house, on one side of the way). And that day that said Martha Carrier was seized, my mother sent me to carry some beer to the folks that were at work in the lot, and when I came within the fence there was a voice in the bushes (which I thought was Martha Carrier's voice, which I know well) but saw nobody. And the voice asked me what I did there and whither I was going, which greatly frighted me, so that I run as fast as I could to those at work and told them what I had heard. About an hour and [a] half, or two hours after, my mother sent me again upon the same occasion, to the workmen abovesaid. Coming home, near the place abovesaid where I heard that voice before, I heard the same voice, as I judged, over my head, saying I should be poisoned within two or three days, which accordingly happened, as I conceive. For I went to my Sister Allen's farm the same day, and on Friday following about one half of my right hand was greatly swollen and exceeding painful, and also part of my face, which I can give no account how it came, and continued very bad some days. And several times since I have been troubled with a great weight upon my breast, and upon my legs when I have been going about, so that I could hardly go, which I have told my mother of. And the last Sabbath Day, was seven night, I went to meeting very well in the morning and went to my place where I used to sit (the ministers not being come). And Richard Carrier, son of abovesaid Martha, looked very earnestly upon me and immediately my hand, which had formerly been poisoned, as abovesaid, began to pain me greatly, and I had a strange burning at my stomach, and then was struck deaf, that I could not hear any of the prayer nor singing till the two or three last words of the singing.

She believed, of course, that Richard Carrier had "overlooked" her, given her the evil eye. Her hysterical deafness was one consequence. The "strange burning" in her stomach was probably the lower body pain with which the *globus hystericus* typically begins. And since the pain in her hand followed so immediately on Richard Carrier's look, one wonders whether it too may not have been psychogenic. One wonders even to what extent her earlier pains may have been a consequence of her aural hallucination of Martha Carrier. In any case, it is clear that some of the citizens of Andover had been living in fear of the supposed occult powers of Martha Carrier for a period of up to seven years before her trial.

A little over two weeks after Martha Carrier's arrest, on July 15, another Andover woman, Ann Foster, was arrested, but little is known about her except for her confessions.

It was John Ballard, an Andover constable, who had served the warrant and warned the witnesses in the Martha Carrier case, and although the documents are missing he may have done the same in the Foster case. At any rate, Ballard's wife had been "this several months sorely afflicted and visited with strange pains and pressures."[14] He thought her bewitched, and thus had several of the hallucinating girls of Salem brought to Andover to see whose specters were afflicting her.[15] As a consequence Mary Lacey, Sr., and Mary Lacey, Jr., the daughter and granddaughter of Ann Foster, were arrested on July 20. Both confessed. The next day three sons of Martha Carrier were arrested, and they confessed as well.

It was a week later, on July 28, that a warrant was issued for the next citizen of Andover, Mary Bridges, Sr. This time the accuser was not one of the afflicted girls of Salem but Timothy Swan, of Andover. From that time on the names of the Salem girls are only infrequently found in indictments against citizens of Andover. That town had developed its own group of hallucinating afflicted persons, who were responsible for the overwhelming majority of the Andover accusations. The names one sees most often in the indictments, besides that of Timothy Swan, are Rose Foster, of Andover; Abigail Martin, of Andover, "aged about sixteen years";[16] Sarah Phelps, of Andover; and Martha Sprague, alias Tyler, of neighboring Boxford, "aged sixteen years."[17] Among them they accused an extraordinary number of persons, and most of those whom they accused confessed. But before we look at the confessors we should look at two more cases in which, because the persons did not confess, the magistrates accumulated sufficient evidence so that we can tell what had brought them under suspicion.

The first is that of Mary Parker, who was arrested toward the end of August. Besides the behavior of afflicted persons, who went into seizures at the mention of her name and were "recovered . . . out of their fits"[18] by the touch of her hand, and besides the evidence given by confessors, there were three witnesses against her. John Westgate testified that "about eight years since" he had been at the public house of Samuel

Beadle when John Parker was among those present. Goodwife Parker then

> came into the company and scolded at and called her husband all
> to naught, whereupon I, the said deponent, took her husband's
> part, telling of her it was an unbeseeming thing for her to come
> after him to the tavern and rail after that rate. With that she came
> up to me and called me rogue, and bid me mind my own business,
> and told me I had better have said nothing. Sometime afterwards
> I, the said deponent, going from the house of Mr. Daniel King,
> when I came over against John Robinson's house I heard a great
> noise coming from towards Mr. Babbidge his house. Then there
> appeared a black hog running towards me with open mouth as
> though he would have devoured me.

He fell on his hip, driving his knife into it, and had to crawl home with the hog worrying him all the way. He had a "stout" dog with him that ran from the hog, "leaping over the fence and crying much, which at other times used to worry any hog well or sufficiently, which hog I then apprehended was either the Devil or some evil thing, not a real hog, and did then really judge or determine in my mind that it was either Goody Parker or by her means, and procuring fearing that she is a witch."

It seems an idle tale, or would seem so in most contexts. But it shows how little it took for a colonial American to convince himself that his neighbor's wife was a witch, and how his fear of her, festering over eight years, would be enough to bring him into court to testify that she was what he had feared her to be.

The second witness, John Bullock, had helped to get Goodwife Parker home when she had been lying out of doors in winter in what was apparently a catatonic state, since the man carrying her "let her fall upon a place of stones, which did not awake her, which caused me to think she was really dead." But when they got her home and "were taking off her clothes to put her into bed, she rises up and laughs in our faces." Martha Dutch confirmed Bullock's testimony and added "that I have seen said Parker in such a condition several other times." Again, it seems an idle tale, and one's first reaction is to wonder why it was offered as testimony in a witchcraft case. Apparently Bullock and Dutch believed that Mary Parker's catatonic seizures were evidence that she possessed occult powers. Once more one has to be impressed at how little it took to make people afraid of their neighbors.

The third witness was Samuel Shattuck, a Quaker who was a hatter and dyer in Salem Town. He testified that in the year 1685 Goodwife Parker, wife to John Parker, Mariner, came to my house and went into the room where my wife and children were and fawned upon my wife with very smooth words. In a short time after, that child which was supposed to have been under an ill hand for several years before was taken in a strange and unusual manner, as if his vitals would have broke out, his breast bone drawn up together to the upper part of his breast, his neck and eyes drawn so much aside as if they would never come to right again. He lay in so strange a manner that the doctor and others did believe he was bewitched. Some days after some of the visitors cut some of his hair off to boil, which they said, although they did [it] with great tenderness, the child would shriek out as if he had been tormented. They put his hair in a skillet over a fire which stood plain on the hearth, and it was thrown down, and I came immediately into the room as soon as they were gone out of the room, and could see no creature in the room. They put it on again, and after it had boiled some time the abovesaid Goodwife Parker came in and asked if I would buy some chickens.

Shattuck's visitors had themselves been practicing malefic witchcraft here, since boiling the victim's hair was a charm intended either to harm the witch or compel her presence. Since it turned out on later investigation that Goodwife Parker had had no chickens to sell, it must have been considered a success, in spite of the spectral casting down of the skillet on the first attempt.

Here as elsewhere it should be noted that New England witchcraft cannot be considered a temporary insanity confined to 1692. Shattuck's suspicions of Mary Parker dated back seven years, to a time when she had lived in Salem Town. Why hadn't he prosecuted her then? Perhaps he was one of Professor Konig's "opponents of law"; certainly he had been willing to take the law into his own hands. Or perhaps he had realized that although his suspicions were strong his evidence was incomplete. Nobody had heard Mary Parker curse the child, or seen her work a charm against it, or even look at it fixedly with an evil eye. And if you took a witch to court, and the court did not put her to death, surely she would find some way to have her revenge. But in 1692, when the Court of Oyer and Terminer was doing its best to rid the country of witches, and when the afflicting specter of Mary Parker had appeared in the hallucinations of three of her present neighbors (Sarah Phelps of Andover, Hannah Bigsby of Andover, and Martha Sprague of Boxford), Samuel Shattuck was willing to come forward and offer his testimony.

Our third case is that of Samuel Wardwell, and in some ways it is

The indictment of Mary Parker of Andover for "witchcraft and sorceries wickedly, maliciously, and feloniously . . . used, practiced, and exercised at and in the Town of Andover . . . in, upon, and against one Sarah Phelps of Andover." Courtesy of Massachusetts Historical Society.

the most interesting, if only because it is so very insubstantial. His specter had appeared in several persons' hallucinations, afflicting Martha
Sprague of Boxford. He had been "much addicted" to fortune telling,
so much so that several of his neighbors were clearly in awe of his supposedly occult abilities in predicting the future. And he had boasted
"that he could make cattle come to him when he pleased."[19] When he
was first examined he confessed "that he had been foolishly led along
with telling of fortunes, which sometimes came to pass. He used also
when any creature came into his field to bid the Devil take it, and it
may be the Devil took advantage of him by that." He went on to provide an account of meetings with the Devil, and of making a covenant
with him. But he later repudiated his confession. Whether he had ever
actually practiced malefic magic remains in doubt, of course. But the
evidence we have seen against him so far is "specter" evidence and evidence about his practicing white magic. So it would be a little surprising
to learn that he, Mary Parker, and Martha Carrier were the three citizens of Andover who were executed for witchcraft if it were not for the
fact that there was another kind of evidence against him. His name, like
that of Martha Carrier and Mary Parker, turns up repeatedly in the
testimony of the Andover confessors.

   John Hale, whose *Modest Enquiry into the Nature of Witchcraft* is
the most reliable contemporary account of the Salem trials, tells us that
the "matter was carried on . . . chiefly by the complaints and accusations of the afflicted . . . and . . . by the confessions of the accused, condemning themselves and others."[20] Of the forty-three Andover names
on Boyer and Nissenbaum's list of accused witches, it is not known how
seven pled. Of the remaining thirty-six, only six denied the accusations;
thirty confessed. If Hale and Calef are correct in saying that there were
"about fifty"[21] confessors altogether, that would mean that Andover
supplied at least 60 percent of them. Whether they are correct or not, it
is clear that the number of Andover confessors is out of all proportion
both to the relative size of the community and to the number of the
Andover accused.

   One can find several motives for the Andover confessions in the surviving documents. Two of the confessors clearly enjoyed the attention
paid them in their hearings. Mary Lacey, Jr., responded readily to the
magistrates in her several examinations, frequently supplying colorful
details for which she had not been asked. It was she who volunteered
that "Goody Carrier told me the Devil said to her that she should be a
queen in Hell,"[22] a detail that so impressed the Massachusetts magistrates and ministers that it found its way into Cotton Mather's account

of the Carrier case in *Wonders of the Invisible World*. She later joined the ranks of the afflicted persons, although she does not seem to have initiated any accusations. William Barker, Sr., also enjoyed confessing, so much so that courtroom appearances were not enough for him: John Hale prints a confession "which he wrote himself in prison, and sent to the magistrates to confirm his former confession to them."[23]

A very different motive for confession is found in the case of Sarah Wilson, Sr. When the Reverend Increase Mather interviewed several of the confessing Andover women in prison, she told him "that, knowingly, she never had familiarity with the Devil; that, knowingly, she never consented to the afflicting of any person, &c. However, she said that truly she was in the dark as to the matter of her being a witch. And being asked how she was in the dark, she replied that the afflicted persons crying out of her as afflicting them made her fearful of herself."[24]

Neither her examination nor her confession survives, but it is easy to reconstruct what happened. Affliction took two main forms. In the first, the afflicted person went into seizures and hallucinations at the glance of the accused person, and could be recovered by her touch. The cause of the affliction was then believed to be the evil eye. In the second form the afflicted also went into seizures and hallucinations, complaining that the "specter" or spirit of the accused was the cause of her convulsions, or was pinching, pricking, biting, or choking her. Goodwife Wilson had seen the awe-inspiring behavior of the afflicted persons in her presence, and, hearing their accusations and unable to think of any other cause, was afraid that she might possess the evil eye without being aware of it, or that her spirit might be responsible for the afflictions without her knowledge.

A third motive for confession was that by the time arrests became general in Andover, it was clear that confessors were not being executed. As the Reverend Francis Dane, the senior minister of Andover, wrote to an anonymous "reverend sir," "I fear the common speech that was frequently spread among us, of their liberty if they would confess, have brought many into a snare" (i.e., of false confession).

But by far the greatest reason for the large number of confessions at Andover appears to have been the bullying of the accused by their own friends and relatives. A particularly chilling instance was discovered by Increase Mather when he interviewed Martha Tyler in prison. She told him

> that when she was first apprehended she had no fears upon her, and did think that nothing could have made her confess against herself. But since she had found, to her great grief, that she had

wronged the truth and falsely accused herself. She said that when she was brought to Salem her brother Bridges rode with her, and that all along the way from Andover to Salem her brother kept telling her that she must needs be a witch, since the afflicted accused her and at her touch were raised out of their fits, and urging her to confess herself a witch. She as constantly told him that she was no witch, that she knew nothing of witchcraft, and begged him not to urge her to confess. However, when she came to Salem she was carried to a room where her brother on one side, and Mr. John Emerson on the other side, did tell her that she was certainly a witch, and that she saw the Devil before her eyes at that time (and accordingly the said Emerson would attempt with his hand to beat Him away from her eyes); and they so urged her to confess that she wished herself in any dungeon rather than to be so treated. Mr. Emerson told her, once and again, "Well, I see you will not confess! Well, I will now leave you, and then you are undone, body and soul, forever." Her brother urged her to confess, and told her that in so doing she could not lie, to which she answered, "Good brother, do not say so, for I shall lie if I confess, and then who shall answer unto God for my lie?" He still asserted it, and said that God would not suffer so many good men to be in such an error about it, and that she would be hanged if she did not confess, and continued so long and so violently to urge and press her to confess that she thought, verily, that her life would have gone from her, and became so terrified in her mind that she owned, at length, almost anything that they propounded to her; that she had wronged her conscience in so doing; she was guilty of a great sin in belying of herself, and desired to mourn for it so long as she lived. This she said, and a great deal more of the like nature; and all with such affection, sorrow, relenting, grief, and mourning, as that it exceeds any pen to describe and express the same.[25]

Indeed, Andover became notorious for the ease and thoroughness with which family and community bonds were broken in the face of witchcraft accusations. Brattle speaks of the "husbands who, having taken up that corrupt and highly pernicious opinion that whoever were accused by the afflicted were guilty, did break charity with their dear wives upon their being accused and urge them to confess their guilt."[26] Calef says of Andover, "Here it was that many accused themselves of riding upon poles through the air, many parents believing their children to be witches, and many husbands their wives."[27] And Andover's senior minister, Francis Dane, lamented that "the conceit of specter evidence as an infallible mark did too far prevail with us. Hence we so easily parted with our neighbors of honest and good report, and [church] members in full communion. Hence we so easily parted with our children, when we knew nothing in their lives, nor any of our neighbors to suspect them. And thus things were hurried on, hence such strange breaches in families. . . ."[28]

Why did Andover's family and community loyalties break down so thoroughly in the face of witchcraft accusations? It may not be possible, of course, to find a fully satisfactory explanation. Perhaps it was their very devotion to Puritan ideals of communal unity which made Andover citizens prefer to think their wives, children, and neighbors witches rather than accept the idea that, as Martha Tyler's brother put it, God would permit "so many good men to be in such an error about it."

Factional hostility has been the most persuasive of the recent explanations of the Salem trials. But it does seem clear, in the light of Andover's experience, that we cannot account for those trials by suggesting that Salem had a history of factional hostility and Andover had not. Even without the Andover experience, it ought to be clear that factional hostility does not in itself provide a comprehensive explanation for the Salem trials. There are departments in twentieth-century American universities with as long and as vicious a history of factional hatreds as any to be found in Salem, and the parties to these hatreds accuse each other of all sorts of absurdities, but witchcraft is not one of them. If we want to understand what happened at Salem, we shall have to begin by acknowledging as causes of the trials some of the ways in which seventeenth-century American culture was different from our own.

III

The first, or one might say the underlying, cause was that seventeenth-century Americans, like seventeenth-century Europeans, believed in witchcraft. That is to say, they believed it possible to affect the course of events, including doing good or evil to other persons, through occult means. Belief in witchcraft was virtually universal, but the practice of it was limited, because it was seen not simply as an appeal to occult forces but to specifically anti-Christian occult forces. Therefore it was practiced only by certain kinds of people: the ignorant, who did not understand that their charms or spells were anti-Christian, and the powerless, the desperate, and the malicious, who did not care. None of these kinds of people are apt to put themselves on the historical record, and most of them are apt to try to keep themselves off it, so we hear of colonial American witchcraft only when it reached the attention of the authorities. But this happened far more frequently than most American historians, or even most historians of American witchcraft, have recognized. Frederick C. Drake lists fifty-eight "cases and incidents" of witchcraft in the American colonies in the eighteen years from 1645 to 1662,[29] and when we remember that colonial records, especially outside New England, are very incomplete, it seems clear that witchcraft cases were a regular feature of American colonial experience. Only some of these cases, of course, were instances of the actual practice of witchcraft; many of them were instances of the fear of it. But if we keep in mind that the "cases and incidents" in the surviving records must be only a very small proportion of the total number, it seems clear that belief in and fear of witchcraft were endemic in the American colonies. From the evidence of the surviving documents it also seems clear that white witchcraft was commonly practiced and that black witchcraft was not uncommon. We have one instance of openly avowed black witchcraft above, in the boiling of the Shattuck child's hair. Without the near-universal belief in witchcraft and the regular practice of it, it is hard to see how witchcraft could have remained a capital crime, as it did in both England and English America until a generation after the Salem trials.[30]

But in the typical colonial witchcraft trial only one or two persons were accused. What distinguishes the Salem trials from all the others is their scale. The total number of the accused is unknown, but a conservative estimate would put the figure over 200. Calef claims that it was more than 350.[31] Nineteen people were hanged, and one was pressed to death for refusing to plead to his indictment. In one sense, then, when we ask the causes of the Salem trials, we are really asking why, on this occasion, a fairly common kind of judicial proceeding got out of hand. Community studies will not help us much here because the accused, the accusers, and the judges of the Court of Oyer and Terminer came from many different communities. Nor will the various hostility theories help us, although servile hostility, sexual hostility, regional hostility, and factional hostility may all be useful in an analysis of why particular persons were accusers or accused. A number of explanations can be found, however, all of them more or less familiar.

Let us start with John Hale's statement that the "matter was carried on . . . chiefly by the complaints and accusations of the afflicted . . . and . . . by the confessions of the accused, condemning themselves and others." "The complaints and accusations of the afflicted" depended chiefly on their hallucinations of the "specters" of the accused, that is, on so-called spectral evidence. The Boston clergy advised the court early, and throughout the proceedings, not to place too much weight on spectral evidence, and it is clear that the court did not take this advice seriously enough. Why they did not do so can only be a matter for conjecture, because no record was kept and no report made of the court's deliberations.[32] One possible explanation may lie in the characters of the magistrate who conducted most of the preliminary examinations, John Hathorne, and of the chief justice, William Stoughton. Both of them, through most of the proceedings, seem to have been much more anxious to obtain evidence of guilt—any kind of evidence of guilt— than to weigh the evidence impartially. It is not only possible but probable that with a different leadership the proceedings would have turned out very differently.

As for confessions, it was here that the Salem court's procedure differed from that of all other colonial American courts, as Drake has pointed out,[33] and from all English courts as well. The ordinary procedure was to execute confessors, since confession was often the best possible proof of guilt in witchcraft cases. The Salem court did not bring them to trial; it even stayed the executions of condemned witches who subsequently confessed. Again we do not know the reasons for the court's procedure. They may have been following Cotton Mather's early advice that "lesser criminals be only scourged with lesser punishments, and also put upon some solemn, open, public and explicit renunciation of the Devil."[34] Or they may have been attracted to the drama of redemption that the confession presented, and reluctant to execute those they had redeemed. Or they may have been hungry for guilt, and pleased that the confessors incriminated not only themselves but others. In any case, the court's policy toward confessors was a major cause of the escalation of accusations.

And of course, as many scholars have pointed out, 1692 was a time of extraordinary troubles for Massachusetts. She had finally and irrevocably lost her Old Charter, which had been the very basis of her identity. There were serious troubles with the French and the Indians on the frontier. It was precisely the sort of time in which even the best of men are apt to feel that unnamed evils are abroad in the land, and that it would be a public service to root them out.

We cannot know, in our present state of knowledge, which of these causes were the more compelling. But we can recognize that the causes of the Salem trials were extraordinarily complex. No single explanation is going to sweep them under the historical rug; we can expect the debate over them to continue.

NOTES

1. John Demos, "Underlying Themes in the Witchcraft of Seventeenth-Century New England," *American Historical Review*, 75 (1970): 1311–26; Richard Slotkin, *Regeneration through Violence* (Middletown, Conn.: Wesleyan University Press, 1973), ch. 5; Paul Boyer and Stephen Nissenbaum, *Salem Possessed* (Cambridge, Mass.: Harvard University Press, 1974); Linnda R. Caporeal, "Ergotism: The Satan Loosed in Salem?" *Science*, 192 (Apr. 2, 1976): 21–26; David Thomas Konig, *Law and Society in Puritan Massachusetts* (Chapel Hill: University of North Carolina Press, 1979), chs. 6 and 7; Lyle Koehler, *A Search for Power* (Urbana: University of Illinois Press, 1980), chs. 10–13; Cedric B. Cowing, "The Roots of Salem Witchcraft." I am indebted to Professor Cowing for his kind permission to read his essay in typescript and to refer to it here.

2. Paul Boyer and Stephen Nissenbaum, *The Salem Witchcraft Papers*, 3 vols. (New York: Da Capo, 1977), pp. 83; 112; 249, 259–60; 357; 611; 797–98, 963; 162–63, 176; 824, 842. This collection is cited hereafter as *SWP*.

3. Boyer and Nissenbaum, *Salem Possessed*, p. 209.

4. See n. 2.

5. Boyer and Nissenbaum, *Salem-Village Witchcraft* (Belmont, Calif.: Wadsworth, 1972), pp. 376–78.

6. If one takes the table of contents of *SWP* as a revised list, some omissions and errors are corrected there, but new omissions and errors are introduced. Either list would do for the present purposes, but the later one would have to be corrected.

7. Richard P. Gildrie, *Salem, Massachusetts, 1626–1683* (Charlottesville: University of Virginia Press, 1975), and Boyer and Nissenbaum, *Salem Possessed*.

8. Gildrie, *Salem*, p. 179.

9. Philip J. Greven, Jr., *Four Generations: Population, Land, and Family in Colonial Andover, Massachusetts* (Ithaca, N.Y.: Cornell University Press, 1970), pp. 269–71.

10. See, for example, the Andover and Salem examinations of Elizabeth Johnson, Jr. (*SWP*, pp. 503–5).

11. *SWP*, pp. 185–86. Because of the extreme irregularity of spelling, punctuation, and capitalization in the legal documents, I have modernized all three.

12. The testimony of Martha Carrier's neighbors is in *SWP*, pp. 189–94.

13. *SWP*, pp. 444–46.

14. Ibid., p. 513.

15. The account of Ballard's sending to Salem for witchfinders is to be found both in Thomas Brattle's "Letter" and in Robert Calef's *More Wonders of the Invisible World*, in George Lincoln Burr, ed., *Narratives of the Witchcraft Cases* (New York: Barnes & Noble, 1959), pp. 180–81 and 371–72. Both Brattle and Calef seem to have been working from very incomplete evidence, as their brief accounts of Andover demonstrate.

16. *SWP*, p. 788.

17. Ibid., p. 786.

18. The legal documents of the Mary Parker case are in *SWP*, pp. 629–37.

19. The legal documents of the Samuel Wardwell case are in *SWP*, pp. 783–89.

20. Burr, *Narratives*, p. 421.

21. Ibid., pp. 416, 373.

22. The legal documents of the Mary Lacey, Jr., case are in *SWP*, pp. 520–29.

23. Hale, *Modest Enquiry* in Burr, *Narratives*, p. 419.

24. An account of Mather's visit, presumably from Thomas Brattle's papers, is in the *Massachusetts Historical Society Collections*, 2d ser., 3: 221–25.

25. Ibid.

26. Burr, *Narratives*, p. 181.

27. Ibid., p. 372.

28. *SWP*, p. 882.

29. Frederick C. Drake, "Witchcraft in the American Colonies, 1647–62," *American Quarterly*, 20 (1968): 694–725. A recent article on the widespread existence of various kinds of occultism in colonial America is Jon Butler, "Magic, Astrology, and the Early American Religious Heritage, 1600–1760," *American Historical Review*, 84 (1979): 317–46.

30. For the Old Charter law, see Section 94 of the *Body of Liberties*, reprinted in Edwin Powers, *Crime and Punishment in Early Massachusetts* (Boston: Beacon, 1966), pp. 533–48. The English law in effect at the time is 1 *Jacob*. Cap. 12.

31. Burr, *Narratives*, p. 373.

32. For a discussion of the court's and the clergy's disagreements on this issue, see Chadwick Hansen, *Witchcraft at Salem* (New York: George Braziller, 1969), especially those passages indexed under "spectral evidence."

33. Drake, "Witchcraft," p. 725.

34. Cotton Mather, "Letter to John Richards," *Collections of the Massachusetts Historical Society*, 4th ser., 8: 397.

3

The Dark Ages
of American Occultism, 1760-1848

JON BUTLER

IN THE PAST FIFTEEN YEARS a quiet historiographical change has thoroughly altered the scholarly view of occult belief and practice in post-Renaissance American and European society. In the 1950s in America, scholars only reluctantly included Catholicism and nothing about occultism in their surveys of American religious history. Now we have just completed the first stage of an important advance in outlining and assessing the scope of occult practice in the American religious configuration. The appearance of Robert Ellwood's *Alternative Altars: Unconventional and Eastern Spirituality in America* in the University of Chicago Press History of American Religion Series and the critical reception given to R. Laurence Moore's *In Search of White Crows: Spiritualism, Parapsychology, and American Culture* and Howard Kerr's *Mediums, and Spirit-Rappers, and Roaring Radicals: Spiritualism in American Literature, 1850–1900* demonstrate the legitimacy occult studies have obtained in the last decade. In turn, these works complement other publications on occult practice in the European past, of which the most prominent are Keith Thomas's *Religion and the Decline of Magic* and the numerous studies by Frances Yates, the most recent being her *Occult Philosophy in the Elizabethan Age*.[1]

We are now in the second stage of scholarly work on occultism in American society. Publications in this stage typically fill gaps in the knowledge acquired in the first stage but also provoke interpretive disagreement. This essay attempts to do both. By describing the range and origins of American occult practice between 1760 and 1850, it probes the survival and rebirth of occult practice in the heretofore neglected period between the eighteenth-century Enlightenment and the rise of spiritualism after 1848. The essay also offers a model for understanding relationships between occult religious practice and mainstream denominationalism in America. Although occult practice may indeed be an "excursus religion," as Robert Ellwood argues, it may not be quite the "alternative religion" it seems. For whites it usually developed out of a strong commitment to Christianity, while for blacks it originated in African sources and sustained and reinforced both Christianity and existing Afro-American culture. Finally, in answer to the criticism that the discovery of occult practice in American religious history may be interesting but not significant, the essay suggests quite the opposite. The origins of occult activity speak directly to the issue of international influence in American religious development, and the range of occult practice, coupled with the remarkable lack of communication among different forms of occult practice and their practitioners, speaks directly to the problem of class and race as barriers to the development of a homogeneous American religious system in antebellum society.[2]

Until now scholars have concentrated on three major periods in the evolution of occult practice in America. I have described the earliest period in "Magic, Astrology, and the Early American Religious Heritage, 1600–1760," in the *American Historical Review,* 84 (1979). This period was distinguished by the appearance, then decay, of alchemy, Rosicrucianism, and Christian Cabalism among English intellectuals and German Christian mystics and pietists and by the importation of occult folk practices by European migrants in the seventeenth and eighteenth centuries. A second period that has interested scholars encompasses the origins and development of American spiritualism between 1848 and 1900. The third concerns the influence of "Eastern" ideas, especially Buddhism and Hinduism, on American religion, especially after 1880.

All of these studies neglect the century between 1760 and 1848. In those ninety years slaves in mainland America collectively utilized African occult beliefs for the first time; lower-class and illiterate Americans sustained occult practices imported earlier or had them reinforced by newly arriving European migrants; and literate middle-class and upper-class whites, most of whom already were adherents of mainstream Christian groups, exhibited significant interest in Swedenborgian ideas, then flocked to hear spiritualist lecturers and consult occult mediums in the wake of the Fox sisters' "toe rappings" of 1848.

Beginning our discussion with the rise of occult practice among American blacks may seem peculiar. Like certain other subjects— Catholicism, Judaism, occultism itself—a description of religion among

American blacks traditionally follows descriptions of religion among American whites as an appendage. But, in a study of American occultism, real benefits derive from beginning with the origins of black occult practice in America. It is the one place where historians have always acknowledged the presence of occult practice without hesitation. It takes us to the heart of a major problem concerning relationships among religious belief, religious practice, and the social process. And it touches the critical issue of relationships between occult and Christian practice in American society.

If we wanted to uncover occult practice anywhere in America between the French and Indian War and the Civil War, the most obvious place to look would be among American blacks, both slave and free. All the available literature documents the presence of occult practices so thoroughly that here we can only describe its range in slave society. John Blassingame describes how slaves feared witches and sorcerers not only because they believed in such things but because such persons existed on numerous plantations. W. E. B. DuBois places the conjurer at the center of a healthy black culture because of his importance in maintaining healthy slave bodies. It was the conjurer, DuBois wrote, who "early appeared on the plantation and found his function as the healer of the sick, the interpreter of the unknown, the comforter of the sorrowing, the supernatural avenger of wrong, and the one who rudely, but picturesquely, expressed the longing, disappointment and resentment of a stolen and oppressed people." Slave cemeteries dating from the early nineteenth century contain visual evidence of African occult practices, and slave narratives contain innumerable references to voodoo, use of amulets to ward off disease, and resort to conjurers to settle slave disputes. Black occult medical practitioners ministered to both whites and blacks—one of many testaments to the complex and ambivalent relationships of Afro-American culture to white society and white persons and to the delicate and sophisticated role black occult practitioners played in sustaining that culture. And, of course, these practitioners survived slavery. Gilbert Osofsky described Harlem in the 1920s as abounding in " 'spiritualists,' 'herb doctors,' 'African medicine men,' 'Indian doctors,' 'dispensers of snake oils,' 'layers-on-of hands,' 'faith healers,' 'palmists,' and phrenologists who performed a twentieth-century brand of necromancy there"—and stressed that these practitioners proffered crafts that were well rooted in the slave and African past.[3]

But when and under what circumstances did black occult practice first emerge in America? In 1972, Gerald Mullin argued that historians have so frequently treated slavery as a static topic that they have lost sight of the way it changed between 1619 and 1865. The problem is especially important in the study of slave religion. As we have seen already, historians have long acknowledged that black occultism was important in sustaining the Afro-American subculture of antebellum America. But only the most paternalistic historian would assume that religion and religious practice among American blacks remained constant and unchanging for 250 years despite the monumental changes that altered slavery in those same years. Among whites, mainstream Protestantism shifted from Puritanism in the seventeenth century to evangelicalism and deism in the eighteenth century and encompassed Unitarianism, revivalism, and transcendentalism in the nineteenth century. What changed in black religious practice? An answer will tell us when significant occult practice first surfaced among black slaves in the colonies and will point up important constraints that social conditions placed on slave religious practice before the Revolution.[4]

Historians usually discuss the origins of black occultism in the context of African survivals. Blassingame states simply that the "strength and longevity of conjurism and voodooism among the blacks illustrate clearly the African element in their culture" and quotes DuBois, describing the plantation "medicine man" as the major "remaining institution" of African culture in American slavery. Similarly, although Genovese dismisses the argument about African survivals as unsolvable, he too argues forcefully that the "spiritual experience of the slaves took place as part of a tradition emanating from Africa."[5]

But when? Did African religion survive from the very beginning of slavery in the seventeenth century to prosper in the nineteenth? Or might religion among Africans enslaved in America have changed across the centuries, perhaps in remarkable ways, as we would assume would have been true among other peoples in parallel circumstances? More specifically, is it possible that black occultism receded and then re-emerged at certain specific points in the evolution of American slavery?

These queries can be answered affirmatively through a simple two-part model of emerging occult religious practice among African slaves in America. This model suggests, first, that the collective practice of either African or Christian religious rites emerged only after family life and kinship systems developed among surviving slaves. This would date the emergence of a collective religious life for most mainland colony slaves at about 1760, although regional variations in the evolution of

family and kinship systems might place the date as early as the 1730s
and 1740s in places like the Chesapeake. Second, the model suggests
that African occultism usually reinforced rather than contradicted
Christian practice and that Christianization also helped sustain some
African beliefs and practices. This happened because the social functions of each were virtually identical—the fostering of a slave subculture in America.[6]

It is dangerous to argue that American slaves failed to sustain a collective religious life in the colonies before the 1760s. Most anthropologists, sociologists, and philosophers agree that religion is inherent in
mankind, and historians and anthropologists alike traditionally stress
the especially religious character of West African culture (although this
analysis sometimes bears a paternalistic conviction that it is true because these people were primitive and African). Moreover, Genovese
correctly points out that "little is known about the religious beliefs of
the slaves during the seventeenth century or most of the eighteenth century." Therefore, it may be impossible to demonstrate the absence or
weakness of black religious practice because insufficient evidence exists
to point up its strength.[7]

True, we lack much information about many aspects of slave life in
pre-Revolutionary America. Allan Kulikoff's unique work on emerging
black culture in the Chesapeake between 1680 and 1760 resulted from
the most arduous combing of disparate evidence, and Ira Berlin's persuasive model of emerging black culture in the different regions of the
colonies acknowledges the numerous gaps in our perception of early
slave life. Nonetheless, we have come to know remarkable things about
secular life among the early slaves in the past fifteen years. Kulikoff,
Berlin, and others have uncovered the shape of slave imports (negligi-
ble before 1680, extremely heavy between 1680 and 1750), sex ratios
and age distributions (most captives were young adult males), chances
for survival (slim before 1740), and African origins (from diverse cultures, but with a bias toward the area of modern Angola). Contemporary letters of white missionaries and catechists like New York City's
Elie Neau and Francis LeJau and Robert Maule of South Carolina, and
the diaries of slaveowners like the Byrds and Carters of Virginia, reveal
much of the texture of slave life between 1680 and 1760—work habits,
field banter, dress, marriage, sexual practices, and language. In the
North Daniel Horsmanden's *The New-York Conspiracy, or a History
of the Negro Plot with the Journal of the Proceedings against the Conspirators at New-York in the Years 1741–2* (New York, 1744) opens
important vistas on slave labor, slave hatred of merchant owners, daily

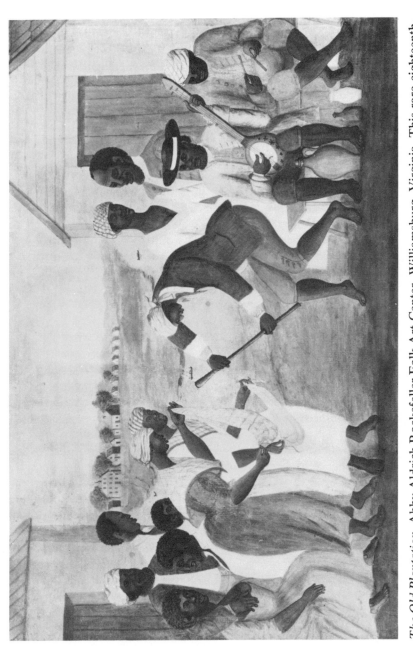

The Old Plantation. Abby Aldrich Rockefeller Folk Art Center, Williamsburg, Virginia. This rare eighteenth-century watercolor illustrates the revival of collective ritual activity among mainland colony slaves after about 1750.

social interchange, slave leisure, and interracial sex in a colony where slave ownership was surprisingly common before 1750.[8]

Yet none of these works reveals much about slave religious practice before 1760. The lack of reference to any Christian practice among them is easy to understand. Marcus W. Jernegan argued in 1916 that slave Christianization did not advance significantly until well after 1760, and Albert J. Raboteau has confirmed this judgment in his recently published *Slave Religion: The "Invisible Institution" in the Antebellum South*.[9]

Does this mean that black slaves in America turned automatically to African religious practices before 1760? Although the argument never has been spelled out fully, not even in Raboteau's recent work, some evidence exists to suggest that this might be true. Blacks planning New York City's 1712 slave revolt allegedly received powder from a free black sorcerer which they believed would make them invulnerable to white weapons when spread on their clothing. The conspirators also allegedly sucked blood from one another's arms to forge a ritual bond among themselves. In South Carolina a white planter complained of "rites and revels" among his slaves, most of whom were recent African imports, and everywhere colonists referred to the growing number of slaves in their midst as heathens and pagans.[10]

Yet English colonists proved exceptionally vague when they described slave religious practices. Gossipy white planters, such as William Byrd II and Landon Carter, chattered on endlessly about nearly all aspects of their slaves' lives except religion, a subject on which they said surprisingly little. When they did make such observations, they seldom mouthed anything except the abstract Christian formulas about paganism and heathenism they learned from their parish clergymen and the widely circulated Anglican tracts on slave Christianization. Other evidence of the collective practice of African ritual in the early eighteenth-century mainland colonies is equally slim. Aside from the 1712 slave rebellion in New York City, no other colonial slave rebellion before 1760 appears to have had religious roots. Indeed, in the 1712 New York City rebellion our knowledge of sorcerers and African ritual actually comes from only one private letter, that of an English military chaplain at Fort George; most New Yorkers appear to have given the subject little thought despite its obvious ramifications. South Carolinians traced the 1739 Stono Rebellion to the simple and obvious secular discontent of the colony's slaves, while New Yorkers laid the alleged plot for a slave rebellion they uncovered in 1742 on French Catholic agitators in Canada rather than on African sorcerers living and working in the city.[11]

In contrast, the great nineteenth-century slave rebellions led by Nat Turner and Denmark Vesey took deep root in black messianic Christianity. And, as Michael Mullin observes, Gabriel Prosser might have succeeded in his 1800 revolt in Virginia had he accepted the support tendered by black occultists working in the slave quarters. Yet the most famous link between blacks and colonial witchcraft is a fraudulent one. Chadwick Hansen has demonstrated that the infamous Tituba, the "black" slave who inducted the daughter and niece of the Reverend Samuel Parris into the occult world and thereby precipitated the Salem witchcraft episode of 1692, actually was a West Indian native and not an African slave. Historians and literary scholars long ignored Tituba's true identity because her behavior so conveniently fit the nineteenth- and twentieth-century stereotypes about Africans they themselves imbibed and even enhanced.[12]

Does this mean that America's slaves lacked religion before 1760? Genovese has suggested that the view is absurd and he may well be right. The question, however, is not whether Africans in America were religious but what kind of religious practices they followed at particular points in their social development. Here it is important to discriminate between the private practice of religion by individuals and collective religious practice involving large numbers of persons pursuing common religious goals. Prior to the formation of family systems and kinship networks by Africans in America, slaves in the colonies may indeed have retained the individual religious beliefs they had formed earlier in Africa. Charles Ball recalled in his slave narrative *Fifty Years in Chains* that his eighty-year-old Maryland grandfather "retained his native traditions respecting the Deity and hereafter." He also kept these traditions to himself, in part because "he was an African of rank in his native land" who only "expressed contempt for his fellow slaves." In this case, then, African social tensions probably constrained both the individual and collective practice of religion in America. Other slaves, especially newly arrived Africans, honored their native religious heritage in a way that precluded future religious practice of any kind. They committed suicide shortly after their capture or arrival in America. Although their numbers were not large, their torment expressed the anguish of their capture and symbolized the helplessness and anomie experienced by thousands of other Africans who continued to live on in America.[13]

This helplessness and anomie also suppressed the collective practice of religion among early slaves in the mainland colonies. The religious systems of both seventeenth-century Africa and Europe survived best in stable social settings. But the holocaust of slavery's first century in America destroyed the foundations of collective religious practice among slaves. The devastating "middle passage" from Old World to New, the prospect of early death in America, the humiliation and resulting anomie produced by the introduction to slavery, and the reality of limited population reproduction in a heavily male-dominated society all took their toll among the early slaves. These conditions were useful to whites in helping to establish slavery in the colonies. But they helped quash the practice of group religion among Africans in America before 1760. Thus, contrary to much theorizing about how traumatic experiences increase religious commitment, the devastation of early slavery appears to have turned its captives away from the collective practice of religion irrespective of its African or European substance.[14]

It is not surprising, then, to notice that the first significant evidence of collective African religious practice among American slaves occurs simultaneously with the first notices of significant slave Christianization after 1760. This happened for two important reasons. First, after about 1740 in the Chesapeake—Virginia and Maryland—or about 1760 in the Carolinas and Georgia, the development of kinship and family systems that was made possible by declining slave mortality, accelerating normalization of the slave sex ratio, and the resulting increase of marriages and children finally made the collective practice of religion meaningful for Africans in America. For the first time they had families to raise, children to teach, and old and new cultural inheritances to transmit. It was in this setting of relative personal and cultural optimism (despite the still important brutalities of slavery) that collective religious practice of any kind first emerged in a significant way among mainland colony slaves.[15]

In this context, African occultism surfaced for the first time on a sustained scale because the continuing importation of Africans as slaves after 1760 brought fresh knowledge of such practices into a population increasingly able to make use of them. Thus the problem of black occultism in America is not so much one of African "survivals," as Melville Herskovits phrased it, as one of importations into a newly receptive setting. Whether dealing with the Virginia runaway of 1745 who had "Scars on his Temples, being the Marks of his Country," and who pretended to cure diseases through African rituals, or the Angolan-born conjurer named Jack Pritchard whom Lawrence Levine describes as having used African rituals to instill courage in Denmark Vesey's conspirators, newly imported Africans who settled in places with relatively well-developed family and kinship systems extended the collective practice of African occultism and rituals to many American slaves who had lost contact with, and perhaps even knowledge of, such traditions. Unfortunately, we know virtually nothing about the rise and fall of particular tribal religious practices in different regions of America at different times. But just as white religious practices changed in America as the population changed—witness the shifts in the religious configuration of eighteenth-century Pennsylvania—so too the configuration of occult practices among Africans in America must have shifted as the composition of the slave population changed between 1619 and 1865.[16]

Paradoxically, the African and Christian religious practices that emerged simultaneously among American slaves after 1760 frequently reinforced each other. The origins and social functions of African occultism made it neither an "excursus religion" nor an "alternative altar" for American slaves. From the perspective of the black laity, the consumers of the religion, if not from the perspective of black or white Christian ministers, African occultism and Christianity provided strikingly similar solutions to crucial slave problems. As Genovese, Levine, Blassingame, and Raboteau have argued, important parallels drew African occultism and Christianity together. As Lawrence Levine writes, "conjurers could be pictured as exotic Old Testament type prophets or magicians . . . [who] at their most powerful . . . commanded great respect from everyone." Since both African occultism and black Christianity also functioned to develop Afro-American culture after 1760—even if neither had been important in creating the family and kinship systems that anchored the culture—the emergence of African occultism after 1760 occurred in a remarkably even and natural way that quite belied its later reputation as something dark, hidden, and secret.[17]

The emergence of African occultism in America provides an important model for understanding important aspects of the maintenance and resurgence of occultism among whites in America between 1760 and 1848. Although I have elsewhere argued that occult practices declined in America after about 1720, a reconsideration suggests that this decline occurred only in certain kinds of occult belief and practice. Alchemy and Rosicrucianism clearly subsided among literate middle- and upper-class Americans in the eighteenth century. But between 1760 and 1865 occult practice survived in more obscure recesses of the American scene and after the Revolution attracted new attention from middle- and upper-class Americans.

After 1760 occult views and practices persisted in several forms among lower-class whites. Many of these views centered on witches and witchcraft. Evidence of their survival abounds in American folklore material used by scholars since the nineteenth century. The leading modern American folklorist, Richard Dorson, has documented witchcraft beliefs in the antebellum period nearly everywhere, including New England, New York, Pennsylvania, the South, and even the West. Evidence of actual witchcraft practice, however, is more difficult to locate. In a study of lower-class social life in Revolutionary Philadelphia, Stephen Rosswurm has uncovered several occurrences that at least point toward possible witchcraft practice in the city. In 1765 the author of an anonymous broadside protesting the Stamp Act placed a "hex" on the Philadelphia commissioner handling the stamps that condemned him to endure rheumatism, pox, and gout if he continued to distribute them. Revolutionary Philadelphia also witnessed several extralegal demonstrations against reputed witches. One such incident allegedly occurred in late June or early July of 1776 and involved the stoning of a woman believed to have practiced witchcraft. Another puts the date of the last known death due to a witchcraft accusation, if not legal execution, in 1787 rather than 1692. In July, 1787, two Philadelphia newspapers reported that a mob carried an accused witch through the city's streets as residents jeered and pelted her with stones, after which she reportedly died.[18]

Astrological beliefs survived more erratically. On the one hand, considerable astrological information still appeared in numerous almanacs published in major American cities throughout the late eighteenth and early nineteenth centuries. Some still included the "anatomy," the figure of a naked man surrounded by the astrological signs that allegedly controlled various body parts and organs. On the other hand, it is extraordinarily difficult to locate astrologers in post-Revolutionary America. The nature and low status of their work together with the social pretensions of city directories, from which most of our knowledge of urban occupations derives, makes discovering astrologers more difficult than finding needles in haystacks. After 1848 American novelists often mentioned fortune tellers and other "mediums" who had practiced earlier in the century. The mammoth modern Philadelphia Social History Project, which has unraveled much of the history of common people in Philadelphia between 1850 and 1870, has located a black astrologer in the

1850 census records. But whether the literary references or notice of the black astrologer in Philadelphia point to the frequent existence of other astrologers earlier in the century simply awaits the verdict of future research.[19]

The divining rod was an occult tool that probably came to America through eighteenth-century German migration and was found in all regions of the new nation by the 1790s. Americans used it in a surprising number of ways—to detect the presence of underground water (when its use was called "dowsing" or "water witching") and to locate any object of value, especially metal ore and buried treasure. Its widespread appearance is especially significant because it underscores the complexity of different levels of belief and practice regarding the occult in late eighteenth- and early nineteenth-century America. Americans who utilized divining rods came from all social classes, but most practitioners who performed the feat appear to have come from the lower end of the economic and social scale. A similar pattern appeared in American folk medicine. For example, upper-class southern whites often utilized herbal medicine and conjuring to cure diseases. But they received these "medicines" from slaves and lower-class whites acting as herb doctors and conjurers. Did the clients really believe that their diseases were cured by magic and conjuring? Or did they accept the cures and reject the magic while remaining indifferent to the beliefs of the practitioners? The answer probably is not as obvious as a cynic might suggest.[20]

Folk medicine became the most important depository of occult activity among whites in post-Revolutionary America. As among black slaves, white Americans endured erratic and still dangerous "professional" medical practices before the Civil War and frequently turned to occult remedies to cure sickness and heal injuries. A 1784 manuscript, the Joshua Gordon "witchcraft book," now located at the South Caroliniana Library at the University of South Carolina, is an important link to occult medical practices among white English settlers in the post-Revolutionary South. Its curing recipes invoked sympathetic magic that used animal feces, urine, and plants to cure sores and rheumatism in humans, sickness in cattle, and the effects of evil spells, including witchcraft, in both. Abundant evidence of additional popular occult cures exists for early nineteenth-century America. In both New England and the southern states folklorists have uncovered numerous examples of "witch doctors" before the Civil War among Americans of English extraction who utilized sympathetic magic and spells to cure diseases and heal afflictions.[21]

Some forms of occult folk medicine continued to come to whites in America through continental European sources. Gerald Strauss and E. William Monter have recorded the persistence of these occult traditions in Europe from the sixteenth through the late eighteenth centuries. In America, Pennsylvanians proved especially receptive to such traditions. Before the Revolution astrological medicine flourished at the Ephrata settlement of German Seventh Day Baptists near Lancaster, while other healers were trained by Christopher Witt in Philadelphia. Witt learned his craft sometime between 1695 and 1710 at Johannes Kelpius's mystical-Rosicrucian settlement along the Wissahickon River outside Philadelphia.[22]

The nineteenth-century German migration to Pennsylvania reinforced the occult practices of the colonial period. Collections of occult remedies for diseases, afflictions, and injuries circulated in both manuscript and printed versions. The latter included *Das Sechste und Siebente Buch Mosis—The Sixth and Seventh Book of Moses*—and several "powow" books that combined occult cures derived from Europe with others reputedly taken from American Indian sources, although the last claim is virtually impossible to verify. Individual occult practitioners are more difficult to identify. Two students of Christopher Witt—a man named Fraily and another named Anthony Larry—practiced their arts in and around Philadelphia past the Revolution and perhaps past the presidency of Thomas Jefferson, while two other Germans, George Dresher and Paul Heym, apparently practiced in the countryside. Again, tracking occult healers and practitioners through the 1850s is extremely difficult, but the Philadelphia Social History Project has uncovered several occult healers in the 1850 and 1860 federal censuses of Philadelphia. The project's census sample includes all German, Irish, and black males but only one-sixth of other white males, which makes it difficult to find "underground" occupations such as occult healers. Still, the sample makes it clear that occult practitioners crossed national and racial boundaries. The 1850 census yields three German "healers" and the black astrologer mentioned earlier, while the 1860 census includes one black "phrenologist," three black herb doctors, and one American Indian "phrenologist"—although just what the census takers meant by the term "phrenologist" is not clear.[23]

More sophisticated forms of occult belief survived among a few middle- and upper-class Americans despite the impact of the Enlightenment. No significant occult literature was printed in eighteenth-century England or America. Although Herbert Leventhal has demonstrated that Yale's Ezra Stiles took intense interest in alchemy and Christian

Cabalism, Stiles isolated these notions in his manuscript notebooks and said little about them publicly. The German or Dutch surveyor and naturalist John William Gerar De Brahm became surveyor general for the southern colonies in 1764. In addition to his surveying reports, De Brahm published four Christian mystical works that hint at alchemical beliefs and worked continuously between 1743 and his death in 1799 on a manuscript with more obvious alchemical biases that he never published. But whether even a few Americans were influenced by De Brahm's works never has been determined. Nor has the American Masonic movement been studied for its occult significance rather than for its more innocent fraternal qualities. In Europe the works of Frances Yates demonstrate its alchemical and Rosicrucian roots. Yet how many American Masons understood and approved these links with the occult remains a fascinating but unexplored topic.[24]

The Swedenborgian movement and its influence are much better understood. Although Swedenborgian proselytizers were in America by 1784, the movement never won a large popular following. Yet the presence of at least one Swedenborgian congregation in all the major American cities and the movement's surprising strength in New England point up important features of the occult renaissance in post-Revolutionary America. As among African slaves, these notions frequently were imported, in this case from Sweden. This probably accounted for Swedenborgianism's failure to win a massive popular following in America. But it also brought Swedenborgianism to the attention of the American aristocratic elite before and after the Revolution. Robert "Councillor" Carter, the Fairfaxes of Virginia, and members of Philadelphia's literary and scientific elite first learned of Swedenborg through Enlightenment connections that drew them to his scientific and technical writings, then to his religious works. As a result, occult notions appeared again in the ranks of college-educated Americans for the first time since Rosicrucian and alchemical interests declined among colonists after about 1680.[25]

Mesmerism performed similar crucial functions for a somewhat different audience. Mesmerism presented itself as a "scientific" rather than occult body of knowledge, and occultists, like the Swedenborgians, bitterly rejected its claims to truth. But these abstract differences were unimportant to many lay persons. For example, American Swedenborgian congregations frequently disciplined members who participated in mesmerist experiments and who acknowledged belief in mesmerist principles. In turn, some Americans came to Swedenborgianism through mesmerism. Whatever grief this confusion brought Swedenborgian

leaders (mesmerists seem to have been unbothered by the confusion),
it was important in a small way to the maintenance and resurgence of
occult notions in America. Like Swedenborgianism, mesmerism won its
following in the American literate middle and upper classes, not among
the poor. It thus further reinforced the visibility of occult beliefs and
spawned other scientific-occult movements—homeopathy, phrenology,
and phalanstery—among the important American middle-class elite.[26]

Thus when the Fox sisters stepped onto the lecture stage, many of the
Americans to whom they spoke were well prepared to accept the legitimacy of occult beliefs. The history of earlier occult religious practices,
however, by no means explains the rise of spiritualism after 1848.
Spiritualism's popularity, evident in the purchase of spiritualist literature and attendance at spiritualist demonstrations, easily surpassed that
of occult beliefs in earlier decades. It may have been rooted in secular
problems, such as the persistence of political and social divisions in
America despite the fervor of Jacksonian reform. Spiritualism also
testified, however, to the persistence of important themes that characterized American occultism in the previous century.

Again, spiritualism bore an international flavor. Although most historians emphasize its uniquely American character, spiritualist periodicals like the *Shekinah* and the *Spiritual Telegraph* eagerly reprinted
articles from continental Europe about spiritualist demonstrations
abroad. Thus the *Spiritual Telegraph* entitled a letter on foreign spiritualist activity in 1858 "The Ocean, a Spiritual Teacher." In the 1850s
American spiritualists also colonized in Europe. They frequently toured
England to help the still infant spiritualist movement there and arranged
to have their works reprinted by English publishers.[27]

American spiritualism also remained within the broad Christian religious spectrum. It was not a self-consciously "alternative" religion
like the nontraditional Eastern and "Zen" movements of twentieth-
century America. True, mainstream Protestant clergymen bitterly opposed spiritualism. They ejected spiritualists from their congregations,
conducted active lecture campaigns against the movement, and attempted to secure state legislation prohibiting spiritualist activities. But
the laity and some ministers who joined the movement saw it as an
extension of Christianity. Episcopal, Presbyterian, and Methodist lay-
persons adopted spiritualist views because they believed spiritualism
represented the most perfect expression of Christianity yet revealed. It
was no accident that a portrait of Jesus served as the frontispiece to
the first volume of the *Shekinah* in 1852 and that it and other spiritualist
periodicals frequently printed articles on figures like Jacob Boehme,

Spirit Voices.

Words and Music written expressly for the Shekinah.

Words by C. D. STUART.

Music by V. C. TAYLOR.

"Spirit Voices." A spiritualist hymn from *The Shekinah* (1853).

George Fox, and Emanuel Swedenborg, who, they claimed, were the forerunners of spiritualism. Here nineteenth-century American spiritualism reasserted the familiar seventeenth- and eighteenth-century occultist claim that the receipt of their previously secret knowledge would lead to the creation of a true and perfect Christian society. In doing so they denied, in the most obvious way, the charge that they had adopted an "occult" religion.[28]

Finally, the rise and growth of American spiritualism after 1848 again demonstrates the importance of class and race as barriers to the development of a homogeneous religious culture in antebellum America. Certainly spiritualism was a national phenomenon. Spiritualist lecturers drew enormous audiences in America's rapidly expanding cities. Spiritualists found eager followers in small-town America as well. In 1853 Warren Chase, a midwestern spiritualist lecturer, reported in the *Spiritual Telegraph* that in Wisconsin, Lake Mills could claim a medium named Augustus A. Ballow; that Waterloo contained two mediums, one "Psycologic," the other a "healing" medium; and that Watertown could also claim two mediums, a "writing" medium and one with no specialty.[29]

But spiritualism never transcended the lines of class and race as it spread across the country. At least in its early years it remained a white, mostly Anglo-Saxon, middle- and upper-class movement of ex-mainstream Protestants. No working relationship ever developed between white spiritualists and black occultists until spiritualism lost favor among prominent whites. This separation is illustrated in the career of Thomas Wentworth Higginson, the literary critic and Unitarian minister who became a spiritualist in the 1850s. Higginson was a committed abolitionist who commanded a black regiment for the Union Army. He wrote a remarkable account of its members and became an important collector of black spirituals. Yet neither Higginson's *Army Life in a Black Regiment* nor his later published defenses of spiritualism evidenced the slightest knowledge of, or concern for, black occultism. Not even Higginson seemed to believe that unlocking occultism's universal foundations might advance American racial equality.[30]

By the 1850s, then, American occultism emerged as a remarkable mirror of American society. Occult practices existed in all the major regions of the country and in all social classes, and had reclaimed at least some of the territory lost in the eighteenth century. Yet their ubiquity also testified to the layered quality of antebellum American society. Occult practices remained stationary and unmoving in their different social strata. Black and white, rich and poor, literate and illiterate, Americans of all kinds adopted occult beliefs and practices in the half-century before the arrival of the Fox sisters. But these beliefs and practices remained severely restricted by class and race. Little in the way of practice or intellectual content seeped through from one layer to the next, and the history of occult practice within each class and race remained essentially separate and unique even while sharing certain parallel features, such as international origins. In this regard, then, American occultism was not nearly esoteric enough to have improved the racial and social integration of American society between 1760 and 1848.

The author wishes to thank Elisabeth Lightbourn of the Philadelphia Social History Project for her help in uncovering references to occult healers in the Philadelphia censuses of 1850 and 1860, and Stephen Rosswurm of Lake Forest College for furnishing references to alleged witchcraft episodes in late eighteenth-century Philadelphia.

NOTES

1. Robert S. Ellwood, Jr., *Alternative Altars: Unconventional and Eastern Spirituality in America* (Chicago: University of Chicago Press, 1979); R. Laurence Moore, *In Search of White Crows: Spiritualism, Parapsychology, and American Culture* (New York: Oxford University Press, 1977); Howard Kerr, *Mediums, and Spirit-Rappers, and Roaring Radicals: Spiritualism in American Literature, 1850–1900* (Urbana: University of Illinois Press, 1972); Keith Thomas, *Religion and the Decline of Magic* (New York: Scribner's, 1971); Frances Yates, *The Occult Philosophy in the Elizabethan Age* (London: Routledge & Kegan Paul, 1979). Other important works include Herbert Leventhal, *In the Shadow of the Enlightenment: Occultism and Renaissance Science in Eighteenth-Century America* (New York: New York University Press, 1976); Russell M. Goldfarb and Clare R. Goldfarb, *Spiritualism and Nineteenth-Century Letters* (Rutherford, N.J.: Fairleigh Dickinson University Press, 1978); Irving I. Zaretsky and Mark P. Leone, eds., *Religious Movements in Contemporary America* (Princeton, N.J.: Princeton University Press, 1974). See also the relevant sections of Eugene D. Genovese, *Roll, Jordan, Roll: The World the Slaves Made* (New York: Pantheon Books, 1974), and Lawrence W. Levine, *Black Culture and Black Consciousness: Afro-American Folk Thought from Slavery to Freedom* (New York: Oxford University Press, 1977). On occultism and popular religion, see Jon Butler, "The People's Faith in Europe and America," *Journal of Social History*, 12 (1978–79): 159–67.

2. Ellwood, *Alternative Altars*, pp. 1–15. For recent sniping at occult studies, see Raymond J. Cunningham's review of Goldfarb and Goldfarb, *Spiritualism and Nineteenth-Century American Letters*, in *Journal of American History*, 66 (1979–80): 139–40. Cunningham writes, "One is tempted

to suggest that perhaps spiritualism had no great significance for Anglo-American letters," then remarks that while the Goldfarbs fail to show that spiritualism "really matters very much," the subject nonetheless might "merit closer attention than it has yet received."

3. John W. Blassingame, *The Slave Community: Plantation Life in the Ante-bellum South* (New York: Oxford University Press, 1972), pp. 32–40; Genovese, *Roll, Jordan, Roll*, pp. 209–32; Gilbert Osofsky, *Harlem: The Making of a Ghetto: Negro New York, 1890–1930* (New York: Harper and Row, 1966), pp. 143–44.

4. Gerald W. Mullin, *Flight and Rebellion: Slave Resistance in Eighteenth-Century Virginia* (New York: Oxford University Press, 1972), pp. ix–xi. This static view of black religion under slavery permeates the works by Genovese and Levine, although each acknowledges that there must have been some change between the colonial and national periods, and even characterizes the recent work by Albert J. Raboteau, *Slave Religion: The "Invisible Institution" in the Antebellum South* (New York: Oxford University Press, 1979).

5. Blassingame, *Slave Community*, pp. 32–33; Genovese, *Roll, Jordan, Roll*, p. 210.

6. One important exception to this model exists in New England. There the small number of slaves and their thorough dispersion in small units among widely scattered white families did produce some significant conversions to Christianity before 1760.

7. For a brief discussion of the problem of defining religion in its historical context with regard to occultism, see Butler, "Magic, Astrology, and the Early American Religious Heritage, 1600–1760," *American Historical Review*, 84 (1979):318–19. Eugene Genovese's superb discussion, "Slave Religion in Hemispheric Perspective," in *Roll, Jordan, Roll*, pp. 168–83, also describes the most important literature on African religious systems.

8. Allan Kulikoff, "The Origins of Afro-American Society in Tidewater Maryland and Virginia, 1700 to 1790," *William and Mary Quarterly*, 3d ser., 35 (1978):229–54; Kulikoff, "A 'Prolifick' People: Black Population Growth in the Chesapeake Colonies, 1700–1790," *Southern Studies*, 16 (1977):391–414; Kulikoff, "The Beginnings of the Afro-American Family in Maryland," in Aubrey C. Land et al., eds., *Law, Society, and Politics in Early Maryland* (Baltimore: Johns Hopkins University Press, 1977), pp. 177–96; Ira Berlin, "Time, Space, and the Evolution of Afro-American Society on British Mainland North America," *American Historical Review*, 85 (1980): 44–78. Kulikoff's work offers the most sustained, detailed analysis of an emerging slave society yet achieved for the American colonies, and Berlin's synthesis is a superb guide to the available literature on pre-Revolutionary slavery.

9. Marcus W. Jernegan, "Slavery and Conversion in the American Colonies," *American Historical Review*, 21 (1916): 504–27; Luther P. Jackson, "Religious Development of the Negro in Virginia from 1760 to 1860," *Journal of Negro History*, 16 (1931): 168–239.

10. Kenneth Scott, "The Slave Insurrection in New York in 1712," *New-York Historical Society Quarterly*, 45 (1961): 43–74; Winthrop D. Jordan, *White over Black: American Attitudes toward the Negro 1550–1812*

(Chapel Hill: University of North Carolina Press, for the Institute of Early American History and Culture, 1968), pp. 20–24, 180–87.

11. The point regarding the lack of comment on slave religion before 1760 is difficult to establish because historians do not frequently utilize what could be called negative proofs. The letter of the Reverend John Sharpe to the Secretary, Society for the Propagation of the Gospel in Foreign Parts, June 23, 1712, is printed in "The Negro Plot of 1712," *New York Genealogical and Biographical Record,* 21 (1890): 162–63. See also Horsmanden, *New-York Conspiracy,* for comments on the 1742 revolt, and Peter H. Wood, *Black Majority: Negroes in Colonial South Carolina from 1670 through the Stono Rebellion* (New York: Alfred Knopf, 1974).

12. The best study of slave revolts is Eugene D. Genovese, *From Rebellion to Revolution: Afro-American Slave Revolts in the Making of the Modern World* (Baton Rouge: Louisiana State University Press, 1980). For the argument on Tituba, see Chadwick Hansen, "The Metamorphosis of Tituba, or Why American Intellectuals Can't Tell an Indian Witch from a Negro," *New England Quarterly,* 47 (1974): 3–12.

13. Charles Ball, *Fifty Years in Chains; or, the Life of an American Slave* (New York: H. Dayton, 1858), pp. 9, 15; William D. Piersen, "White Cannibals, Black Martyrs: Fear, Depression, and Religious Faith as Causes of Suicide among New Slaves," *Journal of Negro History,* 62 (1977): 147–59.

14. The problem of cultural devastation was first and most thoroughly explored in Stanley M. Elkins, *Slavery: A Problem in American Institutional and Intellectual Life* (New York: Grosset and Dunlap, 1963). Accepting Elkins's description of this destruction should not, however, obligate historians to accept his more controversial theory regarding the development of the Sambo personality type among black slaves.

15. These developments are best described in Kulikoff, "Origins of Afro-American Society," and Berlin, "Time, Space, and the Evolution of Afro-American Society."

16. Mullin, *Flight and Rebellion,* p. 40; Levine, *Black Culture and Black Consciousness,* p. 76. This analysis suggests, therefore, that the problem with Melville J. Herskovits's *The Myth of the Negro Past* (New York: Harper and Brothers, 1941) is not that it treated both an unsolvable and irrelevant problem, but that the research was not sufficiently sophisticated because it failed to trace changing "Africanisms" in America across time and space.

17. Levine, *Black Culture and Black Consciousness,* p. 74.

18. Leventhal, *In the Shadow of the Enlightenment,* pp. 77–78; Richard Dorson, *American Folklore* (Chicago: University of Chicago Press, 1977), pp. 35–38; Stephen Rosswurm, "Arms, Culture, and Class: The Philadelphia Militia and 'Lower Orders' in the American Revolution, 1765–1783" (Ph.D. diss., Northern Illinois University, 1979), pp. 46, 48.

19. For a guide to the presence of astrological materials in almanacs in the later colonial period, see Marion B. Stowell, *Early American Almanacs: The Colonial Weekday Bible* (New York: B. Franklin, 1977), and Samuel Briggs, *The Essays, Humor, and Poems of Nathaniel Ames, Father and Son, of Dedham, Massachusetts . . .* (Cleveland, 1891).

20. Leventhal, *In the Shadow of the Enlightenment*, pp. 112–18; Evon Z. Vogt and Ray Hyman, *Water Witching U.S.A.* (Chicago: University of Chicago Press, 1959), pp. 12–22.

21. The Gordon "witchcraft book" is discussed in Butler, "Magic, Astrology, and the Early American Religious Heritage." Information on occult cures can be found in numerous sources, among them Dorson, *American Folklore*, pp. 17–18; Tom Peete Cross, "Witchcraft in North Carolina," *Studies in Philology*, 16 (1919): 217–87; Virginia J. Lacy and David Harrell, eds., "Plain Home Remedies," *Tennessee Historical Quarterly*, 22 (1963): 259–65.

22. Gerald Strauss, *Luther's House of Learning: Indoctrination of the Young in the German Reformation* (Baltimore: Johns Hopkins University Press, 1978); E. William Monter, *Witchcraft in France and Switzerland: The Borderlands during the Reformation* (Ithaca, N.Y.: Cornell University Press, 1976); Leventhal, *In the Shadow of the Enlightenment*, pp. 37, 107–8.

23. Dorson, *American Folklore*, pp. 84–86; Leventhal, *In the Shadow of the Enlightenment*, pp. 37, 107–8; information from the Philadelphia Social History Project was kindly supplied by Elisabeth Lightbourn.

24. Leventhal, *In the Shadow of the Enlightenment*, pp. 129–31; S. Foster Damon, "De Brahm: Alchemist," *Ambix*, 24 (1977): 77–88.

25. Marguerite B. Block, *The New Church in the New World: A Study of Swedenborgianism in America* (New York: Henry Holt, 1932), pp. 73–111; Ellwood, *Alternative Altars*, pp. 84–89.

26. Robert Darnton, *Mesmerism and the End of the Enlightenment in France* (Cambridge, Mass.: Harvard University Press, 1968); Ellwood, *Alternative Altars*, pp. 91–92; Moore, *In Search of White Crows*, pp. 9, 15.

27. *Spiritual Telegraph*, 1 (1853): 19–20, 74–75, 91–95, 196–97, 206–7, 307–8, 367–72; 2 (1853): 23, 48–51, 60–64, 97–98, 106–7, 128–38, 180–81, 232–41, 376–81, 403–5, 426–28, 447–48, 466–67, 484–87, 490–92, 514. International aspects of spiritualism have not yet received further extensive study since the appearance of the surprisingly good work by Frank Podmore, *Modern Spiritualism: A History and a Criticism*, 2 vols. (London: Methuen, 1902).

28. *Spiritual Telegraph*, 2 (1853): 160–64, 346–47, 410–11; Moore, *In Search of White Crows*, pp. 40–64; *Shekinah*, 1 (1852): 105–19; 2 (1853): 49–59, 193–208.

29. For the Chase letters, see *Spiritual Telegraph*, 1 (1853): 249–51, 382–85, 423; 2 (1853): 57–58, 139–41.

30. The class orientation of the spiritualist movement is evident from the observations in both Kerr, *Mediums, and Spirit-Rappers, and Roaring Radicals*, and Moore, *In Search of White Crows*. On Higginson, see Tilden G. Edelstein, *Strange Enthusiasm: A Life of Thomas Wentworth Higginson* (New Haven, Conn.: Yale University Press, 1968), and Thomas Wentworth Higginson, *Army Life in a Black Regiment* ed. Howard Mumford Jones (East Lansing: Michigan State University Press, 1960). Edelstein and other Higginson scholars have had little to say about Higginson's spiritualism and its effect on his life and literary works.

4

The Fox Sisters
and American Spiritualism

ERNEST ISAACS

ON NOVEMBER 26, 1855, a perceptive New York man made an entry in his diary. "What would I have said six years ago to anybody who predicted that before the enlightened nineteenth century was ended hundreds of thousands of people in this country would believe themselves able to communicate with the ghosts of their grandfathers?" asked George Templeton Strong. Here were "ex-judges of the Supreme Court, senators, clergymen, professors of physical sciences, . . . lecturing and writing books" on the confusing and disturbing excitement called spiritualism. Not only these men, continued Strong, but people he saw every day, men and women who are "among the steadiest and most conservative of my acquaintance," acknowledged that they looked on the subject with distrust and dread, "as a visible manifestation of diabolic agency." It was "a momentous fact in history," he concluded, "throwing light on the intellectual calibre and moral tone of the age in which multitudes adopt it."[1]

The New York diarist was not alone in his wonder. Within less than a decade from its beginnings, the mysterious phenomenon of spirit communication had swept over the country and, in its American form, across the ocean to England and the Continent. Its opponents called it fraud, delusion, and demoniacal manifestation, which could bring only hardship, immorality, and suffering. Its proponents called it the basis for modern American spiritualism. Many of them found in it not only scientific proof of life everlasting but also the instrument for producing heaven on earth.[2]

Belief in disembodied spirits and their intervention in human affairs has existed in all cultures. The peculiarly American experience of spiritualism began during a time of rapid social and economic change, both as a response to that change and as a challenge to established patterns of thought. It arose in western New York, which had for a generation experienced emotional religious revivalism and evangelical fervor. The region was populated mainly by New Englanders, many of whom sought a better world both here and hereafter, giving their ardent support to an amazing variety of religious and reform movements. Spiritualists brought to their particular search for a new society a powerful combination of doubt and optimism, of dissatisfaction with the present and confident hope for the future. By proclaiming communication with spirits, they placed themselves outside the orthodoxies in religion. Once having challenged religious orthodoxies, it was a consequential step to reject orthodoxy in science, medicine, economics, and sex. In the process, they exaggerated the main tenets and tendencies of nineteenth-century romantic reform.

Spiritualist doctrines had popular appeal because they offered a clear explanation of the meaning of death and a guarantee of immortality and communication between the living and the dead. Spirit communication would provide the key to a new moral world. Although they drew from it selectively, those spiritualists who sought continuity with the occult tradition also sought to develop a philosophical explanation for the mysterious physical phenomena of spiritual communication. They based their theology, scientific and medical ideas, and social theory mainly on a synthesis of the cosmic systems of three European thinkers: Emanuel Swedenborg, Charles Fourier, and Franz Anton Mesmer.

Spiritualists functioned on two levels: the popular and practical in seances and demonstrations and on a more reflective, philosophical level in their lectures, newspapers, and books. The separation was symbolized by the difference between spirit rapping or materialization in darkened rooms and lectures on Harmonial Philosophy in brightly lighted halls. Those two levels were personified in the careers of the Fox sisters and Andrew Jackson Davis.

American spiritualists date the beginning of their religion as 1848, when Margaret and Kate Fox claimed to hear mysterious rappings. Margaret and Kate and their older sister, Leah, were mediums throughout their lives. Ironically, they never understood the social and religious movement popularly associated with their names nor did they understand their own trance experiences. The unhappy, even tragic lives of Margaret and Kate provide a revealing case study of the claims, investigations, and controversies surrounding nineteenth-century American spiritualism. The contrast between the Fox sisters and Andrew Jackson

Davis explains the uneasy coexistence of deception and comprehensive social analysis in the same movement.

From a background similar in circumstances to the Fox sisters—hard times, an alcoholic father, little schooling—Davis developed a clear understanding of himself and his society. Born in 1826, from the age of twelve he experienced spontaneous trances during which he had visions and heard voices. In 1843, working with a mesmerizer, he began a career of diagnosing disease. Under the guidance of radical Universalist ministers, between 1845 and 1847 he gave a series of fifty-seven lectures that he believed were dictated from the spirit world. The lectures were published in a two-volume work entitled *The Principles of Nature, Her Divine Revelations, and A Voice to Mankind, by and through Andrew Jackson Davis, the "Poughkeepsie Seer" and "Clairvoyant"* (1847). A derivative mixture of Swedenborgian cosmology and Fourierist socialism, it served as the first theoretical inspiration for American spiritualists. After the *Divine Revelations* Davis wrote more than thirty books. His work became increasingly less derivative and more analytical and thoughtful. His most ambitious project of the 1850s, five long volumes, reflected in conception and title his debt to Fourier's vision of earthly utopia. Davis called it *The Great Harmonia*. He insisted that to rid society of slavery, drunkenness, racial injustice, oppression, and war, it was necessary to reject the concept of sin and to insist that humans follow the harmonious principles of nature in order to reach the successively higher stages of development that were inherent in each individual. He celebrated "the grand truth of evolution." For the next fifty years he expanded on all of these topics.[3]

For example, in his writings and lectures on women's rights during the 1850s he insisted on the absolute equality of woman with man. "Woman has ever been the *pet* of man," he explained, "has ever been regarded tenderly and protected as a weak, defenceless, necessary associate—regarded as a useful, beautiful desirable creature." In all societies woman had been "subordinated to man's most limited spheres of interest, and the plaything of his leisure hours, when passion, and not reason, is most likely to sway the soul." Woman, he protested, had been made an angel by poets but ignored as an individual and a co-laborer; she had been made an object of the "most silly attentions from men," and viewed as a "true and tender" sister, helpful wife, affectionate mother, "extolled in history, and worshipped as the sky-born goddess of transcendent virtues." In all of these roles, said Davis, woman was oppressed. "*As a dependent and relative being . . .* woman is universally admired, worshipped, defended. But she is everywhere kept down by political injustice." He insisted on woman's right to vote and be a juror, on her physiological and medical rights, on her right to education and work. "Women must become physicians and members of college-classes," and woman's work must no longer be monopolized by man.[4]

The Fox sisters, like most other mediums, had as little understanding of Davis's social analysis as they did of their own mediumistic experiences. The popularity of spiritualism with millions of Americans was based less on the lectures and writings of Davis than on the phenomena of the seance—communications from the dead through rappings, table tippings, spirit writing, and materialization. For believers and critics alike, the Fox sisters were the founders and most famous seers of the new religion.

Margaret and Kate Fox were the last children of a couple who had been separated for over a decade because of drink. John Fox and his wife had had four other children before the break, and Margaret and Kate came after the partially reformed victim of alcohol had reunited with his wife. The four of them lived in an old frame house that stood in a cluster of similar dwellings known as Hydesville, town of Arcadia, Wayne County, New York. In it the rappings began.

On the night of March 28 Mrs. Fox got up, lit a candle, and walked from the room where they all slept to investigate knockings on the floor of the east bedroom. She could not discover the cause of the knockings that night or on succeeding nights as they grew louder. On the night of March 31 fifteen-year-old Margaret and her twelve-year-old sister, Kate, decided to sleep in the east bedroom. When the noises commenced, Kate began to imitate them by snapping her fingers. As fast as she snapped, the sounds followed in various parts of the dark room, making the same number of raps as the girl did. Then Margaret joined the game, saying, "Now do as I do. Count one, two, three, four. . . ." When the raps did, the girls called their mother. Mrs. Fox ran in, listened, and asked the raps to count to ten, and then to give the ages of her children. When the raps complied, she continued with a barrage of questions. "Are you an injured spirit?" Distinct rap! Mrs. Fox ran to get the neighbors. By this time, recalled Mrs. Fox, "The girls were sitting up in bed, somewhat terrified, and clinging to each other."

The whole experience left the Foxes distraught and the neighbors perplexed. Two weeks after the noises began, Mrs. Fox wrote, "I am sorry there has been so much excitement about it. It has been a very great deal of trouble to us. It is our misfortune to live here at this time." John Fox added a note of despair to his wife's complaint. "Hundreds have visited the house, so that it is impossible to attend to our daily occupations; and I hope, whether it be natural or super-natural, the means will be found out soon." William Duesler summed up the position of the neighbors by saying, "I never believed in haunted houses, or heard or saw anything but what I could account for before but this I cannot account for."[5]

By the middle of April the Fox house became so crowded with curious visitors that John Fox and his wife decided something must be done about it. Since the raps came most frequently when Kate was present, the neighbors began to refer to her as the "medium"—a term as much a part of the language of the traditional occult as the rappings were a part of its manifestations. Her parents decided to send her to Rochester to live with her widowed sister, Anne Leah Fish. But they were disappointed, for as soon as Kate left the sounds began in the presence of Margaret, who was then dispatched to live with her brother David in Auburn. Kate arrived in Rochester and moved into a new house with Leah. As the furniture was being carried in, the raps began. Day by day they increased in violence, disrupting Leah's music classes and forcing her pupils out of the house. Devout Methodist neighbors came to the house and, kneeling with Leah and Kate, prayed for the noises to cease. During the prayer the raps become more violent than ever.

Isaac Post, a Quaker and an old friend of the family, thought of an innovation that made communication between the questioners and the rap much easier. Instead of asking questions to be answered by a rap for the affirmative and silence for the negative, Post recited the alphabet and the spirits rapped for the appropriate letter. (Rapping the alphabet had long been used by those who had to communicate without articulating.) Within a year there would be throughout the region a standard procedure for eliciting spirit messages. The spirits would demand the alphabet by a series of sharp, quick raps, and the medium would begin the alphabet over and over again as the spirits rapped for the letter they desired.

During the spring and summer of 1848 hundreds of people—the curious, the hopeful, those with a will to believe—visited the house on Prospect Street in Rochester. By the early months of 1849 there were hundreds of people in western New York who believed in the spiritual nature of the rappings and other manifestations, and thousands of others throughout the nation ready to believe. But as yet there were only local newspaper accounts and stories spread by travelers. More important for the Fox sisters and the spread of the rappings than either the converts or the proliferation of manifestations was a newspaper editor, Eliab Wilkinson Capron, who arrived in Rochester in November, 1848, to investigate. Leah welcomed him cordially. Along with Isaac Post and others, Capron sat around a table with Leah and Kate. The visitors asked what had become standard test questions—their ages, names of their relatives, and the like—and the spirits answered satisfactorily.[6]

For over a year, according to Capron, the spirits urged the Fox sisters to submit to a public investigation of their spiritual powers. Early in November, 1849, while all three sisters were sitting at a table with Capron, Isaac Post, and George Willets, another ardent believer, the spirits became so insistent on the point that they threatened to leave if the investigation were not held. The spirits gave the girls twenty minutes to decide. They then rapped, "We now bid you farewell." At first the sisters were relieved, but after three or four days they began to miss the excitement and occasionally to break into tears. Visiting the Fox sisters a few days later, Capron and Willets asked if the spirits would rap for them, and "were greeted with a perfect shower of raps on the floor, the walls and the ceiling." Again the question of a public demonstration came up, with Capron and Willets asking the questions. The raps answered that Willets and Capron were the ones to bring the rappings before the public. "You have a duty to perform. We want you to make this matter more public." The raps urged that Capron and Willets should hire Corinthian Hall in Rochester, that Leah and Margaret should be on the platform, and that Capron should give a lecture on the first rappings at Hydesville and the progress of spiritual communication. Willets "should act as business man, door-keeper, &c." Both Capron and Willets objected to Corinthian Hall because it was the largest and most expensive in the city, but the raps answered that objection with a message to the men to charge 25 cents for admission.[7]

On the evening of November 14 nearly 400 people filed into Corinthian Hall. The audience heard the raps throughout the hall, listened to Capron's lecture, and at Capron's suggestion appointed a committee of five to investigate further—a practice that was to become standard for the next fifty years. Capron was triumphant. Not only were three committees unable to find any fraud connected with the Fox sisters, but each night the audience increased in size. The only thing that marred their triumph was a riot that climaxed the three performances. Josiah Bissell felt that the spirits were fraud and humbug combined with a desire by Capron and Willets to make money. Soon after the third meeting began, Bissell walked into the hall with torpedoes, which he distributed among the boys and young men. They acclaimed Bissell chairman of the meeting and exploded their torpedoes. The hall was in chaos as the rioting boys, led by respectable men, took over the meeting, "although others had hired the hall and paid for it," wrote Capron bitterly. "Finding that all attempts to explain the matter further were useless, we left the hall in possession of the rowdies and the police."[8]

Even the riot was not without value, for it caused the press to give more publicity to the meetings. The local papers ridiculed the idea of spiritual communication in general and Capron's meetings in particular, "but still in a way that aroused the curiosity of the people." Publicity was what Capron wanted. Together with Willets, he composed a long letter to Horace Greeley's *New York Weekly Tribune,* telling about the three meetings, the committee reports, and the wondrous nature of the "Singular Revelations" in western New York. This was the first detailed account of the rappings in a New York city newspaper, or in any newspaper with national circulation. It began a floodtide of articles and letters in the *Tribune,* and carried the story of the Hydesville rappings across the country.[9]

The response to the article by Capron and Willets in the *Weekly Tribune* was immediate, since spirits were part of the American tradition. People recalled spirits they had seen and stories they had heard. Greeley, who characterized himself in the phrenological terms then popular as a "person with a large organ of wonder," was one of the few New York editors to take the rappings seriously. Calling for scientific investigations, he editorialized, "We cannot regard with any other feeling than respect that natural instinct of the heart, which in one way or another affirms a world of spiritual existence at no impassible remove from our natural life; and we have little sympathy for such unscientific presumption as passes the verdict 'humbug' upon every fact it does not understand."[10]

In the early months of 1850 partisan publicists began to bring out histories of the western New York rappings. These accounts were combinations of newspaper articles, letters solicited by the authors, and personal narratives by the historian-participants. One of the earliest pamphlets was *History of the . . . Mysterious Noises!* by Dellon M. Dewey, a Rochester printer and book dealer. Dewey became the agent not only for his own book but also for *Singular Revelations* by Eliab Capron and Henry Barron, which by March, 1850, had gone through an original and a revised edition. Even the credulous Greeley felt that the statements in *Singular Revelations* were "of such a nature as to require a very large amount of unimpeachable evidence to sustain them."[11]

With the pamphlet propaganda added to the newspaper publicity, the manifestations increased in both number and complexity. In Rochester Methodist clergyman Asahel H. Jarvis woke up one night and had a conversation with his wife about slavery. He told her he was sorry that John Quincy Adams was not living, since his influence in Congress would be beneficial at that critical moment. As he spoke, he felt a rapping on the bedclothing directly over his breast. A Universalist minister, the Reverend Charles Hammond, contributed to the growing body of rapping literature a detailed account of a seance at the Fox house in Rochester. The three Fox sisters and their mother selected Hammond from among the men assembled in their house, and took him to a back room. They placed a lighted candle on a large table and sat down. In the eerie half-light the sounds began immediately, "and continued to multiply and become more violent, until every part of the room trembled." Suddenly Hammond felt the side of the table next to him "move upward—I pressed upon it heavily, but soon it passed out of reach of us all—full six feet from me, and at least four from the nearest person to it. I saw it clearly; not a thread could have connected it with any of the company without my notice," wrote the amazed clergyman. Meanwhile, the noises grew louder. "The family commenced and sung the 'spirit's song,' and several pieces of sacred music, during which accurate time was marked on the table, caused it to vibrate—a transparent hand, resembling a shadow, presented itself before my face—I felt fingers take hold of a lock of hair on the left side of my head—then a cold, death-like hand was drawn designedly over my face—three raps on my left knee—a violent shaking, as though two hands were applied to my shoulder. . . ." This was enough to convince Hammond. He renounced Universalism, became a believer in the spirits and one of the first writing mediums, transcribing messages dictated by the spirit of Thomas Paine. Hammond's experience was representative, if not typical. The number of mediums continued to increase, and the manifestations became more dramatic, more intricate, and more appealing. By the summer of 1850 there were in Auburn, for instance, more than a hundred mediums in various stages of development; most of them were rapping, some speaking, some clairvoyant, and a few were musical mediums in whose presence their patrons heard the sounds of trumpets, guitars, bass drums, and other instruments.[12]

As the excitement increased, Capron decided that the fame of the Foxes had spread far enough to try for more controlled demonstrations than those in Rochester's Corinthian Hall. The Fox sisters should leave the provinces to try their talents in the metropolis. On June 4, 1850, Mrs. Fox and her three daughters arrived in New York City. The

Leah Fox (A. Leah Underhill). Portrait from A. Leah Underhill, *The Missing Link in Modern Spiritualism* (1885).

Margaret Fox (Margaret Fox Kane). Portrait from A. Leah Underhill, *The Missing Link in Modern Spiritualism* (1885).

Kate Fox (Kate Fox Jencken). Portrait from A. Leah Underhill, *The Missing Link in Modern Spiritualism* (1885).

sisters, Leah in her mid-twenties, eighteen-year-old Margaret, and fourteen-year-old Kate, bore a strong family resemblance. All three of them had long, dark hair, dark eyes, and extremely pale skin—"complexions of a transparent paleness, such as we have observed in persons highly susceptible to mesmeric influences," as one of their admirers put it. Their faces were long and thin, with high foreheads, sharp cheekbones, long noses, and thin lips. Like other young women, they wanted to go to the theater, to hear Jenny Lind, to visit Barnum's Museum and Fowler and Wells's Phrenological Cabinet. They had not the slightest thought of forming a new religion.[13]

Along with Capron, the Fox family moved into a suite of rooms in Barnum's Hotel. Capron advertised the seances and hopefully made ready for a throng of visitors. He established an admission price of one dollar and posted "Rules of Decorum" on the door. Crowds thronged the room—"all varieties of life," reported the *New York Tribune,* "from the sunbrowned Hoosier of the West to the jewelled aristocracy of New York." The country people and New Yorkers differed little in their actions. Once seated around the large table, they all asked the same most difficult test questions they could think of—the names and ages of relatives both living and dead, their own occupations, and whether departed relatives had a message for them.[14]

The spirits were capricious, sometimes refusing to rap at all. The sisters explained the silences and meager or unsatisfactory replies by insisting that they had no control over the spirits. Capron welcomed investigations, whether by individual customers or by committees that the customers appointed. The results of the investigations brought more customers and more investigations, for the skeptics had to admit that they "were unable to detect any motion on the part of the ladies, which could have originated the sounds." Several committees of women had Margaret and Kate disrobe, and the raps beat a staccato while the girls stood in naked innocence. "The production of the sounds is hard to explain," observed one puzzled investigator, "and still stranger is the accuracy with which the ghosts guess of whom one is thinking—his age, his residence, vocation, and the like." The chances were a thousand to one, he concluded, that the correct answers were the results of sleight of hand or the girls' skill in using clues furnished by the facial expression or voice of the inquirer.[15]

Others were troubled less by the means of production of the raps than by the undignified behavior of the spirits. One shocked clergyman felt a hand grasping at his leg, and another had the table on which he was writing move up and down every time he set pen to paper. "All this sounds sufficiently ridiculous and amusing," commented the *Tribune,* "yet the men are parties of high intelligence and respectability." One man explained the ridiculous behavior of the spirits by observing that "there may be as great fools out of the flesh as there are in it." But indignities and caprice aside, the man who had come from Newport, New York, to see the Fox sisters and listen to the rappings summed up the usual reaction: "I went away convinced that what before appeared to me much like a nice plump humbug, deserved investigation by the best minds among us."[16]

After their visits to Barnum's Hotel most of the customers came away, like the Newport man, somewhat confused and skeptical but almost unable not to believe. A few, however, were absolute skeptics who heard not spirits but the raps of money-making humbuggers, and a like number were thorough and ardent believers not only in the honesty of the Fox sisters but also in what the spirits told them.

With the exception of Horace Greeley's *Tribune* and N. P. Willis's *Home Journal,* the New York press accused the girls of "jugglery" and "fraud," and declared that all who believed them were idiots, lunatics, or knaves. The defenders of the sisters were just as convinced as their critics, but they were better known and more influential. Horace Greeley became a thoroughly convinced believer if only a somewhat reluctant and restrained defender in his newspaper. He took the Fox family into his home for three days, and became convinced of *"their perfect integrity and good faith."* Charles Partridge, a wealthy manufacturer, visited the Foxes at Barnum's Hotel and became passionately interested. After the Fox family returned to Rochester in August, Partridge and his wife journeyed there for further seances, where he heard not just rappings but also a terrible creaking noise, as from a ship laboring on a heavy sea, and occasional dull thuds, as if the ship had been struck on its side. To Partridge these noises represented the sounds of a shipwreck he had survived four years earlier. A young girl in his care had been swept overboard, and it was she, the guilt-ridden Partridge believed, who made the sounds at the seances. The awed man took Kate back to his New York City home for daily seances over a period of more than two months. These seances convinced him that he could converse with all of his departed friends and relatives, and with the great men of all time. "Let me caution persons against trifling with this matter," he warned. "I exhort them to investigate it fairly or let it alone." Partridge took his own exhortation seriously, for he soon became the chief financial backer of spiritual investigation.[17]

During their three months in New York the Fox sisters had achieved successes of which they were not aware. As the sisters, their proud mother, and the triumphant Capron left the city and returned to Rochester to plan a tour of the West, they left behind dozens of circles for spiritual communication, hundreds of men and women who believed they were in contact with their ancestors, thousands of people who were curious and interested, and a few wealthy believers who, like Partridge, would be willing to devote their lives and their fortunes to spiritual investigation.

Just as there were leaders of spiritualism, there were leaders of the opposition. The earliest important leader of the fraud and humbug school, James Stanley Grimes, had been a successful lawyer in Boston and New York and a professor of medical jurisprudence at Castleton Medical College. His main interest, however, was not in law but in all of the new and progressive scientific and intellectual currents of his day. An ardent proponent of phrenology, mesmerism, and evolution, he delighted in controversy. Arguing that all the wonders of mesmerism and clairvoyance were natural phenomena that could be explained on "strictly scientific principles," he subjected spiritualism to the same sort of analysis. The "true key" to the written communications from the spirit world that Andrew Jackson Davis and others had been "suffered to enjoy" lay for Grimes in mesmerism: a mesmerized subject could be made to see or hear anything the "operator" might suggest. As for the rappings, Grimes found their source to be nothing but deception. A medium confessed to him that she had learned the art of rapping from the Foxes in Rochester. Hoping to amuse her family, she had produced spirit knockings by a combination of levers activated by pegs in the floor, ventriloquism, and accomplices in the cellar; the first experiment had aroused the entire neighborhood, and she had been unable to admit the farce for fear of disgrace.[18]

Turning to the Foxes, Grimes described them in caustic phrenological terms. He accused Leah of being co-exploiter with Capron of her younger sisters, who had "nothing in their appearance to distinguish them from ordinary country girls," and whose "phreno-organization indicated very little of the ability" to initiate deception. Leah, on the other hand, possessed "a masculine energetic temperament, and an organization of the brain indicating courage, cunning, skepticism, and a ready skill, with a deficiency of ideality, and of those peculiar developments which are commonly supposed to indicate a tendency to spirituality." Their raps, charged Grimes, were made by means of machinery concealed under their clothing, and their success at avoiding detection depended on "the respect for the female sex which prevents examination of their persons." The committees who inspected them were composed mainly of confederates, and other accomplices produced the raps during the examinations. Further, charged Grimes, they could make no noise that under the same circumstances a "skillful juggler" could not; when they were so rigidly scrutinized that deception was impossible, they claimed that the spirits refused to rap and that they had no control over them.[19]

Like nearly all the testimony of the spiritualists themselves, Grimes's explanation depended in the last analysis on the perceptiveness and honesty of the observer and, more important, on his predisposition to belief or disbelief. The explanation of another member of the fraud and humbug school, Charles Chauncey Burr, had a more scientific jargon, more effective backing, and gained wider acceptance. In 1850 Burr and his brother Heman brought out a book entitled *Knocks for the Knockings,* in which he claimed that for two months he spent all his time examining the best mediums in five states "where rappism prevails most," and in no case was there any cause but *"fraud* and *delusion."* To prove his point, Burr claimed that he could produce the "mysterious rappings" seventeen different ways, and through the columns of the *New York Tribune* he invited all those who were interested to come and hear them at Hope Chapel beginning Monday evening, January 13, 1851. He had incorporated the rappings, he explained, into his "lectures on Imagination, Ghostseeing, and the Temperament of Genius."[20]

Horace Greeley appointed himself and the *Tribune* referee of the controversy that ensued. At Greeley's request, a "gentleman of intelligence and truth" who had been investigating the manifestations for more than a year wrote that he had heard raps and seen physical manifestations that were, beyond doubt, dignified and free from fraud. Attacking Burr's favorite method of producing the raps, the snapping of his toe joints, the writer advised Burr that if he could produce the effects he promised in his letter "with his great toes," he should simply "get them patented." Orson Squire Fowler, one of the "Phrenological Fowlers," listened to Burr's noises and concluded that they were no more like the rappings of the Fox sisters "than a church bell is like a Scotch fiddle."[21]

Burr soon got support for his toe-snapping theory from three professors at the University of Buffalo Medical School. This was the first of many investigations of the Fox sisters by groups of academic scientists. In February, 1851, the doctors visited the sisters in Buffalo, heard the raps, and left with what they felt was an explanation that would "serve to prevent further waste of time, money, and credulity (to say nothing of sentiment and philosophy), in connection with this, so long successful imposition."

They sent their explanation to the *Buffalo Commercial Advertiser,* and other papers throughout the country were quick to reprint the story. The Buffalo doctors told their readers that they reached their explanation "almost by a logical necessity," by using the same methods of analysis that they employed in diagnosing diseases, *"the reasoning by exclusion."* First they excluded any spiritual explanation, since there was a possibility that the manifestations could be accounted for in physical terms. Then, since they had been able to find neither, they excluded contrivances in the clothing Leah and Margaret wore and machinery attached to doors and tables. These were examples of "negative evidence," and the expression on Margaret's face provided them with the key to "positive evidence." During the rappings her face showed signs of great effort going on in her body, which indicated to the doctors that she must be moving her muscles. "Hence," concluded the doctors, "the only possible source of the noises in question, produced, as we have seen they must be, by voluntary muscular contractions, is in one or more of the movable articulations of the skeleton." Margaret, they decided, was producing the rappings in her joints.

The doctors' strongest argument came when, "by a curious coincidence," they found a "respectable lady" who could make her knee joints rap by dislocating them. The doctors dealt their final blow to the claims of the mediums by explaining that furniture moved because the "force of the semi-dislocation of the bone is sufficient to occasion the distinct jarring of the doors, table &c., if in contact." The belief that sounds came from different parts of the room they explained as delusion arising from an incorrect appreciation of the laws of acoustics.[22]

In reply to these charges, Margaret and Leah wrote a letter to the newspapers for the first time. Addressing the doctors as "Gents," and observing that they had been referred to as "females" in contrast to the "highly respectable lady," they invited the doctors to investigate their knees before being so certain of the new theory. The next night the doctors began the investigation by asking them to sit on a couch, and to extend their legs and rest their heels on cushions. To produce the raps, Dr. Lee later explained, the mediums needed solid support for their feet. Leah and Margaret sat this way for fifty minutes, urging the spirits to manifest themselves, but the raps did not come until they placed their feet on the floor. By the end of the evening Margaret was in tears. "I need not add that our position was triumphantly sustained," added Dr. Lee, "and that public opinion here is now almost universally on our side." Greeley commented that the doctors made a strong case but "undoubtedly we shall have another version of the matter."[23]

Other versions were not long in coming. Capron found a doctor to challenge both methodology and conclusions of the Buffalo medical men. Hezakiah Joslyn, M.D., claimed that the "erudite Professors" put forth mere conjecture, and that he had facts based on two years of research which would "entirely silence all *toeology* and *kneeology* theories. . . ." Leah admitted it was true that when their feet were on cushions no raps came, but just as true that "if our friendly Spirits retired when they witnessed this harsh proceeding on the part of our persecutors, it was not in our power to detain them." She also challenged the professional competence of the doctors: "As professional gentlemen whose reputations are dear to them, I would like them to tell your readers what conditions our poor joints would be in by this time, after four years of constant service in this almost ceaseless operation."[24]

The work of the Buffalo doctors was manna for Burr. He added knee snapping to toe cracking in his lectures, and drew even larger audiences than before. But his greatest *coup* was in finding a high-ranking defector from the ranks of spiritualism to give added support to the knee and toe theories. In April, 1851, two months after the investigation at Buffalo and a month after the exchange of letters on it had begun to die down, Burr and his brother Heman discovered that in Arcadia, Mrs. Norman Culver, a relation to the Foxes by marriage, was willing to reveal the secrets of the Fox girls. The Burrs had Mrs. Culver make a deposition before a doctor and a minister, and circulated it widely. Mrs. Culver swore that for two years she had believed that the raps were produced by spirits, but now knew it to be a deception. Kate had shown her how to do it with her toes, explaining that it helped to place the feet in warm water before a demonstration. After a week of practice Mrs. Culver was able to produce raps with all the toes on both of her feet and to make as many as 150 raps in a row. "The reign of these imposters is nearly at an end," wrote Burr.[25]

Burr was wrong in predicting that "the reign" of the Fox sisters was over. The publicity he, the Buffalo doctors, and Grimes generated merely served to advertise the mediums, and spiritualism continued to gain adherents. By 1855 probably one million Americans—out of a population of twenty-eight million—identified themselves with the new religion, at least to the extent of giving credence to the phenomena and to the reality of spiritual communication. Well-known, respectable converts—judges, senators, scientists—proclaimed the new revelation.

Public interest in the movement subsided after the mid-1850s, but the Fox sisters continued to attract defenders and to be dogged by investigations and exposés.

The most respectable investigation of the Foxes and other mediums so far was undertaken by a committee of Harvard scientists in 1857. Two years earlier Frederick Willis, a young Harvard theology student, began experiencing visions, trances, and premonitions. The Divinity School suspended him. His mediumistic talents had given Willis entree into the best spiritual circles in Boston; Thomas Wentworth Higginson and others wrote letters of protest, but to no avail. In the aftermath of the Willis case the *Boston Courier* offered $500 to any medium whose manifestations might be accepted as genuine by a scientific committee that included among its members Benjamin Peirce, the nation's leading mathematician, and naturalist Louis Agassiz. Among the mediums invited to participate were Kate and Leah Fox, to whom Agassiz gave special attention. "Our rappings came, if not as profuse as usual, yet abundantly, both low and loud," Leah later recounted, "in spite of our being moved to different parts of the room, of our being placed standing on cushions and on the stuffed spring seat of a sofa, etc." But the committee's brief report of June 29, 1857, spoke less to the evidence of the test seances than to their view of spiritualism: "It is the opinion of the Committee, derived from observation, that any connection with Spiritualistic Circles, so called, corrupts the morals and degrades the intellect. They therefore deem it their solemn duty to warn the community against this contaminating influence, which surely tends to lessen the truth of man and the purity of woman."[26]

Whatever its dangers, spiritualism did not cease to attract important converts. Even among the famous, Robert Dale Owen had a special importance. Nearing the end of a distinguished career as reformer, politician, and diplomat, Owen approached his study of mediumistic phenomena as a freethinker and rational skeptic. In 1856 he witnessed slate writing in Italy and could not explain it without admitting the intercession of some unseen hand. Returning to America, he read, attended seances, and studied carefully. The result was *Footfalls on the Boundary of Another World* (1860), an inquiry into whether communication from another world was a reality or a delusion. If, in fact, the phenomena were spiritual, he explained, there would be an assurance of immortality. *Footfalls* was the first spiritualist book issued by a leading conventional publishing house, and an English edition soon followed from a respected British publisher. Read by people who ignored the books of other spiritualists, it went through several editions in both countries.[27]

Continuing with his researches, in the fall of 1860 Owen spent several weeks living in the home of Leah Fox (now Mrs. Daniel Underhill) and sitting in seances conducted by her and by Kate Fox. During the 1860s he prepared a sequel to *Footfalls*. In December, 1871, *The Debatable Land between This World and the Next* was published simultaneously in the United States and England, receiving respectful reviews not only in the spiritualist press but also in conventional magazines and journals. Leah and Kate had a prominent and honored place in *The Debatable Land*. Owen claimed that spirit raps were absolutely genuine. He described them in great detail and variety. "I have heard them as delicate, tiny tickings, and as thunderous poundings." He had heard raps in the dark and in daylight, indoors and out, on ships and at the seashore. "But in no circumstances have I witnessed this wonderful phenomenon under such varied conditions, and with such satisfactory results," as with Leah and Kate Fox, whose gift was "more marked and more readily to be obtained, than in any other persons. . . ." He was convinced that they had no other motive than "a frank wish that the truth should be ascertained and acknowledged." Owen explained as occult occurrences floating phosphorescent lights, which "usually showed themselves first behind and between Leah and Kate, near the floor. Then they rose; sometimes remaining near Leah's head, sometimes near her sister's." After floating, the lights returned either to Leah or to Kate. Owen testified that neither medium would accept payment from him for any sitting, and that neither was capable of deception.[28]

The book, and Owen's subsequent articles in the *Atlantic Monthly,* produced a revival of interest in spiritualism, and a new willingness to take it seriously. Because Owen's contribution was so great, any future weakness or failure in his investigations would be all the more devastating.[29]

In the summer of 1874 Owen went to Philadelphia to investigate the spectacular and highly publicized materialization of the spirit of Katie King through the mediumship of Mr. and Mrs. Nelson Holmes. Departing from his usual careful investigations, Owen endorsed the Holmeses in the American and British spiritualist press as honest and the materializations as authentic. "I stake whatever reputation I may have acquired after eighteen years' study," he wrote, "upon the genuine character of the phenomena." He prepared for the *Atlantic Monthly* an account of the authenticity of the materialization of Katie King. Six days after his endorsement he informed spiritualist newspapers that he was withdrawing it. A Holmes accomplice admitted to Owen that she had abetted them in their fraud. Even worse, although he telegraphed the editors of the *Atlantic* to stop publication of his article, the message was too late. As a movement, American spiritualism never recovered from the derisive publicity resulting from Owen's failure to detect deception.[30]

The Fox sisters, the movement's inadvertent originators and most famous mediums, never understood it. In their search for respectability, throughout their careers they denounced the radical social ideas of Andrew Jackson Davis, Victoria Woodhull, and other spiritualists who offered strong criticisms of injustice and inequality in American society generally and in women's conditions particularly. For Margaret and Kate the events that began in the spring of 1848 brought little in the way of happiness, independence, or security. Of the three, Leah's life—both public and private—was the least troubled and most stable. Older when the rappings began, she was better educated than her sisters and always more able to understand and accept notoriety and the demands of the curious and ardent. Deserted by her first husband in the 1840s and widowed by the death of her second husband in 1853, in 1858 she married Daniel Underhill, a spiritualist and wealthy New York insurance executive and clubman, and for more than thirty years they lived a relatively quiet life. Her home was often a refuge for Margaret and Kate. Spiritualists who knew all three testified that she was as adept a medium as either of her sisters, but after her marriage she gave only private seances, none professionally and none for money. In 1885 she published *The Missing Link in Modern Spiritualism,* a justification of her sisters and herself and a collection of historical documents that added little new information. Her observation on the problems of mediumship, however, is revealing: "Mediumship is a great mystery." And she affirmed her belief in the existence of spirits, who, she was convinced, had contributed to her happiness.[31]

Difficulty and confusion marked Margaret Fox's life from the 1850s, while she was still at the height of her mediumistic career. In the fall of 1852, while appearing in Philadelphia, she met the famous Arctic explorer Elisha Kent Kane. Like other Philadelphians, he was curious about the rappings, but his reaction at seeing Margaret was one of horror that a young and sensitive girl was being exploited. He became a regular visitor and soon, in addition to pity, developed feelings of responsibility and genuine affection for both Margaret and Kate. He tried to convince them to give up spirit rapping, for although he could not understand how the phenomena were produced, he thought the demonstrations dishonest and immoral. Showering almost constant attention on Margaret, before he left on his second Arctic expedition in May, 1853, he arranged for her support and education at a small school near Philadelphia.[32]

After Kane's death in 1857 Margaret's relationship with him became clouded with a haze of conflicting and untrustworthy testimony. She claimed that with members of her family as witnesses she and Kane had exchanged marriage vows in 1856, thus making her his commonlaw wife. His family denied it. Probably he had vacillated in his intentions, never resolving his conflict between genuine affection for her and fear for his own and his family's social position. He could more easily have overcome his family's objections to her lower-class origins than their abhorrence of her spirit-rapping occupation. Margaret claimed he had left her an annuity that his family refused to pay, and in 1862 she began suit for it. The Kanes agreed to pay the annuity in exchange for Margaret's placing Kane's letters to her in the care of a trustee. Charging that the bargain had not been honored, in 1865 she published the letters as *The Love-Life of Dr. Kane*. Having converted to Roman Catholicism in 1858, from that time on she engaged in spirit rapping infrequently.[33]

In 1884 she did agree to participate in investigations conducted by the Seybert Commission, which was appointed by the University of Pennsylvania to study the claims of spiritualism in compliance with the terms of a bequest from Henry Seybert, a wealthy Philadelphian fascinated with the question of an afterlife. From the beginning the commission encountered serious difficulties. Most private mediums refused to offer their services, and professionals either demanded high fees or insisted on setting conditions inimical to controlled experiment. As a result the investigators had to attend seances under conditions imposed by the mediums.

At their first meeting with Margaret they noted that her feet were concealed by the table and by her long dress. During the ninety-minute session a series of raps gave messages from Seybert to the investigators. At the second session, with Margaret's consent, they made tests while her feet rested on tumblers; when no raps came, she explained that she had no control over the spirits. Repeating what she had said ever since the early 1850s, she told them, "I do not even say the sounds are from Spirits . . . I do not say they are the Spirits of our departed friends, but I leave others to judge for themselves." Later, going into trance, she wrote a message from Seybert that included a phrase in Latin—a language Seybert had not used while living. Finally, with her permission one of the investigators held her feet while very faint raps were heard. "This is the most wonderful thing of all, Mrs. Kane," the investigator told her. "There is not a particle of motion in your foot, but there is an unusual pulsation." Inviting her to a third session, they explained that their efforts so far had convinced them that "the so-called raps are confined wholly to her person, whether produced by her voluntarily or involuntarily. . . ." Margaret declined the invitation, agreeing that the results were unsatisfactory and that another meeting "instead of removing the present belief of the Commission might add confirmation to it."

In 1887 the Seybert Commission issued its findings. Without mentioning the earlier controversies and investigations that had made Margaret's career continuously suspect and her life miserable, the report gave tacit support to the old charges of fraud. Cautiously noting that "our investigations have not been sufficiently extensive to warrant . . . any positive conclusions" about spirit rapping, the report nonetheless observed that "the difficulty attending the investigation of the mode of Spiritualistic manifestation is increased by the fact, familiar to physiologists, that sounds of varying intensity may be produced in almost any portion of the human body by voluntary muscular action." In any event, the report contained abundant and convincing evidence to sustain "the theory of the purely physiological origin of the sounds."[34]

Why Margaret agreed to be tested at this late date is not clear. But her decision does raise at least two questions: Was she seeking—for herself and her sisters—a way of repudiating the physical phenomena of the rappings? And was she seeking a way of finally understanding the nature of the psychical trance experiences in which their pencils wrote messages from the spirits?

Kate Fox's existence was no happier than Margaret's. From the time of the first New York demonstrations of 1850 a series of wealthy patrons had wanted to protect her as they sought solace in her mediumistic activities. Horace Greeley was the first, offering to provide for her education, but Kate left with her family on extended and successful tours organized by Eliab Capron. In 1852 the family moved to New York City, and from that time Kate was more active as a medium than either of her sisters. Her patrons, moved by her youth, innocence, and frailty, took her into their homes. In 1854 the inventor Horace H. Day engaged her for a year at a salary of $1,200 to give free sittings.

For Kate the decade of the 1860s was an active and troubled time.[35]

Between 1861 and 1866 she held nearly 400 seances with Charles F. Livermore, a wealthy New York banker whose wife, Estelle, had recently died. At first Kate conveyed messages by rappings. Soon, like other mediums, she added two new methods of communication: spirit writing and materialization. In a trance state Kate engaged in rapid automatic writing, with either right or left hand and at times with both hands simultaneously, but always from right to left in mirror image. After the forty-third sitting, according to Livermore, "an illuminated substance like gauze rose from the floor behind us, moved about the room and finally came in front of us." Then the substance "assumed the form of a human head," and touched him. After moving around the room, accompanied by loud "electrical sounds," the gauze changed form: "a female hand grasped it, concealing the lower part of a face; but the upper part was revealed; it was that of Estelle—eyes, forehead, and expression in perfection." During the half-hour of Estelle's materialization, Livermore held both of Kate's hands. In later seances Estelle appeared even more clearly and completely, "every feature and lineament in perfection, spiritualized in shadowy beauty." In 1866 Livermore remarried, and although he continued to take a protective interest in Kate, the seances ceased.[36]

The other spirit that materialized most frequently during the Livermore sittings was that of Benjamin Franklin. Indeed, since 1849 Franklin had been for most mediums the most sought after and responsive spirit. Because spiritualists insisted that theirs was a new scientific religion, they frequently compared their phenomena to the mysteries of electricity. They called their method of communication the "spiritual telegraph." In 1853, for example, the *Shekinah* placed Franklin in its gallery of seers. "We are assured that *he* first worked out the problem by which beings in heaven can communicate with the beings on earth through the potential agency of magnetic forces. What spirit gone heavenward would be more likely to have accomplished it?" Franklin continued to materialize for Kate and to send messages that had no resemblance, in style or content, to his writings while alive.[37]

In 1865 both of Kate's parents died. Dr. Edward Bayard brought Kate to Dr. George H. Taylor's Swedish Movement Cure, hoping that the skilled physician and his wife, Sarah Langworthy Taylor, would care for Kate and protect her from the alcoholism that was to plague her for the rest of her life. The Taylors managed to keep Kate from excessive drinking until the summer of 1867, when she left the sanitarium for several months. They sought also to cure Margaret, who stayed with them occasionally.

In November, 1869, Kate began a series of seances with the Taylors that continued at various times for over twenty-two years. The phenomena were dramatic, far beyond simple rappings. Harriet Beecher Stowe, who attended some of the sessions, was convinced that "the phenomina [sic] that accompany her are matters quite beyond doubt *as facts*. It only remains by what theory to account for them." In an attempt to convince George Eliot of the reality and significance of the phenomena, Stowe sent the English novelist an account of a typical session she and her husband Calvin experienced:

I have myself seen some of them in Mrs. Taylor's bed room—occupied as a sewing room till the last moment we held one evening a seance with Katie—Myself and husband Dr and Mrs Taylor my sister and brother. We had her between us holding her hands while the things occurred that I mention. Phosphoric lights arose and floated about among us—They were like the clear light of a glow worm they touched me on my arm and I felt that they had a strong resisting force—one of them struck the table with a loud report like the firing of a pistol—then hands were felt—my husband was told to put his handkerchief in his hand and one of these globes of light rested in it—in this globe was a hand which displayed itself first on one side and then on the other—pencil and paper was taken from my hand and a message written on it. A guitar was raised up over our heads and played on—My husband who is a very stout man weighing two hundred was moved back from the table five feet to the wall chair and all and then placed again at the table. All this was done in a room we were all familiar with—in a boarding house where the rooms above and below and around were all occupied by boarders who knew nothing of what we were doing, and while Katie was held between two of us—[38]

Two of the Taylors' young children had recently died. They materialized during the seances, as did other Taylor relatives. But the messages from them, Benjamin Franklin, and other spirits reveal much more about Kate than they do of the spirit world. Surely Kate's trance writings were a bewildered expression of another personality, of her desperate attempts to control her alcoholism and her life. They were Kate's unconscious messages to her conscious self. On May 7, 1870, for example, Kate left the Taylors' for an engagement with a fashionable family on Fifth Avenue and returned, according to Sarah Taylor, "sick and crazy with brandy." The next morning Kate wrote in mirror image, "Oh! how I tried to enter the circle last night in order to protect this poor girl, but I couldn't, for the spirits were dark and powerful.

Prof. K." On May 25 Robert Dale Owen got Kate to promise that she would not drink for six months, but three days later she and Margaret got drunk. The next day, in a trance, Kate wrote, "Katie ought to have minded her mother and not gone with her sister to that place. We hope that she will keep away now. Olin." A few days later, after another drinking session on Fifth Avenue, she wrote, "Curses will follow those people! To give her drink and keep her overnight! I know all! Pity them, I do not. You had better let them know that you know it. B. F." And on August 7, 1871, Kate made a moving plea for herself: "Look not coldly upon Katie at any time. She has much to contend with and our sympathies go out to her. B.F."[39]

People who cared about Kate and sought to help her agreed on her conscious personality. "She is apparently without a nature of her own but is only a medium of reflecting others. Sensitive, wilful, irritable, affectionate she fulfils my idea of a fay or wood sprite," observed Harriet Beecher Stowe. "I have known Kate Fox for years," Robert Dale Owen wrote. "She is one of the most simple-minded and strictly impulsive young persons I have ever met: as incapable of framing, or carrying on, any deliberate scheme of imposition as a ten-year-old child is of administering a government."[40]

On October 7, 1871, Kate left New York on a voyage to England. The day before she sailed, the spirit of one of the Taylor children wrote through her hand, "Katie, we will all follow you with our protection, and now God bless you and return you a well and happy girl." Charles Livermore paid for her passage and sent sympathetic English spiritualists a request to treat her gently. "Miss Fox, taken all in all, is no doubt the most wonderful living medium. Her character is irreproachable and pure," he explained. "I have received so much through her powers of mediumship during the past ten years which is solacing, instructive and astounding, that I feel greatly indebted to her, and desire to have her taken good care of while absent from home and friends." Livermore described Kate in the same terms that Stowe and Owen used. "That you may more thoroughly understand her idiosyncracies, permit me to explain that she is a sensitive of the highest order and of childlike simplicity. . . ."[41]

English spiritualists gave Kate a warm welcome, and she began giving private seances immediately. In England, as in America, highly respected men and women of letters and science defended Kate's honesty and insisted on the spiritual nature of the phenomena produced in her presence. When in 1872 she married Henry D. Jencken, a successful international lawyer and legal scholar, the guests heard loud raps during the wedding breakfast. Jencken was an ardent believer and wrote articles for the English spiritualist press. Their first child, Ferdinand, was born in 1873, and the family testified that he exhibited great mediumistic powers at the age of three months. In 1874 Kate returned to America, bringing her son with her. She stayed at Leah's where her second son, Henry, was born in 1875. Shortly thereafter she returned to the Taylor sanitarium, and from July to March gave another series of seances. She then returned to England, where Margaret, who had been waging a losing battle with alcohol, joined her in 1876. In 1881 Kate's husband died, but she and Margaret remained for a time in England.

After Kate returned to America in the spring of 1885, her drinking problem became more acute. In August, 1886, she was arrested in Rochester for drunkenness; in May, 1888, she was again arrested and her boys taken from her by the Society for the Prevention of Cruelty to Children. Sympathetic spiritualists helped Kate get her children back and care for them; Isabella Beecher Hooker, a radical women's rights advocate and sister of Harriet Beecher Stowe, was particularly responsive. Margaret sent a letter from England to American newspapers blaming spiritualism for her sister's misfortune. "I presume my absence has added to my darling sister's depressed state of mind," she informed the *New York Herald*. She denounced spiritualists as "fanatics" and spiritualism as "a curse and a snare."[42]

Thus began the exposé of forty years of mediumship. There had been earlier exposés, but this one, coming from Margaret herself, threatened to be the crushing blow. Margaret returned to America and explained to reporters who met her on her arrival that she and Kate had always made the rappings by throwing their big toes out of joint. On October 21, 1888, Margaret demonstrated the technique to a large audience at Music Hall. She charged that Leah had forced Kate and herself to keep up the spirit-rapping fraud, and denounced her for exploiting and tyrannizing them. Kate sat in the audience, giving full assent to Margaret's explanation. Leah refused to make any public comment. Reuben Briggs Davenport, one of the sponsors and promoters of the Music Hall demonstration, hurriedly wrote a book triumphantly titled *The Death-Blow to Spiritualism: Being the True Story of the Fox Sisters*. He prefaced it with a statement signed by Margaret and Kate: "We hereby approve of Mr. Reuben B. Davenport's design to write a true account of the origin of Spiritualism and of our connection therewith, and we authorize him to make proper use of all data and material that we furnish him."

Spiritualists denounced Margaret's exposé as the ravings of a poor besotted woman who would do anything for money. Opponents of spiritualism claimed that Margaret had given "the death-blow" to a dishonest and immoral farce. A lecture tour by Margaret, managed by the men who had arranged her Music Hall demonstration, proved to be a financial failure. Swearing that she had been tricked into making the false exposé by unscrupulous men, she recanted a year later. A new lecture tour, during which she reaffirmed her belief in spirits, also failed. Both she and Kate sank deeper into poverty, humiliation, and drink.[43]

On November 1, 1890, Leah died. She was mourned by spiritualists throughout the world. Two years later, on July 2, 1892, Kate died; she was survived by her sons, neither of whom had developed the mediumistic talents that their early performance had seemed to promise. During the last few months of her life Margaret lived on the donations of sympathetic spiritualists. She died on March 8, 1893, and was buried near Kate and Leah at Greenwood Cemetery in Brooklyn. Appropriately, during the long funeral services the spirits of Benjamin Franklin and Horace Greeley, among others, spoke through mediums.[44]

Andrew Jackson Davis was not at all surprised by the exposé and recantation of Margaret and Kate Fox. Since the 1850s he had insisted that the phenomena of the seance were unreliable; to have meaning, he said, spiritualism and Harmonial Philosophy must have expression in social reform. When the New York legislature prohibited magnetic and mental healers from practicing medicine, Davis enrolled in the United States Medical College in New York, encouraging other healers to do the same so that they could be licensed. He was fifty-four years old. After graduating in 1883 with degrees in medicine and anthropology, in 1885 he moved to Watertown, Massachusetts, where for the next twenty-five years he treated patients whether or not they were able to pay.[45]

In his conclusion to the report of the Seybert Commission, Horace Howard Furness voiced a lament that historians have echoed many times since. "Unfortunately," he wrote, "in my experience, Dante's motto must be inscribed over an investigation of Spiritualism, and all hope must be abandoned by those who enter on it."[46] Although the temptation is strong to follow Furness's warning, some clear conclusions are possible. Paradoxes haunt the lives of the Fox sisters. As mediums they engaged in one of the few professions in which women outnumbered men.[47] Yet as they struggled unsuccessfully to come to terms with their experience, they rejected the thoughtful analysis of the condition of women offered by spiritualists like Andrew Jackson Davis, whose writings provided a philosophical basis for reform. For Margaret and Kate Fox, spiritualism brought only confusion and misery after the excitement of their early celebrity. The evidence of hundreds of seances indicates that they had an unusual capacity to sense and reflect the thoughts, feelings, and wishes of others. That capacity, over which they had no control, frightened them. Nor did they understand what happened to them in trance, or whether their trance writing might not be, in fact, the product of some occult force.[48] Clearly the messages Kate wrote were pleas of distress from her unconscious self. In their rappings and materializations they practiced deception, yet in all their various efforts succeeded best in deceiving themselves. The most famous mediums in a movement they could not understand, all three sisters often disclaimed any spiritual cause for their rappings. In their long careers there is no convincing evidence of genuine spirit communication; yet millions of Americans believed in the rappings of the Fox sisters and, through them, in the existence of spirits.

NOTES

1. Allan Nevins and Milton Halsey Thomas, eds., *The Diary of George Templeton Strong*, 4 vols. (New York: Macmillan, 1952), 2:244–45. A portion of the research for this essay was supported by a grant from California State University for a semester's creative leave.

2. For excellent recent work on the history of spiritualism, see especially Howard Kerr, *Mediums, and Spirit-Rappers, and Roaring Radicals: Spiritualism in American Literature, 1850–1900* (Urbana: University of Illinois Press, 1972); Lewis Perry, *Radical Abolitionism* (Ithaca, N.Y.: Cornell University Press, 1973); Mari Jo Buhle, "Feminism and Socialism in the United States, 1820–1920" (Ph.D. diss., University of Wisconsin, 1974); and R. Laurence Moore, *In Search of White Crows: Spiritualism, Parapsychology, and American Culture* (New York: Oxford University Press, 1977).

3. The main sources for Davis's early life are, in order of usefulness, William Fishbough's introduction to *The Principles of Nature, Her Divine Revelations, and A Voice to Mankind, by and through Andrew Jackson Davis, the "Poughkeepsie Seer" and "Clairvoyant"* (New York: S. S. Lyon and W. Fishbough, 1847); Andrew Jackson Davis, *The Magic Staff: An Autobiography* (New York: J. S. Brown, 1857); Davis, *The Great Harmonia: Being a Philosophical Revelation of the Natural, Spiritual, and Celestial Universe*, 5 vols. (New York and Boston: various publishers, 1850–55), vol. 2, *The Teacher* (Boston: B. B. Mussey, 1852); Davis, *Memoranda of Persons, Places, and Events: Embracing Authentic Facts, Visions, Clairvoyance, Spiritualism* . . . (Boston: W. White, 1867); W. N. Slocum, "Andrew Jackson Davis," in *Carrier Dove* (Oakland, Calif.), Oct., 1886.

4. Davis, *The Great Harmonia*, vol. 4, *The Reformer* (Boston: Sanborn, Carter, & Bazin, 1855), pp. 231–42.

5. For a brief comprehensive account of the Fox family, see Ernest Isaacs, "Anne Leah, Margaret, and Catherine Fox," in *Notable American Women 1607–1950: A Biographical Dictionary*, 3 vols. (Cambridge, Mass.: Harvard University Press, 1971), 1:655–57. For Fox family background and the alcohol problem of the entire family, see William George Langworthy Taylor, *Katie Fox, Epoch Making Medium, and the Making of the Fox-Taylor Record* (New York: Putnam's, 1933), pp. 154–58; Eliab Wilkinson Capron and Henry D. Barron, *Singular Revelations: Explanation and History of the Mysterious Communion with Spirits, Comprehending the Rise and Progress of the Mysterious Noises in Western New York . . .*, 2d ed. (Auburn, N.Y.: Capron and Barron, 1850), pp. 10–12; Dellon M. Dewey, *History of the Strange Sounds or Rappings, Heard in Rochester and Western New York, and Usually Called the Mysterious Noises! . . .* (Rochester, N.Y.: Dewey, 1850), pp. 14–18; *New York Weekly Tribune*, Dec. 8, 1849; Eliab Wilkinson Capron, *Modern Spiritualism: Its Facts and Fanaticisms, Its Consistencies and Contradictions . . .* (New York: Partridge and Brittan, 1855), pp. 33–39. The signed statements of Mrs. Fox, John Fox (Apr. 11, 1848), and William Duesler (Apr. 19, 1848) are reprinted in Capron and other early histories of spiritualism.

6. *Spirit of the Age*, July 28, 1849, pp. 54–55; Capron, *Modern Spiritualism*, pp. 54, 57–66, 74–79; Dewey, *History of the Strange Sounds*, pp. 19–21; Jarvis to Capron, in Capron and Barron, *Singular Revelations*, pp. 38–39, 41, 53–54.

7. Capron, *Modern Spiritualism*, pp. 88–98; Dewey, *History of the Strange Sounds*, p. 23; *Putnam's Monthly Magazine*, 1 (1853):60–62.

8. Capron and Barron, *Singular Revelations*, pp. 46–49; William Turner Coggshall [Coggeshall], *The Signs of the Times: Comprising a History of the Spirit-Rappings in Cincinnati and Other Places . . .* (Cincinnati: Coggshall, 1851), pp. 20–21; Augustus Porter Hascall to Capron, Feb. 13, 1850, in Capron and Barron, *Singular Revelations*, pp. 82–83.

9. Capron and Willets to Greeley, *New York Weekly Tribune*, Dec. 8, 1849.

10. *Weekly Tribune*, Dec. 15, 1849, Jan. 19, 1850.

11. *Weekly Tribune*, Jan. 26, 1850.

12. E. W. Hazard to *Binghampton Republican*, Jan. 27, 1850, in Dewey, *History of the Strange Sounds*, pp. 27–32; Capron, *Modern Spiritualism*, pp. 99–100, 113.

13. For engravings, see Taylor, *Katie Fox, Epoch Making Medium*; George Lawton, *The Drama of Life after Death: A Study of the Spiritualist Religion* (New York: Henry Holt, 1932); and A. Leah Underhill, *The Missing Link in Modern Spiritualism* (New York: T. R. Knox, 1885). For the Fox sisters in New York, see *Philosophy of Modern Miracles . . . by a "Dweller in the Temple"* (New York: Stringer & Townshend, 1850), p. 13; *New York Daily Tribune*, June 5, 1850.

14. *Daily Tribune*, June 21, 1850; "S." to editor, *Daily Tribune*, July 15, 1850.

15. *Daily Tribune,* June 5, 1850; "O." to editor, *Daily Tribune,* June 27, 1850.

16. C. Smith to editor, *Daily Tribune,* July 12, 1850; *Diary of George Templeton Strong,* 2:15–16.

17. Capron, *Modern Spiritualism,* pp. 172, 183–86; *Daily Tribune,* June 27, 1850; *Telegraph Papers,* 9 vols. (New York: Partridge & Brittan, 1852–57), 4:257–65; *Weekly Tribune,* Mar. 22, 1851.

18. Ernest Sutherland Bates, "James Stanley Grimes," *DAB* (1934); John D. Davies, *Phrenology: Fad and Science: A Nineteenth-Century American Crusade* (New Haven, Conn.: Yale University Press, 1955), pp. 43, 133–34; Grimes to editor, *Daily Tribune,* July 3, 9, 1850.

19. Grimes to editor, *Daily Tribune,* July 3, 9, 17, 26, 31, 1850.

20. *Daily Tribune,* May 3, 1853; *Spiritual Telegraph,* Sept. 17, 1853; Charles Chauncey Burr and Heman Burr, *Knocks for the Knockings* (1850), quoted in A. H. Mattison, *Spirit Rapping Unveiled!* (New York: J. C. Derby, 1855), pp. 176–77; Burr to editor, *Weekly Tribune,* Jan. 18, 1851.

21. *Weekly Tribune,* Jan. 18, 1851; "H." to editor, *Weekly Tribune,* Jan. 25, 1851; J. L. Scott to editor, *Weekly Tribune,* Feb. 1, 1851; J. B. Campbell, *Pittsburgh and Allegheny Spirit Rappings: Together with a General History of Spiritual Communications* (Allegheny, Pa.: Purviance, 1851), pp. 62–64.

22. Austin Flint, Charles Lee, and C. B. Coventry to *Buffalo Commercial Advertiser,* Feb. 18, 1851, quoted in Capron, *Modern Spiritualism,* pp. 309–18. The doctors explained that "the muscles inserted into the upper and inner side of the large bone of the leg (the tibia) near the knee joint, are brought into action so as to move the upper surface of the bone just named laterally upon the lower surface of the thighbone (the femur), giving rise, in fact, to a partial dislocation. . . . the return of the bone to its place is attended by another loud noise. It is practicable, however, to produce a single sound by moving the bone out of place with requisite quickness and force, and allowing it to slide back slowly, in which case it is noiseless."

23. Ann L. Fish and Margaretta Fox *to Buffalo Commercial Advertiser,* quoted in Capron, *Modern Spiritualism,* p. 313; Charles H. Lee to Greeley, *Weekly Tribune,* Mar. 1, 1851.

24. Joslyn's deposition was in a letter from Capron to Greeley, *Weekly Tribune,* Mar. 15, 1851; Ann L. Fish to *Buffalo Commercial Advertiser,* reprinted in *Weekly Tribune,* Mar. 29, 1851.

25. *Telegraph Papers,* 1 [1852]:140–44; deposition of Mrs. Norman Culver in Burr to editor, *Weekly Tribune,* June 7, 1851.

26. Emma Hardinge, *Modern Spiritualism: A Twenty Years' Record of the Communion between Earth and the World of Spirits* (New York: Hardinge, 1870), pp. 173–81; *New York Times,* Apr. 24, July 3, 1857; *Boston Courier,* July 2, 1857; *Boston Commonwealth,* Mar. 21, 1868.

27. Richard W. Leopold, *Robert Dale Owen: A Biography* (Cambridge, Mass.: Harvard University Press, 1940), pp. 321–28, 382; Howard Kerr, *Mediums, and Spirit-Rappers, and Roaring Radicals,* p. 108; Robert Dale Owen, *Footfalls on the Boundary of Another World* (Philadelphia: Lippincott, 1860), pp. 3–6; Owen, "How I Came to Study Spiritual Phenomena. A

Chapter of Autobiography," *Atlantic Monthly*, 34 (1874):578–90.

28. Leopold, *Robert Dale Owen*, pp. 329–34, 364–86; Underhill, *The Missing Link*, pp. 326–60; J. W. Edmonds to John F. Gray, Oct. 12, 1871, enclosed with Gray to Owen, Oct. 13, 1871, Ferdinand J. Dreer Collection, Pennsylvania Historical Society; Owen, *The Debatable Land between This World and the Next* (Philadelphia: Lippincott, 1871), pp. 342–48.

29. Leopold, *Robert Dale Owen*, pp. 387–99.

30. Ibid., pp. 400–416; Frank Podmore, *Modern Spiritualism: A History and a Criticism*, 2 vols. (London: Methuen, 1902), 2:97–99; Kerr, *Mediums, and Spirit-Rappers, and Roaring Radicals*, pp. 113–16; Alan Gauld, *The Founders of Psychical Research* (New York: Schocken Books, 1968), pp. 80–81.

31. Underhill, *The Missing Link*, p. 403 and *passim*.

32. This material is based on Isaacs, "Anne Leah, Margaret, and Catherine Fox," *Notable American Women*, 1:655–57.

33. Ibid.

34. Podmore, *Modern Spiritualism*, 2:193–96; University of Pennsylvania, *Preliminary Report of the Commission Appointed by the University of Pennsylvania to Investigate Modern Spiritualism . . .* (Philadelphia: Lippincott, 1887), pp. 21–22, 35–49; *New York Times*, Aug. 22, 1887. See also Earl Wesley Fornell, *The Unhappy Medium: Spiritualism and the Life of Margaret Fox* (Austin: University of Texas Press, 1968).

35. For these years, see Taylor, *Katie Fox, Epoch Making Medium*; Epes Sargent, *The Proof Palpable of Immortality* (Boston: Colby and Rich, 1875); Margaret Fox Kane to Robert Dale Owen, Dec. 20, 1866, and Kate Fox to Owen, Feb. 14, 1872, both in Dreer Collection, Pennsylvania Historical Society.

36. Owen, *Debatable Land*, pp. 482–502.

37. *Shekinah*, 2 (1853):49–66.

38. Harriet Beecher Stowe to George Eliot, Feb. 9, 1872, Berg Collection, New York Public Library. Material from this letter is used with permission of the Stowe-Day Foundation and the Berg Collection; Howard Kerr kindly brought this and other Stowe letters to my attention.

39. Taylor, *Katie Fox, Epoch Making Medium*, pp. 142, 154–58; Henri F. Ellenberger, *The Discovery of the Unconscious: The History and Evolution of Dynamic Psychiatry* (New York: Basic Books, 1970), pp. 83–85, 129, 693, 781–83.

40. Stowe to Eliot, Feb. 9, 1872; Owen, *Debatable Land*, p. 498.

41. Arthur Conan Doyle, *The History of Spiritualism*, 2 vols. (New York: George H. Doran, 1926), 1:94–95.

42. *New York Herald*, May 27, 1888.

43. On the exposé and subsequent recantation, see *New York Herald*, May 5, 27, Sept. 24, 1888; *New York World*, Oct. 21, 22, 1888; *New York Times*, Oct. 22, 1888; *Open Court* (Chicago), Nov. 8, 1888; *Religio-Philosophical Journal*, Oct. 20, 1888; *Banner of Light*, Oct.-Dec., 1888, Jan., 1889.

44. On the last years, see *Religio-Philosophical Journal*, Nov. 15, 1890; *New York Herald*, July 3, 1892, Mar. 9, 10, 1893; *New York Times*, Mar. 10, 1893.

45. Robert W. Delp, "Andrew Jackson Davis: Prophet of American Spiritualism," *Journal of American History*, 54 (1967):54; *Boston Globe*, Jan. 14, 1910.

46. University of Pennsylvania, *Preliminary Report*, p. 159.

47. Moore, *In Search of White Crows*, ch. 4.

48. See Raymond Prince, ed., *Trance and Possession States* (Montreal: R. M. Bucke Memorial Society, 1968), especially pt. I.

5

The American Theosophical Synthesis

ROBERT S. ELLWOOD, JR.

THEOSOPHY AND AMERICA

THE MODERN THEOSOPHICAL MOVEMENT, centering around the Theosophical Society founded in New York in 1875, has had a large part in
articulating the modern occult experience. It played a significant role in
the independence movements and cultural renaissances of such countries as India, Sri Lanka, and Ireland. Its voluminous writings and
multitudinous spiritual progeny—other movements like Anthroposophy, I Am, much of modern Gnosticism and astrology—have done
much to standardize and popularize Oriental and Hermetic teachings
in America in the late nineteenth and twentieth centuries.

Theosophy, with its far-traveling lecturers and widely accessible literature, brought alternatives to conventional Western spirituality to
places where the voice of strictly academic scholarship would be little
heard, but where there were those in the 1880s and 1890s who yearned
for a spiritual synthesis attuned to the expansive, idealistic, and increasingly pluralistic temper of the day. Their thirst had been stimulated by
the idealism and orientalism of Swedenborgians, transcendentalists,
spiritualists, and mesmerists. But it was not yet slaked. Theosophy
offered questors in cities large and small guidance and an intellectual
and organizational structure as they essayed this integration.

Thus the *Theosophic Messenger* of January, 1900, lists some seventy-
one branches of the society. They were not only in such fertile fields for
the esoteric as Boston, New York, and Los Angeles. Theosophical out-
posts were also found in such communities as Council Bluffs, Honolulu,
Sheridan (Wyoming), and Pierre (South Dakota). The White Lotus
Lodge in Pierre, for example, reported "very interesting and instructive

meetings every Saturday." This group had at the time of reporting gone through seven Theosophical manuals and was engaged in discussion of a chapter on karma.[1]

Today most of the lodges of 1900 are gone and others have come into existence. But Theosophy—now represented in the United States by at least three independent Theosophical Societies—goes on, never surging dramatically in membership, never dying out. Its work of presenting Eastern wisdom to the West has now been supplemented by that of a number of other organizations, such as the Vedanta Societies of the Ramakrishna Mission, transcendental meditation, and numerous yoga and Zen groups. Yet Theosophy remains, the custodian of the crystalized essence of the "Ancient Wisdom" behind them all, or, by less pretentious definition, the caretaker of a synthesis of several major currents of nineteenth-century spirituality. Our task in this study will be briefly to identify those currents and indicate how the world view of Theosophy brought them together.

The principal emphasis will be on Theosophy in 1875–78, the years between the founding of the society by Helena P. Blavatsky and Henry Steel Olcott and the departure of those "Theosophical Twins," as Olcott liked to call them, for a long sojourn in India where the movement underwent much development and suffered several vicissitudes. But we are here chiefly interested in the American aspect of things. Those four American years, which include the publication of Blavatsky's massive first book, *Isis Unveiled,* sufficiently indicate the relation of the Theosophical idea to the American background.

NOTES ON THEOSOPHICAL HISTORY

Theosophy is a continual process of synthesis, intended to draw truth from many wells and express the spiritual unity of humankind. Its view of the world's religions is a striking attempt to correlate them without reductionism or chauvinism, its history involves chapters set in both East and West, and in its two principal founders two very unlikely people of highly disparate backgrounds were brought together.

Helena Blavatsky (1831–91) was born of high Russian aristocracy. Her father was a Russian Army officer of German descent. Her mother, related to the ancient and princely Dolgorouky house, was a popular novelist whose stories inevitably centered on women suffering at the hands of callous men. Helena spent much of her childhood in the home of her maternal grandfather, a provincial governor of the czar. She was

Helena Petrovna Blavatsky ("HPB"). Courtesy of the Theosophical Society in America.

Henry Steel Olcott. Courtesy of the Theosophical Society in America.

an imaginative and strong-willed child who would tell long and involved stories about the present and past lives of the stuffed animals in her grandfather's private museum, and would sometimes hide and force the household with its regiment of servants to spend hours looking for her. As an adolescent she once burned her foot in scalding water rather than go to a viceroy's ball. But at eighteen she impulsively married N. V. Blavatsky, vice-governor of Erivan in Armenia and a widower more than twice her age. Helena soon left him to travel widely, studying spiritualism and magic and what lay behind them around the world. The details of her life between her marriage in 1849 and her arrival in New York in July, 1874, on a pilgrimage to observe spiritualism in its modern homeland, are not entirely clear.[2]

In October, 1874, she met Henry Steel Olcott in Chittenden, Vermont, at the home of the dour Eddy brothers, where sensational alleged spiritualist manifestations were drawing crowds nightly. Olcott was writing newspaper articles about them, which he later published in book form.[3] The Russian lady was perhaps attracted as much by the presence of the energetic journalist with spiritualist interests as by the spirits. The odd match took; Olcott, already estranged from his pious wife, made contact anew with the flamboyant pilgrim upon his return to the city. By the end of the following year he was sharing an apartment with her (though not, he makes clear, a bedroom). Olcott spent much time in the company of his enigmatic companion, astounded by her mysterious psychic "phenomena," amused by her colorful personality and racy conversation, initiated by her and her invisible mentors more and more deeply into the lore of Brahmavidya or "Eastern Spiritualism," whose practice was as far above the Western as heaven above earth.

The background of Henry Steel Olcott (1832–1907) contrasts mightily with that of the wandering Russian noblewoman. He came out of the sturdy middle class of small-town, democratic America. As a youth he spent some time on an uncle's farm in Ohio, where he witnessed some of the early manifestations of spiritualism and dabbled in mesmerism. He served the Union during the Civil War as an investigator of fraudulent suppliers, and afterward made his way in New York City through the practice of law combined with writing and journalism. When Madame Blavatsky entered his world, he was outwardly a successful and sociable man-about-town. But a failed marriage was behind him, and apparently he could not well contain an unmet inner yearning that in the end was to take him to far exotic places, to com-

merce with the "invisible government of the world," and to high office
in a new and controversial worldwide organization.

HPB—as she liked to be called (she hated the pomposity of "Madame")—quickly made a reputation for herself in the New World with
her pungent personality and articles on spiritualism, in which she directed acerbic attacks against its frauds while with equally forceful
sorties she defended those she regarded as genuine mediums. Understandably, the "Lamasery," as Olcott termed their apartment on West
47th Street, became a magnet for the city's coterie of seekers, esotericists, and Bohemians. It was the site of innumerable fascinating col-
loquia, uproarious parties, and informal lectures on the mysteries of
the ages, all of which is incomparably recorded in the first volume of
Olcott's delightful *Old Diary Leaves*.[4]

Given the Victorian penchant for organizations replete with charters,
slates of officers, and lofty principles, we are not surprised to note that
some of the Lamasery group determined on September 7, 1875, to
organize a society devoted to their interests. This was the Theosophical
Society, formally launched with the president's inaugural address on
November 17. The first president was Olcott; HPB became corresponding secretary, the only exoteric office she ever held in the society. While
she was certainly the catalyst of the movement, she had neither interest
in nor temper for administration.

The Theosophical Society of 1875–78 was a remarkably diverse
group. Early members included Thomas Edison, inventor of the electric light, and Abner Doubleday, supposed inventor of baseball. There
was at least one minister, a Unitarian. A lively handful of skeptical Irish
and Italian immigrants mixed with learned autodidacts such as Alexander Wilder, a self-taught physician and classicist of many parts, and
independently wealthy gentlemen-scholars like Charles Sotheran. Olcott tells us of a house-painter member learned in Greek philosophy.
The nascent society also attracted a congregation of spiritualists, but
they did not stay with it long.

Indeed, the Theosophical Society itself sustained vital life no more
than a few months in its 1875–78 manifestation. But as public response
dwindled, the inner circle, particularly Olcott and Blavatsky, with the
aid of Wilder, the Irishman William Q. Judge, and a few others, quickly
moved into another work. That was the writing and editing of HPB's
first book, *Isis Unveiled*. Not long after its publication and unexpect-
edly successful reception in 1877, Blavatsky and Olcott left for India
at the end of 1878, where the fortunes of Theosophy were to rise, fall,
and rise again even more dramatically than in America.[5]

BASIC THEOSOPHICAL TEACHING

What kinds of ideas were the Theosophists thinking and talking about during the years between the founding of the society and the departure for India? What can we learn of them from the massive manifesto of that period, *Isis Unveiled*? While the original Theosophical Society was intended as an open forum for speakers on a wide range of philosophical and esoteric topics, HPB from the beginning also saw it as a vehicle for imparting the Ancient Wisdom she believed it was her calling to present anew to the world.

Isis Unveiled, like the informal account of her talk and work given in such sources as Olcott's *Old Diary Leaves,* seems at first glance to be more than anything else a farrago of anecdotes about magic around the world, especially as practiced by witch-doctors and shamans in out-of-the-way places, together with sharp and often surprisingly sophisticated jabs at the prelates and scientists who refuse to perceive such marvels save as they are those of their own camp. But as the lengthy work continues, one finds that gradually a position emerges: behind the religions of the world lies a "monomyth," in Joseph Campbell's later term. The monomyth concerns the making-up of the universe and the individual human by the conjoining of three principles: matter, an invisible energizing spirit, and immortal consciousness. It tells us that true seership and magic are possible if based on knowledge of those principles. It also recounts the spiritual evolution of the universe.

This wisdom is reconstructed with the particular help of Neoplatonism, the Cabala, and certain texts from India. While holding that the same outlook is latent in the "myths" of conventional Judaism and Christianity, *Isis Unveiled* engages in much polemic against the institutionalized forms of the latter faith, which does little to raise the book above the usual nineteenth-century standards for such invective. At the same time, perhaps from the perspective of her own role as an oft-abused wanderer, Blavatsky comes across as very protective toward such subjects of bigotry as Jews and the victims of seventeenth-century witch-hunts.[6] She accepted the opinion of Gibbon that the ancient Gnostics were "the most polite, the most learned and most wealthy of the Christian name," and characteristically defended them against the abuse of the church fathers.[7]

This ancient wisdom did not die out "with the Philaletheians of the last Eclectic school." Rather, "The Gnosis lingers still on earth, and its votaries are many, albeit unknown."[8] She mentions in this connection a labyrinth of secret societies, Sufi, Druze, Hermetic, Rosicrucian, and the Brotherhood of Luxor in Egypt, as among those of sufficient visibility that they can at least be named.[9] Olcott was a student of an adept of Luxor during his early days with Blavatsky, but later, as their interests became more Eastern, he was transferred to the Indian section of the Universal Mystic Brotherhood.[10]

Here are a few features of the teaching communicated by Madame Blavatsky from the Ancient Wisdom and the Universal Mystic Brotherhood.

1.   The magic and mystery the author has uncovered around the world and down through the ages point not to strictly supernatural powers but, rather, to laws and forces as natural as gravitation but far less well known. It is these powers which seers and shamans understand. More specifically, there is an energy which flashes through all things. Call it aether, akasha, the Hermes-fire, the vril of Bulwer-Lytton, the odic force of Reichenbach, or the animal magnetism of Mesmer discussed by Schopenhauer,[11] it can be wielded by those who know its secrets to work wonders that seem to defy natural law. But actually it is nothing more than the stuff of spirit or form or potential life-energy, natural in its own way but of a very different nature than matter, for when life has leverage over matter its sovereignty is never in doubt, as the marvelous working of our own bodies demonstrates.

2.   The universe, then, is permeated with two substances, spirit and matter. Spirit is primary in that it is closer to the nature of the ultimate source of both streams, God, the Universal Mind and Universal Soul, and in that it bears the ideas which give form to matter. But matter is very important; it can attain highly sublimated forms, for even thoughts as they take form in the material brain and send out subtle waves—the aura—are material. Consciousness derives from the union of spirit and matter, and so reflects God, the unity from which both derive.

Although this teaching about spirit and matter is quite complex and far more subtle than a crude dualism, early Theosophy often presented a pronouncedly antimaterialistic face that emphasized the priority of spirit and the divine spark within each expression of life. This was chiefly a necessity of its trenchant debate with what Blavatsky and other Theosophists saw as the blatant materialism of the science of their day, hardly better than the shallow orthodoxy of the churches. Thus Alexander Wilder, who actually wrote the preface to *Isis Unveiled,* recalled Plato's allusion to the body as a grave and life in it as a dream.[12] But Theosophy moved quickly ahead to theurgic Neoplatonism, and discovery that the corpse is electric and can write the scenarios of its own dreams.

3. This basic universal truth is contained in the myths and legends, and veiled in the conventional religious teachings, of all peoples. Thus in *Isis Unveiled* we read of the "mystic primordial substance" as the biblical Spirit of God, the Egyptian Kneph, the mead of the gods in the Eddas, the primordial water out of which Oannes or Dagon taught the Chaldeans the world was made, the alkahest of the alchemists.[13] The view that the world's faiths have subtler interconnections than we might have supposed has led to unconventional interpretations of their origins and history as well. We are told that Jesus was actually a leading light of a sect of "new nazars," very much on the fringes of Judaism, who practiced Chaldean theurgy and who instructed his followers in a Buddhistic doctrine brought from India. That was not an opinion likely to sit well with traditional Christians. But very controversial theories quite comparable to it have recently been revived in the scholarly world on the basis of far more information about Hellenistic religion than was available in the 1880s.[14]

Theosophy was syncretistic (a word often unjustly maligned), affirming that the "ancient wisdom" was to be found, at least in bits and pieces, worldwide. Theosophists were then open to the spiritual paths of many traditions. Yoga, alchemy, even (in the later Liberal Catholic Church) Catholic sacramentalism could play their part in one's infinite journey. Moreover, one was open to the companionship of a great assembly of spiritual friends and mentors, for it would stand to reason that other beings in other places might be ahead of us on the great path. The well-known theosophical belief in a hierarchy of highly evolved Elder Brothers guiding the evolution of the world and the development of select individuals did not mature until a later generation than the 1880s. But its seeds were there: Olcott and Blavatsky received correspondence and even visits in the astral body from adepts of Egypt or India, and Blavatsky is said by Olcott to have written much of *Isis Unveiled* as a sort of amanuensis for Tibetan masters working through her. The juxtaposition of deep-diving philosophy, comparative religion, and rather spectacular talk about adepts is highly characteristic of Theosophy.

4. This universe composed of matter, spirit, and consciousness is in a continual process of evolution, an idea that brought Theosophical thought together with its Platonic, Cabalistic, and Eastern sources into engagement with modern Darwinism. That was not necessarily to the

latter's advantage: "It is an easy task to show that the cosmogonical legends all over the world are based on a knowledge by the ancients of those sciences which have allied themselves in our day to support the doctrine of evolution; and that further research may demonstrate that they were far better acquainted with the fact of evolution itself, embracing both its physical and spiritual aspects, than we are now."[15] Theosophy teaches that evolution is holistic, involving both biological organisms and the subtler entities of the realm of spirit. Moreover, in its echoes of the Gnostic myth of the fall of the children of light into the realm of matter, the ancient wisdom suggests that those evolutions have been separate until relatively recently, when they were conjoined to produce the human consciousness which reflects the divine.

Evolution, both individual and planetary, is really a series of initiations and so analogous to those of mystery schools, and to rebirths. By this striking concept, alluded to over and over in Theosophical writing, what in profane hands was a mere "natural selection," acquired in occultist eyes the status of an immense rite when its esoteric significance was understood. It is that side of things which the masters know, and which gives them power and wisdom; it is through their own series of initiations they have grown to great spiritual stature.

5.   Finally, once again let it be emphasized that for the early Theosophists such "sciences" as astrology, clairvoyance, or control of physical appearances through "mayavic" power were quite important. This was not only for their own sake, but even more because they represented employment of the subtle force whose reality and control they were learning. The popular forms of these arts were considered to be of little worth, mere fragments of the grand vision of the wise, but not to be despised or explained away as they were by those who knew not what they represented.

A related matter was Theosophical belief in an alternative line of evolution to that represented by the human, the "devic," which culminates in majestic demigods who control nature. These are correlated with the devas of Vedic India, the elementals of alchemical lore, and in their junior ranks with the fairies, gnomes, and elves of folklore.

NEOPLATONIC OCCULTISM

What is the background of this remarkable syncretism seeking to become a synthesis? The weightiest influence was clearly later Neoplatonism. The more occultist theurgic wing of Neoplatonism, which overwhelmed it in the end, stems not so much from Plato and Plotinus themselves as from later savants like Proclus and Iamblichus. They were swayed by the practice as well as, like Plato, the vision of Greek, Egyptian, and Chaldean mysteries and magic, and no doubt ultimately by shamanism. Theurgic Neoplatonism has ever run like an underground river beneath the terrain of Western civilization, perennially sending up fresh wellsprings of esotericism and "alternative" spirituality.

The lore of theurgic Neoplatonism can be seen behind the systems of the medieval Cabalist, magician, alchemist, and Manichee. In the Renaissance, Neoplatonism was virtually reborn to a brief but potent career as a major spiritual force aligned with the Age of Discovery's new awareness of the distant, the past, and the inward. But the passions of the Reformation and the cooler eye of the new science again sank the Chaldean river beneath the surface. Its early modern legacy remains in the voluminous tomes of the Florentine symposium, of Paracelsus and what Frances Yates has called the Rosicrucian Enlightenment. That legacy is part science, part alchemy and astrology, and part mysticism; of it the best that can be said (and this is not to be despised) is that its visionaries far more closely united the spiritual quest to the scientific quest for the knowledge which is power than has seemed possible since.

But though Neoplatonic occultism may have sunk underground, it did not go out of existence. The Age of Reason produced a spiritual counterculture represented by the likes of Cagliostro, Saint-Germain, the Illuminati, and the more esoteric aspects of Freemasonry. As though following some law of compensation, this counterculture countered with excessive credulity the wingless rationalism of the intellectual establishment. But it was patronized by some very well-placed persons, and kept Chaldea alive for romantic reconstruction in the next century. That revamping was done under the influence of two eighteenth-century scientist-philosophers who were well aware of the richest ancient and Renaissance Neoplatonist thought, and who both impelled what can justly be called social movements as well as intellectual causes: Emanuel Swedenborg and Anton Mesmer.

Swedenborg, seeking to explain spiritual matters with the exactitude of scientific discourse, revived the ancient doctrine of correspondences: he saw spiritual realities as prior to material; everything visible exists because it is the end-product of a spiritual force and reflects patterns laid in the spiritual world. Mesmer, a pioneer in hypnotism and psychosomatic medicine, sought to explain his findings through the concept of "animal magnetism," a subtle, universal force-substance that can give life and vitality. Its application through hypnotic techniques can cure illnesses; its awakening can also, Mesmer taught, open latent powers of perception transcending space and time: telepathy, clairvoyance, precognition, psychokinesis. Mesmer believed that much of what seers and mystics of the past did was valid, though for reasons previously not understood. On this basis Blavatsky later highly praised the Viennese doctor, calling mesmerism the most important key to magic and, indeed, the true base of all that appears magical or miraculous.[16]

In the nineteenth century the underground river became a torrent. Occult Neoplatonism was deepened by German idealism and spiritual evolutionism: Fichte, Schelling, and Hegel, interpreted by Coleridge to the English-speaking world. The tradition was given a new effervescence by the romantic exaltation of feeling as cognitive, especially the feelings of wonder, mystery, and expansion of awareness into the infinite so well given scope by its occult lore. Of the romantic and idealist philosophers, *Isis Unveiled* cites with particular appreciation Schopenhauer's *Parega und Paralipomena* (1851) on "animal magnetism" (which the German affirmed), on the priority of spirit (as will) over manifestation, on nature as "the infinite illusion of our senses."[17] On the other hand, it is interesting to note that HPB speaks of the metaphysical systems of Hegel and Schelling as "gigantic failures," unable to stem the rising tide of materialism.[18] That task would presumably require the deeper-set levees of mystery, miracle, and light from the East.

This judgment reflects well the predicament of Neoplatonism in the last century. It is easy, from the perspective of a century later, to view the era as virtually awash with the residue of Platonism, from the systems of the philosophers to the spiritualism and mentalism of popular culture. That was, however, hardly the way the century saw itself. Whether Christian, romantic, or Neoplatonist, spiritual-minded commentators as well as ordinary reformers saw little about them but crass materialism. As science moved decisively in a mechanistic direction, and philosophical culture lay torn between the German idealism and romanticism with which the age had begun and the ever-strengthening acids of scientific positivism, they perceived themselves, like HPB, as fighting a desperate rearguard action against all that is inimical to the spirit. Yet popular culture, when not conventionally religious, was ever receptive to the influx of idealist notions ultimately from the Platonic tradition, whether guised as Chatauqua transcendentalism, spiritualism, Theosophy, "New Thought," or even the liberal Christianity of Schleiermacher or Maurice.

THE GNOSIS IN THE NINETEENTH CENTURY

Despite the diversity of shapes, a core of ideas held this lineage together, especially in its forms more explicitly alternative to mainstream
Christianity. There is first a rigorous dualism of spirit and matter, more
sharply conceived than that of conventional faith, and with it belief in
the original goodness of spirit and the priority of spirit to matter. The
theme of occult initiation is also important, and so is a tendency to
legitimate the teaching by looking to ancient or distant examples. We
have observed that those themes were prominent in Theosophy.

Belief in the original goodness of spirit and its priority to the matter
into which it has fallen is an idea generally associated with Gnosticism.
Movements as diverse as Theosophy, Jungian psychology, and existentialism, having in common little more than an emphasis on intrapsychic
reality and the alienation of the individual psyche from its cosmic
environment, have been spoken of as modern Gnosticism. But often
these views fall short of embracing such distinctively Judaeo-Christian
Gnostic teachings as the "lower" Old Testament God, the rule of
malign planetary archons, and the uncrucified Savior.

Much confusion in the delineation of modern Gnosticism has resulted
from failure to distinguish carefully between Judaeo-Christian Gnosticism and the "pagan Gnosticism," or better Hermeticism, of the *Corpus
Hermeticum* brought to Florence as early as 1460. Hermeticism had no
small influence on Renaissance thought and so indirectly on modern
occultism. But its compacted correspondences and initiatory stages interlocking earth and heaven point to a rather more optimistic spiritual
world than Christian Gnosticism with its unimaginably remote unknown
God, its entrapped souls, and its universe riddled with malevolent
pseudo-gods. Outside the manuals of patristics scholars, who knew of
it only as among the heresies roundly denounced by the church fathers,
Judaeo-Christian Gnosticism was little regarded prior to the eighteenth-
century discovery of two original sources, the *Pistis Sophia* and the
Book of Jeu. But in the later eighteenth century Gnosticism began to
exert a distinctive intellectual pull. One example is its place in the
thought of William Blake. Kathleen Raine in her monumental study
Blake and Tradition opines that the poet had undoubtedly read of
Gnostics in Johan Lorenz von Mosheim's *Ecclesiastical History* (available in English in 1765) and Joseph Priestley's *Early Opinions Concerning Jesus Christ* (1786), and that this reading influenced, at the
least, Blake's belief that the temporal world had been created not by the

supreme God but by a satanic demiurge. The extent of influence of authentic Gnosticism, however, is uncertain; Blake was also familiar with the emanationism of Hermeticism and the Christian Neoplatonists and Cabalists from Paracelsus to Fludd, whose meditations could have led him to similar conclusions concerning the temporal order. His powerful poem "The Tyger" is believed to have been written in the excitement of his reading of Everard's translation of *The Divine Pymander* of Hermes Trismegistus.[19] Blake was called a Gnostic by his acquaintance Crabb Robinson, but we know not whether he would have applied the epithet to himself.

Almost a century later Madame Blavatsky took up again the cause of the Gnosis. Scattered through *Isis Unveiled* are affirmations of most of its principles, though their existential pessimism is much mitigated by her making them equivalents of more sanguinely expressed Eastern, Hermetic, and Cabalistic doctrines.

Gnosticism, she said, "taken in its abstract sense," in its doctrines of the illusory body of Christ suffering, its Unknown Abyss with No Name, its emanations, its lower God as an inferior being who does not contain the fullness of wisdom, represents a Western manifestation of that wisdom. She even set up in *Isis Unveiled* a chart showing that parallel entities under different names are posited in the Indian, "Chaldean," and Gnostic Ophite systems.[20] She quite justifiably took pains to show that these soteric schemes, far more than the "orthodox" ones, gave equal place to feminine and masculine principles.

She also affirmed that the suffering of Christ was spiritual rather than physical, and the atonement allegorical, for the Christos is really a collective term for the higher souls of all creatures on earth with which they are inwardly groaning to unite, and the passion of Jesus is an allegory of the initiatory ordeal beings must undergo to complete this transformation.[21]

Blavatsky derived her historical knowledge of Gnosticism chiefly from C. W. King's *The Gnostics and Their Remains,* first published in 1864. This was the first substantial book in English on the subject, though dependent on the original scholarship of French and German investigators, especially M. Jacques Matter's *Histoire Critique du Gnosticisme* (Paris, 1828). But King's work was the first to bring to the English-speaking public such fairly sensational new discoveries as the *Pistis Sophia* text.[22] King held that Gnosticism originally came from India, and indeed commented that every Christian heretical notion can be traced to "Indian speculative philosophy as its genuine fountainhead." Second to India, Egypt was the derivation of this river. In this, doubtless caught up in the excitement of nineteenth-century advances in Indology, King goes beyond Matter, who was content to stress Pythagorean, Platonic, and especially Persian origins. (The French scholar pointed particularly to the celestial hierarchy and cosmic dualism of the Zend-Avesta.) It might be added that Henry Mansel, in his long-respected work *The Gnostic Heresies* (1875), cites King's Indic theories without extensive discussion but with apparent approval, and finally posits "Buddhism modified by Platonism" as one of the three main sources of Gnosticism, along with "Platonism modified by Judaism" and "Persian dualism."

King compared, for example, the Valentinian system with the hierarchies of cosmic buddhas of Vajrayana in Nepal, probably on the basis of the texts which had been published earlier in the century by Csoma de Körös, the intrepid Hungarian scholar and traveler. King's concept of Buddhism seems to have been of a doctrine of divine emanations ending in terrestial creatures, who could then be reabsorbed into God by means of wisdom and asceticism. Although the possibility of Indic ideas in Gnosticism is not to be dismissed, King certainly overstated the case in seeing mystic India as the source of esoterica everywhere. In particular, we now know that the Vajrayana systems to which he referred were too late to have affected first- and second-century Gnosticism in the Mediterranean. Madame Blavatsky used King's hypothesis as one prop of her belief that India, and beyond it mysterious Tibet, were the present sources and reservoirs of the hidden and immemorial wisdom she was returning to the world.

TRANSCENDENTALISM

Let us now turn to the American precursors of Theosophy. If Swedenborgianism and transcendentalism were not, strictly speaking, antecedents to the Theosophy of Blavatsky and Olcott, they certainly helped prepare its way to acceptance by many souls. Popular movements that had their roots in these perspectives, especially spiritualism, were directly involved in the formation of Theosophy.

Marguerite Block, in her history of American Swedenborgianism, speaks of a "Swedenborgian wave" in the 1840s that washed through intellectual America and watered the early flowers of transcendentalism.[23] Certainly reflection on Swedenborgian themes in the ambiance of the expansive New World gave much impetus to the latter's inception. Mysticism has often been a response to cribbed or deteriorating social situations; transcendentalism was instead the irrepressible vigor of an optimistic and growing new society reaching spiritually into the Infinite. Understandably, then, in what Catherine Albanese has called transcendentalism's "kinetic revolution," thinkers like Emerson made motion into virtually an absolute, a form of perfection in itself—a concept that could later justify both the infinite evolution through infinite worlds of the "cosmic pilgrim" in Theosophical thought and the peripatetic careers of its leading lights.[24] Transcendentalism revived again the ancient Neoplatonic doctrines of correspondence and the priority of spirit. The soul, it taught, has a separate destiny from the body, a destiny in which it must leave behind all that confines and find its kinship with the unbounded Oversoul. This realization is found by plunging inward, discovering from one's soul itself one's true nature. There one learns inwardly, as did the initiates of the ancient mysteries, that movement is grace, for one is only a transient here—one has come from realms of light and will return thither.

SPIRITUALISM

Soon enough America was ready for a more concrete expression of the separateness of spirit from its fleshly envelope. That expression emerged in the late 1840s as spiritualism, a movement that took the country by ghostly storm in the 50s. John Humphrey Noyes, of the Oneida Community, once remarked that spiritualism was "Swedenborgianism Americanized." This is hyperbole, but contains more than a modicum of truth. We would cover the truth fairly well by saying that spiritualism is Swedenborgian ideology, mixed with an experimentation with transic states inspired by mesmerism that easily led to mediumship of Swedenborg's spirits, and set before the backdrop of Native American shamanism. To the whole Neoplatonist tradition as transmitted by Swedenborg, spiritualism owes the motif of the separate destiny of the soul, and to Swedenborg also its characteristic stress on the afterlife as a place for growth and education rather than for the forensic judgment preached by the orthodox religions of the day; from Mesmer and shamanism it borrowed the experiential techniques so eagerly seized and wielded by an audacious, self-confident new society.

Spiritualism also revived the experience of sacred meaning in immediate access to the distant and the past. The spiritualist experience actually began (a decade or so before the famous "Rochester rappings" of the Fox sisters, which launched the national movement) within

Shaker communities. Their holy meetings were attended, as were later seances, by biblical figures and worthies like Mother Ann Lee of the first Shaker generation. The temporal span between a significant past— whether (in spiritualism) the lifetime of departed loved ones or the remote past of sacred time—Mircea Eliade's *illud tempus*—is thus annihilated, and in the present holy hour of the seance or meeting that past is brought into immediate contact with the now.

When Madame Blavatsky began attending the Chittenden evening seances with Olcott, remarkable figures from Russia and Caucasia began to appear along with the Native American guides and little girls common to American spiritualism. Space was banished, even as in Theosophy time was to be devoured by its ancient wisdom in gulps that made those of geology seem puny, as teachers from temples along the ancient Nile or Ganges spoke of aeons measured by Hindu kalpas and pralayas.

Transcendentalism also encouraged legitimation in the distant and the past, as had its forerunner Swedenborg. The Stockholm sage had spoken of a "Lost Word," which seemed to represent both primeval innocence and a transformative philosopher's stone. In a passage that reminds one strongly of the Stanzas of Dzyan, said to have been preserved in inner Asia and with which Blavatsky opened *The Secret Doctrine*,[25] the Swede referred to an arcane scripture preserved in the same region: "The ancient Word, which existed in Asia before the Israelitish Word, is still preserved among the people of Great Tartary. In the spiritual world I have conversed with spirits and angels who came from that country. They told me they had possessed from the most ancient times and still possessed a Word; and that they performed their divine worship in accordance with this word which consisted of pure correspondences."[26]

The orientalism of the transcendentalists is well known. The vague but evocative notion that a wisdom of incalculable antiquity and depth beside which the best of the West is but child's play could be found in Asia, though now somewhat to the south of Great Tartary, is reflected in the famous lines from *Walden* which speak of the *Bhagavad-Gita,* "since whose composition years of the gods have elapsed, and in comparison to which our modern world and its literature seem puny and trivial." As he reads that "stupendous and cosmogonal philosophy," Thoreau tells us, "the pure Walden water is mingled with the sacred water of the Ganges."[27]

Somewhat later outflowed Walt Whitman's "Passage to India," which sums up even better the inward meaning that the East, and now

especially India and the enigmatic Tibet beyond it, were to have for
Theosophists and their kin. The poet sang not only of "Passage O soul
to India!" but also of "Passage to more than India!" The India then
basking in the high noon of the British Raj was not the India those
seekers sought. It was less India as a place than India as an idea, a
dream, a spiritual treasure-house of wonder and wisdom older and
stronger than any the triumphant West in its shrill pride could compre-
hend. Yet there were those who would seek it out, and within a decade
of Whitman's poem, written to celebrate the opening of the Suez Canal,
Olcott and Blavatsky were sailing through that marvel of nineteenth-
century engineering to find what was greater even than it. Already in
Isis Unveiled the wisdom of India had been used extensively to legitimate the critique of modern science and religion, as had that of the
Greeks, Egyptians, and Chaldeans, and from then on it was employed
still more.

The passage of the Theosophical Twins to India and more than India
was like a pilgrimage, and so like an initiation. More explicit concepts
of initiation—and experiences of them—were part of the nineteenth-
century esoteric background that preceded Theosophy. Spiritualists like
Andrew Jackson Davis and D. D. Home reported remarkable inner
initiations that bear a striking similarity to those of archaic shamanism.
(The initiation of each man occurred shortly after his mother's death
and began with hearing her voice call him in the middle of the night. In
the case of Davis, the summons was followed by marvelous flight over
mountainous terrain toward encounters with high and solemn spirits,
including the shade of Swedenborg.)

Interest in initiation of a more occultist sort was fostered by the
novels of Edward George Bulwer-Lytton, especially *Zanoni* (1842),
which greatly influenced Blavatsky and other early Theosophists.
Bulwer-Lytton (whose son, the poet and romantic imperialist Robert
Bulwer-Lytton, was, curiously, viceroy of India at the time of the advent
there of the Theosophists) took occultism seriously and drew substantially from the writings of such men as Éliphas Lévi, architect of the
French occult revival, in his portrayal of Mejnour, a mysterious, highly
initiated surviving member of a Rosicrucian fraternity, and his disciple
Zanoni.[28]

Closely intertwined with this sort of occultist lore, and with the roots
of modern Theosophy, is the world of Freemasonry. The importance
of Masonry as a cultural and spiritual force has declined in the twentieth century. But in the eighteenth, when it was founded in its modern
form, Masonry was a major influence for the dissemination of emergent

political and spiritual ideas, and for the assembly of people of progressive temperament. Politically it was usually aligned with anticlericalism and bourgeois reformism. Spiritually it favored a version of the Neoplatonist heritage derived ultimately from the "Rosicrucian Enlightenment" but deeply dyed with deism. From the former it borrowed a proclivity for initiations and legitimation through putative lineages from ancient mystery orders. From the latter it took an ethical emphasis and a general sense of affinity with "reason" and "science."

In the nineteenth century Masonry became steadily more bourgeois and nonradical on both the political and religious fronts, especially in the English-speaking world where the preponderance of Masons lived. But though any deeply felt occultism may have gone out of it, Freemasonry still made much of its ties with ancient and medieval mysteries; it was still in ambiguous relation to orthodox Christianity and maintained more than a little of the language and symbols of the Neoplatonist alternative tradition. Masonry was the obvious model to which one who wished to create new and perhaps more serious vehicles for the ancient wisdom looked. Theosophy was not the only such attempt, nor was it the most overtly Masonic. It soon lost whatever it once had of such Masonic externals as formal initiations and secret handshakes. It rejected the Masonic principle of sexual separation, even to the extent of later establishing "Co-Masonry," an order of the Masonic sort in which men and women participated together. But its meetings were called lodges, and the idea of successive "degree" initiations is deeply implanted in the Theosophical consciousness—even though Theosophists usually experience these transitions inwardly rather than ritually.[29]

The several strands whose interweaving made up Theosophy are well represented in the books Olcott tells us HPB used often in the composition of *Isis*.[30] These include King's *Gnostics*; Hargrave Jennings's curious *The Rosicrucians*;[31] S. F. Dunlop's singular *Sōd, the Son of the Man*,[32] a spiritualist historical inquiry, from which the material about Jesus as a nazar magician was derived; Moor's pioneer *Hindoo Pantheon*;[33] various works of the occultist Éliphas Lévi, of the Indologist L. Jacolliot, and of scholars, scientists, or philosophers of the rank of Max Muller, T. H. Huxley, Herbert Spencer, and John Tyndall—persons with whom HPB did not always agree but whose books she consulted.

The mind of Helena Blavatsky was eclectic, not to say disorganized, and she was woefully unschooled in the scholarly and philosophical methods of the academy. Much the same could be said for many, though not all, of the early Theosophists. But their concerns were far from trivial. The colorful gossip and scandal which always accompanied

HPB and the Theosophical movement, and which to this day unduly
fill historical treatments of it, have often obscured the facts that Theosophy was a response to certain of the central deep-level issues of the day,
and that it managed to interest some of the brightest and most idealistic
people in its milieu, even more in Europe and India than America.

The significant conundrum to which Theosophy was a response,
judging from what seem to be the deep themes of *Isis Unveiled,* is this:
the great conflict between science and religion, which so preoccupied
intelligent late Victorians, could never be resolved in the terms in which
it was being fought. Science could not be defeated by religion because
of the way in which it set the field and the rules of the game. It generally
raised the challenging new problems—Darwinism, empirical psychology—to which the adversary could only respond defensively, it provided the "hard" data upon which the argument had to be fought, and
increasingly its methods of verification were the models by which critics
insisted all truth claims must be judged.

But, on the other hand, nineteenth-century science could not justly
claim that its hard-won knowledge was truly comprehensive, and *Isis*
seems to have been perceptive enough to intuit the Achilles heel that
falsified any claim that it was. Science's very dedication to the objective
models of natural law which seemed then to offer the best verification
results meant that it methodologically excluded from any coherent part
in the fabric of reality that which lay behind the objective eye: subjective consciousness. Neither in the observer nor in the universe did consciousness fit; yet, as the idealists had so lately proclaimed, for us humans it ought to be the most obvious reality of all.

Religionists were willing, of course, to argue loudly for consciousness
in self and universe, for soul and God. Yet the ossified spiritual institutions of the day were poorly equipped to take advantage of the weak
link in the mail of a foeman whose armor was otherwise so shining and
demeanor so priestly. As HPB did not fail to point out, the parochialism
of churches, their concern for peculiar dogmas and consequent failure
to align themselves with the spiritual quest of humankind as a whole,
made them a laughingstock to those who, in an expansive new age, were
increasingly aware of the majestic antiquity and awesome pluralism of
religion as a total human concern, rather than as a stock-in-trade of one
or another sacerdotal shop.

Theosophy's program was through rational but not reductionistic
means to restore consciousness as a pervasive presence to the world
described by science, and to liberate religion to enjoy its worldwide
heritage and its ultimate compatibility with all that science discovers.

To do so it must, HPB believed, draw models for reality undogmatically but forcefully from the wisdom of those the wisest in spirituality's worldwide past. Something had once been known, she was convinced, that was lost amid the rise of competitive religion and one-dimensional science in historical times. We have seen what some of those models were, and what the more immediate sources for them were in traditions she thought best in touch with that past and its hidden but living present. The details are perhaps less important than the program in understanding the appeal of Theosophy, and its initial emergence as a synthesis attempting to contain an epochal crisis in the human spirit.

NOTES

1. *Theosophic Messenger,* Jan. 1900.
2. According to Madame Blavatsky's own account, she spent much of those years in a worldwide quest for spiritual lore that culminated in Tibet in the late 1860s. There, at the roof of the world, she received occult initiations. Her cousin, Count Witte, once Nicholas II's prime minister, tells us in his memoirs that the family rebel traveled about Europe with an opera singer and tried her hand at business in Odessa. But his account, written in old age many decades later, contains enough obvious lapses of memory to make us hesitant to put complete faith in the great statesman's recollections of his notorious relative. (He has the Theosophical Society founded in England instead of New York.) Other stories make Helena Blavatsky tour Europe as a concert pianist or ride bareback in a Turkish circus. She was in England in 1851, and back in Russia in 1858–63 and 1867, but for the other years there is limited independent documentation. Tantalizing hints exist. After late 1861 or 1862 she had a baby boy named Yuri with her—an extant Russian passport of 1862 attests to this—but the child died in 1867. She kept a notebook of travels in the Balkans, apparently in 1866 or 1867. She was a friend of the basso Agardi Metrovitch, with whom Witte linked her, and was with him at various times in their wanderings. For further discussion of this fascinating life, see Marion Meade, *Madame Blavatsky: The Woman behind the Myth* (New York: Putnam, 1980). See also the relevant material in a more cautious and hermeneutically sophisticated work, Bruce F. Campbell, *Ancient Wisdom Revived: A History of the Theosophical Movement* (Berkeley and Los Angeles: University of California Press, 1980), especially pp. 4–6.
3. Henry Steel Olcott, *People from the Other World* (Hartford, Conn.: American Publishing Co., 1875; reprinted, Rutland, Vt.: Charles E. Tuttle, 1972).
4. Henry Steel Olcott, *Old Diary Leaves, First Series: America 1874–1878* (Adyar, Madras, India: Theosophical Publishing House, 1895, 1941). Despite the title, these are not diary reprints but reminiscences penned some years after the events. The subsequent five volumes carry Olcott's recollections of Blavatsky and Theosophy up to 1898.

5. The reasons for the journey to India and its meaning are explored in my *Alternative Altars: Unconventional and Eastern Spirituality in America* (Chicago: University of Chicago Press, 1979), ch. 5.

6. In view of recent attempts to link Theosophy and the writings of Madame Blavatsky with the rise of anti-Semitism and Nazism, a word should be said about Blavatsky's attitude toward Jews and Judaism.

It is true that some Theosophists have been anti-Semitic, but it is also true that once the Nazis came to power they persecuted German Theosophists viciously. Certainly the Nazis appropriated in their muddled way terms and concepts from such racist occultist groups as the Thule Society and the Germanen Order, as they did from any source they could use, whether fairly or not, to construct what passed for the intellectual expression of a virulently antirational cause. Certainly occult groups like those in turn borrowed terms and concepts from Theosophy as well as from other nineteenth-century esoteric sources. The Theosophical concept of root races and historical cycles, removed from its proper level of abstraction, can too easily lend itself to the use of those who wish to speak of races whose time has come and of others whose time has run out.

But it should also be noted that whenever Theosophy in a pure form and self-identified Theosophists, like Annie Besant in India or George Russell (AE) in Ireland, have been conspicuously involved in such social causes as the independence movements and cultural renewals of India, Sri Lanka, or Ireland, they have been on the side of democracy and responsible reform. So, in a different way, have the bulk of American Theosophists.

Regarding Judaism, first let it be noted that Blavatsky pays that faith a considerable tribute by her extensive use of the Cabala. She apparently judged no Christian intellectual or mystical system its equal. Olcott tells us: "I have known a Jewish Rabbi pass hours and whole evenings in her company, discussing the Kabbala, and have heard him say to her that although he had studied the secret science of his religion for thirty years, she had taught him things he had not even dreamed of, and thrown a clear light upon passages which not even his best teachers had understood" (*Old Diary Leaves, First Series,* p. 206).

In pursuance of her comparativist and Gnostic revival programs, Blavatsky speaks of the God of the Israelites as a Moloch or as a lower demiurge. These passages have been seized upon by those who wish to show her feeding fuel to anti-Semitism. But of the abominable god Moloch she claims only that "in their early days," before the prophets who denounced such deities, the Israelites had worshipped a god of the type of Baal, Moloch, Hercules, or Shiva—the archaic agricultural god. See H. P. Blavatsky, *Isis Unveiled,* 2 vols. (Wheaton, Ill.: Theosophical Publishing House, 1972; facsimile of first edition, New York: J. W. Bouton, 1877), 2:524.

Making the God of the Old Testament a lower and less reliable deity than the utterly transcendent Lord of Light who is the true Father is simply a part of the Gnostic package. The doctrine is not necessarily anti-Semitic; the Cabala contains real echoes of the same vision, and modern scholarship has moved strongly toward the view that Gnosticism, far from reflecting Gentile anti-Semitism, largely arose among Jews who perhaps suffered under an ancient version of Freud's problems with the God of Moses.

Finally, Blavatsky tells us: "But we should not regard the Israelites with less favor for having had a Moloch and being like the natives. Nor should we compel the Jews to do penance for their fathers. They had their prophets and their law, and were satisfied with them. How faithfully and nobly they have stood by their ancestral faith under the most diabolical persecutions, the present remains of a once-glorious people bear witness. The Christian world has been in a state of convulsion from the first to the present century; it has been cleft into thousands of sects; but the Jews remain substantially united. Even their differences of opinion do not destroy their unity" (*Isis Unveiled*, 2:526).

7. *Isis Unveiled*, 2:249.

8. Ibid., p. 402.

9. Ibid., pp. 306ff.

10. Olcott, *Old Diary Leaves, First Series*, pp. 75–76.

11. *Isis Unveiled*, 1:125.

12. Ibid., p. xiii.

13. Ibid., p. 133.

14. Ibid., 2:129–34. See Morton Smith, *Jesus the Magician* (New York: Harper and Row, 1978).

15. *Isis Unveiled*, 1:134.

16. Ibid., p. 129.

17. Ibid., pp. 58–60; 2:158.

18. Ibid., 2:369.

19. Kathleen Raine, *Blake and Tradition* (Princeton, N.J.: Princeton University Press, 1968), 2:12–16.

20. *Isis Unveiled*, 2:170.

21. Ibid., pp. 158–59.

22. William Emmette Coleman accused Blavatsky of having borrowed some forty passages from King. The latter author himself, however, seems not unduly worried by the alleged plagiarism, judging from the tone in which he alluded to her in the introduction to the 1887 edition of his works. "Buddhism" is used here as Blavatsky often used it, in its root sense of "Wisdomism": "There seems reason for suspecting that the Sibyl of *Esoteric Buddhism* drew the first notions of her new religion from the analysis of the *Inner Man*, as set forth in my first edition. I may therefore promise to myself the gratitude of those 'clear spirits' (the Miltonian phrase) who are busying themselves 'by searching to find out God,' for now making known to them a still more profound theosophy, whose revelations definitely settle hardest problems relating to our mental nature, and the world beyond the grave. Investigators of the same order as the *Esoteric Buddhists* will find here a Gospel ready made to their hand—so full of great truths, so original in its conceptions, that it would seem to flow from no human source; and must carry conviction of its divine origin to every mind that shall be adapted by its nature for the reception of the *good seed*" (C. W. King, *The Gnostics and Their Remains*, 2d ed. [London: David Nutt, 1887], p. ix). A summary of William Emmette Coleman, "The Sources of Madame Blavatsky's Writings," can be found in V. S. Solovyoff, *A Modern Priestess of Isis* (London: Longmans, Green, 1895; reprinted, New York: Arno Press, 1976), Appendix C.

Bruce F. Campbell has gone to the trouble of checking a substantial sample of the some 2,000 plagiarisms Coleman alleged to have found in *Isis Unveiled*. Campbell concludes that they do exist but are nearly all on the level of phrases and sentences in the midst of longer unplagiarized discourses, and so in a work of some 1,400 pages probably do not represent more than 5 percent or so of the total. He contends, however, that 2,000 entries is nonetheless plagiarism on a large scale and challenges the traditional Theosophical interpretation of the source of the book. Campbell, *Ancient Wisdom Revived,* pp. 33–35.

23. Marguerite Block, *The New Church in the New World* (New York: Henry Holt, 1932), pp. 158–59.

24. Catherine L. Albanese, *Corresponding Motion: Transcendental Religion and the New America* (Philadelphia: Temple University Press, 1977).

25. H. P. Blavatsky, *The Secret Doctrine* (Adyar, Madras, India: Theosophical Publishing House, 1888; 6th Adyar ed., 1971).

26. Emanuel Swedenborg, *The True Christian Religion* (London: Everyman's Library, 1936), p. 335.

27. Henry David Thoreau, *Walden* (New York: New American Library, 1942), pp. 198–99.

28. See Sten Bodvar Liljegren, *Bulwer-Lytton's Novels and Isis Unveiled* (Cambridge, Mass.: Harvard University Press, 1957).

29. For a fascinating account of occult Theosophical initiations, see Charles W. Leadbeater, *The Masters and the Path* (Adyar, Madras, India: Theosophical Publishing House, 1925, 1965).

30. Olcott, *Old Diary Leaves, First Series,* p. 207.

31. Hargrave Jennings, *The Rosicrucians* (London, 1870, 1887; reprinted, New York: Arno Press, 1976).

32. S. F. Dunlop, *Sōd, the Son of the Man* (London and Edinburgh, 1861).

33. E. Moor, *The Hindoo Pantheon* (1810; new ed. annot. W. O. Simpson, Madras, 1864).

6

The Occult Connection?
Mormonism, Christian Science,
and Spiritualism

R. LAURENCE MOORE

EVERYONE KNOWS that the prestige of science grew by leaps and bounds in the nineteenth century and that the process of secularization, however secularization is defined, profoundly affected American culture in its first one hundred republican years. However, a number of recent studies have suggested that the triumph of the modern scientific perspective over the popular imagination has been exaggerated.[1] The Christian religion made adjustments to science and to Darwin, but liberal theology scarcely eliminated the competition of various kinds of Bible-oriented fundamentalism.[2] Moreover, the obvious attention that many Americans gave to occult and esoteric science, particularly in the last quarter of the nineteenth century, suggests that the popular enthusiasm for something called science often embraced activities that professional scientists regarded as absolutely inimical to their goals.

The aim of this essay is to provide an estimate of the appeal of occultism in nineteenth-century America by examining the permeation of magical and esoteric ideas into three religions that were launched during the nineteenth century: Mormonism, Christian Science, and spiritualism. The possible significance of the investigation was suggested to me by the charges of opponents that those religions threatened a recrudescence of astrology, Cabalism, witchcraft, and related forms of satanically inspired belief.[3] According to many nineteenth-century assessments, Joseph Smith, Mary Baker Eddy, and the Fox sisters appealed to the dark and magic-craving side of human nature. They promised to make their followers privy to extra-ordinary forces in the universe that sensible people had decided either to leave alone or to dismiss as pre-Enlightenment fantasies.

Our investigation calls for caution because occultism was usually bandied about in the latter part of the nineteenth century as a pejorative term. None of the groups I propose to examine accepted for a moment the charge that it was occult (although each vigorously directed the charge at the others). Historians can try to detach themselves from the confused charges and countercharges that historical actors made and use their own notion of what constitutes occult and esoteric belief to settle the truth of those charges. But they cannot completely escape the implication of the observation that superstition is a label for the other person's religion. From somebody's point of view, all systems of thought, whether Roman Catholicism or the modern physics of quarks and gluons, are tainted with occult associations.

Most religions are inescapably implicated in practices associated with popular notions about occultism if someone chooses to make the connections. Historians of religion are always going to have trouble holding firm the distinction drawn by Frazer, Malinowski, Durkheim, and others, between a religious confession of human impotence before superior powers and magical, occult attempts to control nature by tapping hidden sources of power.[4] The important question, then, is not whether this or that religious group was truly occult, despite the denials of the group, but what factors made the charges plausible in a given historical context. Nothing in this essay is meant to suggest that Mormonism, Christian Science, and spiritualism are best understood as occult systems utterly removed from any common themes that one finds among other American religious groups. The aim is rather to investigate the practices that allowed many people to promote that conclusion and to suggest some implications of those practices for American cultural history.

To begin this enterprise, we might dwell briefly on one group founded in the late nineteenth century that freely embraced the label "occult," Madame Blavatsky's Theosophical Society. As the closest approach to a systematically occult group in nineteenth-century America, it suggests some guidelines for judging what tendencies in Mormonism, Christian Science, and spiritualism made them vulnerable to the charge of occultism.[5]

The leaders of the Theosophical Society claimed to be "heirs of a greater knowledge concerning the mysteries of Nature and humanity than modern culture has yet evolved."[6] They presumed to know age-old secrets, gleaned in part from the study of ancient texts, in part from the development of a higher spiritual consciousness that transcended and made irrelevant the perceptions of our normal senses. Although Blavatsky and her successors wrote books about Theosophy, only initiation into the secret rites of the society and advancement through a series of stages reminiscent of Masonic lodge degrees provided a full understanding of the highest truths guarded by Theosophy. Occult knowledge was most assuredly not for everyone. Because of the presumed power that occult knowledge commanded over natural phenomena, a knowledge that made practical occultism and magic the same thing, a number of doctrines had to be kept secret. Those who attained information about magical techniques without having first received wisdom were potentially very dangerous people.

In intention, and usually in practice, the early Theosophical Society was a hierarchical, even authoritarian, movement that turned its back on general social concerns. It invited its members to pursue a higher form of personal, spiritual growth than they could by following the normal patterns of American life. As with most previous Western enterprises self-consciously dedicated to the study of occult things, Theosophic wisdom rested on a pantheistic metaphysics that linked it to Neoplatonism, Christian Gnosticism, and various religious traditions of Asia. That emphasis, along with a cosmic "harmonial" theme that in some interpretations reduced evil to an illusion, affronted ministers in virtually all Christian pulpits.

If these things, taken together, characterize occultism and esoteric philosophy, and it seems to me that they do, then Mormonism, Christian Science, and spiritualism don't come very close to an "ideal type" of occultism. However, we can still ask whether they contained enough bits and pieces of occult systems to offer historians a critical perspective on statements that have stressed the imperialistic success of modern science. Moreover, given the highly charged antagonisms directed at nineteenth-century American groups that tried to keep their activities secret, we can usefully ask why groups that strenuously rejected the occult label nonetheless consciously adopted practices that left them vulnerable to the charge. Traces of an occultist tradition may survive and prosper not because men and women crave atavistic answers to what is unknowable, but because the tradition continues to make sense and have uses to people who live within the cultural frameworks of the nineteenth and twentieth centuries.

The standard accounts of Mormonism make it difficult to take seriously the author of a book titled *Occultism: The True Origin of Mor-*

monism.[7] Many of the philosophical underpinnings of Mormonism either derived from Protestantism or were peculiar in ways that had nothing to do with occult traditions. Mormons, for example, did not challenge the reliability of our common sensory awareness in reaching the highest levels of wisdom. For the most part they were eager to confirm their faith by citing evidence received through ordinary sensory channels—hence the importance they assigned to the statements of those who allegedly witnessed the golden plates. They even taught that our ordinary senses would continue to serve us in the life to come. Arguably, the Mormon religion espouses a more materialistic metaphysics than any in the history of Christianity. The Mormon God is reduced neither to a pure principle nor to a pantheistic abstraction. He has flesh and bones. Far from teaching a doctrine of ultimate oneness, Mormons believe that individual human beings may become gods.

Nonetheless, nineteenth-century critics of the Mormons insisted that elements of occultism surrounded the discovery and translation of the Book of Mormon. After all, the Book of Mormon was purported to be an ancient text and, in a fashion, a repository of lost wisdom. To find it, Joseph Smith received assistance from the spiritual world, an assistance that marked him off as a man of extra-ordinary powers. To translate it, he had to use two peep stones, the Urim and the Thummin, devices easily linked in the popular mind to the lore of necromancy.[8] As if these things weren't enough, Smith later claimed to translate an ancient Egyptian manuscript that fell into his hands in 1835. This was published in 1842 as the *Book of Abraham.*

In many ways these connections with occultism were merely superficial. Smith's fascination with Egypt, as Fawn Brodie demonstrated in her important biography of him, was rooted in the popular culture of the 1830s.[9] Since nothing in the content of Smith's "translations" suggested intellectual links to Hermes Trismegistus, Giordano Bruno, or Paracelsus, no one has yet turned Joseph Smith into a very convincing alchemist or Rosicrucian. However, the connections become more suggestive when one considers the initiatory rites developed by the Mormon church and the uses made of those rites to protect the inner secrets of the group. Eber Howe, who wrote one of the earliest in a series of seemingly endless Mormon exposés, attributed Joseph Smith's success to the "propensity for the marvelous in the human mind." Howe's attempt to get at the truth, he said, had been made difficult because Mormonism "has from its birth been so studiously vailed [*sic*] in secrecy, and generally under a belief that the judgments of God would follow any disclosures of what its votaries had seen or heard." "The half," he warned his readers, "is yet untold."[10]

Throughout the 1830s Mormon leaders vigorously denied that they ran a secret society. The Book of Mormon explicitly condemned secret societies. According to a statement issued by the twelve apostles in 1841, "there are no mysteries connected with godliness and our holy religion, but what are pure, innocent, virtuous, just, and righteous."[11] Few of Mormonism's critics, however, were convinced by this and many similar denials. They listened instead to Daniel Kidder, who wrote: "In the whole history of the delusion there never has occurred a single instance of a frank development of their peculiar tenets before an un-initiated audience. The elders are expressly instructed not to declare anything more than the first principles to those who are unbelievers, 'leaving the further mysteries of the kingdom' until afterward."[12] Or to Benjamin Ferris, who said: "The Mormon hierarchy has all the effi-ciency of a secret society: its members are initiated into different de-grees; take oaths of allegiance to the Church, of vengeance upon their former persecutors, and of denunciations upon themselves in case of apostasy; and have signs and pass words by which they recognize each other in any part of the world."[13]

Without any question, Mormon leaders did deliberately hold back information about their activities from the general public. In fact, they concealed many things from their own followers. Motives as usual were mixed, and the historian must acknowledge that the strategy of secrecy was to a certain extent pursued as a simple expedient to avoid persecu-tion. In explaining why he had for a time kept "secret the circumstances of having received the Priesthood," Joseph Smith referred correctly to "a spirit of persecution which had already manifested itself in the neighborhood."[14] Sidney Rigdon, who was the second most important figure in the Mormon church during the 1830s, justified secret meet-ings by saying: "If we had talked in public, we should have been ridi-culed more than we were. The world, being entirely ignorant of the testi-mony of the Prophets, and without knowledge of what God was about to do, treated all we said with pretended contempt and much ridicule, and had they heard all we said, it would have made worse for us."[15]

The reality of the savage persecutions that the Mormons encountered in Missouri during the 1830s certainly explained the Mormons' most notorious experiment with secrecy, the organization of the Daughters of Zion, or, more simply, the Danites. This terrorist band, formed by Sampson Avard, adopted an elaborate set of secret rituals and oaths whose purpose was to conceal the names of its members and the extent of its activities. As historians have learned, the strategy worked extremely well; they have subsequently been unable to find out much about it. The extent to which Smith and other church leaders encouraged (or discouraged) Danite activities is not even clear. We need not worry here whether the public denunciations against the Danites made by Mormon leaders ("pure friendship always becomes weakened the very moment you undertake to make it stronger by penal oaths and secrecy") served to cover over secret plots against the "Gentile" inhabitants of Illinois and Utah.[16] It is only necessary to note that not everything the Mormons did in secret carried overtones of occultism.

However, other developments in the Church of Jesus Christ of Latter-day Saints suggest that secrecy within the Mormon organization was not merely, or even primarily, a response to persecution. Since the alleged secrecy was within a short time used to justify the persecution, it clearly had other meanings and functions within the church. For example, when Joseph Smith began in the 1830s to organize the church hierarchy and established the Aaronic and Melchizedek priesthoods, he was in effect delineating stages that marked an ascending order of spirituality. Those toward the top of the order held keys to rather special powers. They could, for example, perform healing miracles. Although these powers seem to have been fairly widely distributed (in the beginning Joseph Smith was not the only Mormon to receive revelations), not everyone in the church stood on an equal plane with respect to spiritual enlightenment. The Mormon hierarchy, in a way that sharply contrasted with the hierarchies of any of America's Protestant churches, implied an ascending order of spiritual consciousness and power.

Some members of the Mormon church, then, were prepared to learn the full truth of God's revelations before other members. The concealment of the plural wife system provided the clearest application of this principle. When the Mormon church made official its policy of encouraging polygamy in 1852, no one was surprised. But when the unofficial practice of polygamy by church leaders became widely recognized in the 1840s, a good many Mormons who purposely had been left in the dark were shocked. B. H. Roberts, the Mormon church historian, believed that Smith received the revelation about polygamy in 1831 but, waiting for the further spiritual development of his followers, concealed it from all but a few of his closest associates.[17] From the beginning of his leadership, Smith clearly distinguished between communications "to be received only by the spiritual minded" and those that could be known at present even "to the weakest of the Saints."[18] To his enemies this selective disclosure constituted a high-handed authoritarianism. To Smith it was dictated by a new dispensation whose full truth would blind and confuse everyone but himself. The truth about "the glories and privileges of the Saints," known to Smith and a few associates, would one day be known to all Mormons, but not until they were further tested and then initiated into lesser mysteries.

The secret temple rituals, which Joseph Smith did not fully elaborate until the Nauvoo period, became, of course, the major path of initiation. Knowledge of these rituals separated Mormons not only from one another but from everyone else. The ceremonies of endowment and baptism of the dead excited a great deal of anxious curiosity among non-Mormons. The oldest charge against occultism, which in Christian eyes had made heretics of its practitioners, was that it concealed a conspiracy against the standing order—against what most people agreed was proper government, proper religion, and proper morals. That was precisely the charge that Mormon apostates aimed at the temple rituals. Their efforts to outdo one another in describing lascivious and traitorous behavior among the Mormons were truly remarkable. Apostates claimed that they had participated in the rituals because of curiosity and the alluring promise of greater spiritual understanding. According to one account, "Men, who proud that they had a secret, and desirous that every one should know that they had it, uttered dark hints. They exhibited a singular kind of an under-garment which they constantly wore. This was fantastically marked and given them in the Temple. They promised this endowment to their awe-struck disciples, as the full fruition of the blessing of heaven, etc., etc., etc. As to what it really was, all was perfectly hidden; as all who received the initiation were bound by the most fearful penalties not to reveal any thing of the matter." Rather than spiritual enlightenment, the apostates claimed, the ceremonies had revealed to them plots directed against the political and moral order of the United States.[19]

The temple ceremonies have been the subject of considerable disagreement. For our purposes, they do appear to tie Mormonism in a specific way to Masonry, which was a movement with roots in Western occult traditions. On March 15, 1842, Joseph Smith ignored his own prohibition against secret societies and participated in the installation of a Masonic lodge in Nauvoo. Within twenty-four hours Smith had risen to the sublime "degree"; and within six months, 286 Mormons had been inducted into the Nauvoo lodge, more members than all the other Illinois lodges had put together. Although Judge James Adams, Smith's friend and the deputy grand marshall of the Illinois Masonic lodge, sponsored the Nauvoo installment, irregular proceedings, particularly the rapid advancement of candidates, soon got the Mormon Masons into trouble. The ultimate suspension of the Nauvoo lodge from the Masonic movement forms one part of the story of the widening rift between Mormons and Gentiles that led to the Mormons' expulsion from Nauvoo.

While often treated as a curious footnote in Mormon history, Smith's attraction to Masonry deserves close attention. Smith only sporadically participated in lodge events and undoubtedly regarded entrance into the Masonic network, which included prominent Illinois politicians and judges, as one way to buy protection.[20] Nonetheless, he clearly drew his temple rituals from Masonic practices. The parallels between Masonic and Mormon ceremonies and oaths, the latter developed only after Smith became acquainted with Masonry, could not have been coincidental. Neither could the Masonic symbolism that became intrinsic to Mormon design—the Masonic square and compass cut into ritual garments, the beehive, the all-seeing eye. In suggesting that Mormonism found in Masonry a genuinely occult connection, one must emphasize that Masonic rituals, as they were developed in the eighteenth century, were many times removed from the Cabalistic and occult practices of the Renaissance. With some exceptions most Masons probably showed only ceremonial interest in reaching the forms of higher knowledge sought, for example, by the Rosicrucian orders. Fawn Brodie certainly spoke too strongly when she asserted that the adoption of the temple ritual "transformed the Mormon Church into a mystery cult."[21]

Nonetheless, we should not modify Brodie's language to the extent that we lose her point. The occult associations suggested by the Nauvoo lodge and the temple rites had serious consequences. In the nineteenth century people who already feared the alleged conspiratorial aims of the Masons saw the founding of the Nauvoo lodge as proof of their worst fears about Joseph Smith.[22] To many Christian ministers, Mormonism's occult connection through Masonry was proof of its godless attempt to overturn the standards of Christian scripture. The subsequent quarrels between Mormons and Masons did nothing to shake that conviction.

Ezra Booth, one of the first Mormon apostates, seized upon words appropriate for an attack on witchcraft and magic to describe his former fascination with the Latter-day Saints: "The magic charm of delusion and falsehood had so wrapped its sable mantle around me, as to exclude the light of truth and secure me a devoted slave. But thanks be to God! the spell is dissipated."[23] Booth chose his words to inflict as much damage as possible, and his writings distorted the truth about Mormons in virtually every particular. For all that, his implied connection between Mormonism and magic had strong links. When some twentieth-century Mormon writers tried to explain the similarity of Masonic and Mormon ritual on the basis of a common source rather than on Smith's plagiarism, they argued that Smith was made privy to knowledge that had been lost, not merely from the time of Solomon's Temple but since the expulsion of mankind from the Garden of Eden.[24] Without any question, Joseph Smith had founded his religion on the assertion that he had in uncommon ways recovered meanings and wisdom from the distant past.

Mary Baker Eddy's first husband happened to be a Mason. Briefly but happily married to George Glover, she remained forever grateful for the help she received from his brother Masons when Glover died. Later, membership in a Masonic lodge was the single organizational affiliation that was not ruled incompatible with membership in the Christian Science mother church. However, Eddy's gratitude toward the Masons never prompted her to imitate their ritual. Although some links to occult sciences were strikingly present in the church she founded, those links had nothing to do with Masonry. Rather, it was the peculiarities of her extreme version of philosophical idealism that allowed Eddy's critics to charge her with occultism.[25]

Mary Baker Eddy must have thought it uncommonly bad luck that *Science and Health* was published in the same year, 1875, that Madame Blavatsky founded the Theosophical Society. Thereafter, she was never able to change the minds of her critics who thought that the two women had a great deal in common. She wanted no association with Blavatsky, who returned the favor by calling Christian Science a form of crude occultism similar to spiritualism. Nonetheless, the fact that some of Eddy's followers became Theosophists (and vice versa) was sufficient evidence to many that a common appeal joined Christian Science not only to Theosophy but also to spiritualism, Rosicrucianism, Mormonism, and the "fantastic and crude dogmas savoring of . . . the mystic East."[26] The intent in suggesting these connections was not always hostile. To Eddy's dismay, some Hindu swamis, who began to tour America after the Chicago World Parliament of Religions in 1893 (a parliament that accorded a great deal of attention both to Christian Science and to Eastern mysticism), attested to startling similarities "that exist between the fundamental principles of modern Christian Science and those of that ancient system of philosophy known in India as Vedanta."[27]

One of the earliest known pictures of Mary Baker Eddy. Historical Picture Service, Chicago.

These were not the only associations that Eddy denied. Throughout her long career as a religious leader, she adamantly refused to acknowledge an intellectual debt to anyone. When she described herself as the "discoverer of Christian Science," she allowed a certain ambiguity to cloud the issue of whether divine inspiration had aided her. Her doctrine, as she put it, was "hopelessly original."[28]

It was not, of course. The most important debt Eddy owed, a debt clear even in her denials, was to her teacher, Phineas Parkhurst Quimby.[29] Quimby's ideas can in turn be related to the intellectual universe of Andrew Jackson Davis and his version of Harmonial Philosophy. On a more sophisticated intellectual plane, one might even suggest parallels that connect Eddy to the metaphysical assumptions of the transcendentalists and especially to the philosophy of Emanuel Swedenborg. No scholar has yet adequately examined the impact of the Swedish philosopher upon popular versions of philosophical idealism in nineteenth-century America. But doubtless his American followers helped prepare the way for the reception of Christian Science.[30] Swedenborg's theories about the mystical interconnections of all things and his Doctrine of Correspondence, ideas suggestive of Renaissance magic and alchemy, were related to an idea, found in Davis, Quimby, and Eddy, that physical illnesses are reflections merely of discord in man's spiritual force or principle. A spiritual disturbance causes a corresponding material imbalance to appear as disease, which can be cured by mind.[31] Eddy built a church organization that was distinctly her own. But her version of the idea that sin and evil are illusions cannot be set down as an original contribution to philosophy.

In her teachings Eddy attempted to undermine our usual reliance on ordinary sense perception to receive truth and on ordinary language to communicate it. Eddy followed Quimby, who followed Swedenborg, in teaching that biblical words had a spiritual interpretation differing from their literal meaning. She wrote: "We have learned in Christian Science that when reading the Scriptures if you substitute the spiritual significance of a term for its material definition, or the bare word, it will elucidate the meaning of the inspired writer." "I read the inspired page," she added elsewhere, "through a higher than mortal sense."[32] To make plain the hitherto unknown "inner" sense of the words of the Bible, Eddy added a glossary of spiritual meanings (a Key to the Scripture) to the sixth and subsequent editions of *Science and Health*. The connection between her glossary and Swedenborg's *A Dictionary of Correspondences, Representatives and Significatives Derived from the Word of the Lord* (first printed in Boston in 1847) is clear enough.

Unlocking the spiritual significance of a word did not, of course, wholly solve the problem of communicating a nonobvious truth. Whatever care Eddy took in revising and perfecting each edition of *Science and Health* ("a misplaced preposition would change the sense and misstates the science of the Scriptures"), she believed that the printed word could never seem spiritual to the uninitiated reader. "The English language," Eddy regretted, "or any other language with which we are familiar, is inadequate to fully convey a spiritual meaning with material terms."[33] Seekers who wanted to progress in the wisdom of Christian Science had to pay for a series of lessons taught by an authorized instructor.

All of these points suggest that Eddy's early followers were attracted to a style of thought that Edward Tiryakian has identified with "esoteric culture."[34] According to Tiryakian, such a culture relies on commonly available religious texts—the Bible, the Torah, *Science and Health*—but insists that the meaning of these is not exhausted by an ordinary reading. Furthermore, the esoteric group advertises itself as possessing a unique understanding of the secret and real meaning in the text and adopts a parlance that to the outside world must necessarily seem obscure. Eddy prided herself in thinking that Christian Science healing could be both logically and practically demonstrated. In contrast, she said, Theosophical mysteries were like the excavated cindered human bodies of Pompeii—they fell into dust the moment that air touched them.[35] But whatever she said, her epistemological views were not unlike those of P. D. Ouspensky, a twentieth-century occultist. He said: "The idea of a knowledge which surpasses all ordinary human knowledge, and is inaccessible to ordinary people, but which exists somewhere and belongs to somebody, permeates the whole history of the thought of mankind. . . . Magical or occult knowledge is knowledge based upon senses which surpass our five senses and upon a capacity for thinking which surpasses ordinary thinking but it is knowledge translated into ordinary logical language, if that is possible or in so far as it is possible."[36]

The parallel between occultism and Eddy's church goes beyond a shared attitude toward the limitations of ordinary sense perception and language. Eddy maintained around herself an inner circle of trusted students who often met in secret. Her enemies insisted that she obtained money for Christian Science lessons "by pretending that she had important secrets relating to healing the sick which she had not theretofore imparted."[37] She in turn replied much like the early Mormon leaders: the early private sessions of the church were necessary to protect her followers from persecution and ridicule. Only "advanced Scientific students" were ready for some of the truths she had to impart.[38] Whatever the justification, the hierarchical nature of Christian Science wisdom set novices apart from adepts. And Eddy not only maintained strict control over who was authorized to teach Christian Science lessons but forbade any of her teachers from trying to convey the contents of those lessons to the general public.[39]

If Eddy had been worried merely about the confusion and misunderstanding that her teaching could arouse in inadequately prepared students, she might have avoided some of the portrayals of herself as a dangerously superstitious woman. But Eddy made the explicit claim that the end result of Christian Science teaching was power—indeed, the shamanistic power to heal, which Mircea Eliade has called "the most archaic and most widely distributed occult tradition."[40] Where there was power to do good, there was power to do evil. "Why we take so few students," Eddy wrote, "is because of the great danger there is in promiscuously teaching metaphysics, or the power of mind to do good, lest it abuse that trust, forsake metaphysics, and this developed mental power becomes the . . . extracts and essences of evil."[41] To the newspaper editorialists who were hostile to Eddy, this statement clearly implicated her in an attempt to devise a system of black and white magic.

Such criticism grew particularly strong because of Eddy's obsessive concern with what she called "malicious animal magnetism," the use of mental powers to cause disease and illness in others rather than to heal. Eddy always argued that malicious animal magnetism was the opposite of Christian Science and was part of the illusion her philosophy wished to dispel. Nonetheless, the behavior that resulted from her belief in malicious animal magnetism contributed with legitimate reason to her reputation as an occultist. For example, in the spring of 1878 a suit was filed in Salem against Daniel Spofford, a former student of Eddy who was bitterly estranged from her. The charge against him was that he had practiced harmful mesmerism against a Christian Scientist, Lucretia L. S. Brown. The charge was dismissed, but not before the press had branded it an attempt to resurrect the Salem witchcraft trials. Eddy's chapters on "Demonology" in the early editions of *Science and Health* indeed warned that "the peril of Salem witchcraft is not past, until that error be met by Truth and Science."[42]

The summary dismissal of the case did not discourage Eddy from continuing to make strong public warnings. In 1882, when her third and last husband died, Eddy told a *Boston Globe* reporter that he had been the victim of mental malpractice. The activators of the fatal poison, which she claimed was applied mentally without any physical contact with Dr. Eddy, were again alleged to be former Eddy students. In Eddy's mind, largely because of the growing popularity of her doctrines, the dangers of mental malpractice never thereafter slackened. Quite the contrary: "The mild forms of animal magnetism are disappearing, and its aggressive features are coming to the front. The looms of crime, hidden in the dark recesses of mortal thought, are every hour weaving webs more complicated and subtle. So secret are its present methods, that they ensnare the age into indolence, and produce the very apathy on this subject which the criminal desires."[43]

Eddy's personal sufferings from malicious animal magnetism became well known. She publicly maintained that her crusade for Truth made her the brunt of mental attacks from those who had vested interests in the continued domination of Error. However, she and her followers tried to keep secret the steps that they took to ward off the effects of malicious mental malpractice. According to one unfriendly reporter, Eddy organized "watches" to turn the effects of evil thoughts back upon particular enemies. She would gather students in a room and have them "treat in thought" someone she suspected of causing harm to herself. "Say to him," she instructed, "your sins have found you out. You are affected as you wish to affect me. Your evil thought reacts upon you. You are bilious, you are consumptive, you have liver trouble, you have been poisoned by arsenic, etc."[44]

Somewhat startling confirmation of these practices was provided in a memoir written by Adam H. Dickey, Eddy's private secretary during the last three years of her life and for a time chairman of the board of directors of the mother church. The memoir was a considerable embarrassment to the church, but for Dickey it fulfilled his promise to Eddy that he would prove after her death that she was "mentally murdered."[45] Her failure to prevent the occurrence was not, by Dickey's account, for want of trying. She turned her household into a mental fortress, dividing the night into four mental watches. Each was assigned to different mental workers, all residents of the house, who had specific instructions about how to counteract the "evil influence of mental mind directed against our Leader and her establishment during their hours." The typewritten instructions designated in numerical order which phases of error they were supposed to combat. Since Eddy had a horror of excessive snowfall, she even directed her watchers one winter to "make a law that there shall be no more snow this season." After Eddy experienced one particularly severe mental attack, Dickey reports that she told her staff: "You don't any of you realize what is going

on. This is a dark hour for the Cause and you do not seem to be awake
to it . . . I am now working on a plane that would mean instantaneous
death to any of you."[46]

In view of such words and practices, critics of Christian Science
understandably doubted whether the movement reduced demonology,
as it claimed, to "a record of dreams."[47] In a telling sentence Eddy
wrote, "Let the age that sits in judgment on the occult methods of her
period sanction only such as are demonstratable on a scientific principle, and productive of the greatest good to the greatest number."[48]
Eddy obviously considered the "occult methods" of Christian Science
worthy of sanction. Surprisingly, however, in view of her implied distinctions, Eddy's publications often advertised competing "occult methods." When Warren Felt Evans published *Esoteric Christianity and
Mental Therapeutics* in 1886, Christian Scientists attacked it. Ignoring
its claim to have stripped the veil from the "ancient mystic brother-
hoods," they accused Evans of forcing Christianity "into the farcical
grooves of Occultism." They reproached him for saying that he gave
readers only the principles "which it may be proper openly to promul-
gate to the world at large in the present state of the mind of man."[49] Yet
throughout the 1890s the book was prominently advertised in Christian
Science publications as being available from the Christian Science Publishing House. Other recommended titles included J. H. Dewey's *Christian Theosophy,* Swedenborg's *Correspondences,* and the *Bhagavad-
Gita.* If the intellectual connection suggested by these advertisements
was a mistake, someone within the Christian Science empire was ready
to capitalize on it.

Eddy's attempt to make Christianity (or religion) scientific was
scarcely a unique enterprise. The claim to have established a scientific
basis for faith was universal to the new nineteenth-century religions.
Clearly, science had many popular meanings. The science that Eddy
promoted had little to do with the laboratory procedures being developed in the physical and biological sciences.[50] When Eddy spoke of experimental proof or systematic demonstration and exactitude, she was
not thinking like a Faraday or a Darwin. She borrowed words from an
empirical tradition that she in fact wanted to challenge. In this respect,
the connection that people made between Theosophy and Christian
Science was absolutely correct.

The hostile criticism of spiritualism, another American movement
that began in the mid-nineteenth century, also stemmed in part from
confusion over what sort of science the movement promoted or encour-

aged. I have argued elsewhere that spiritualism gained a popular following (a following that far exceeded the numbers attracted to Mormonism
and to Christian Science) because it claimed to prove the reality of life
after death by the methods of commonsense empiricism.[51] Insofar as
spiritualism sparked a separate religious movement, it did so without
sponsoring secret initiation rites. A person who attended a seance was
not normally expected to undergo special preparatory instruction, nor
was the goal of attendance to achieve a higher plane of spiritual awareness. The few simple truths of spiritualism could be grasped and communicated in ordinary ways. Although many seances were private
affairs conducted by a regular circle of sitters, interested people in the
nineteenth century could easily find their way to a medium. Those who
went to a seance were encouraged to go away from it and tell their
friends and neighbors exactly what they had seen and heard. Spiritualist
leaders made no attempt to conceal their message or to exclude casual
observers from their central ritual.

Yet none of the endlessly repeated, emphatic endorsements of public demonstration saved spiritualism from attacks seeking to link it to
demonism and occultism. The latter linkage became extremely common
after 1875, for, as everyone knew, Madame Blavatsky and Henry Steel
Olcott had been spiritualist publicists before moving up to the "higher"
concerns of Theosophy. Other "esoteric philosophers" suggested an
overlap, for they did not hesitate to publicize as real all the things that
reportedly happened in the parlors of spiritualist mediums. Both Theosophists and spiritualists made distinctions between their movements,
and the more esoteric Theosophists urged the more banal spiritualists
to outgrow their childish fascination with material phenomena.[52] However, since some prominent American mediums, including Emma Hardinge Britten, responded to Theosophy's call to take up the study of
"higher" spiritual realities, many newspapers concluded that spiritualism and occultism were the same thing.

The rhetoric adopted by spiritualist leaders to deny occult associations was usually uncompromising. In their own version of a warfare
between ancients and moderns, spiritualists proclaimed themselves as
firmly on the side of the moderns. Blavatsky and her followers, they
warned, were promoting a dangerous retrogression into the "darkness
of Egypt and the Middle Ages." Theosophy sought to recreate the "old,
old story" of a priesthood who used secrets to hold mankind in "mental
bondage and consequent physical slavery." In India, where Blavatsky
moved her headquarters, centuries of occult philosophies had resulted
in an antiprogressive, "nearly stagnant semi-barbarous condition." The

alleged claims of spiritual gurus had made the people of Asia "the victims of ignorance, superstition, poverty, spiritual and political tyranny, and physical degradation."[53]

In contrast to all these lamentable consequences of occult quests, spiritualism encouraged followers not to be "helplessly led by the nose by these blind guides, into the quagmires and bogholes of . . . exploded superstitions and long forgotten dreams of our 'ignorant forefathers.' "[54] The movement "reduced the verbiage of Occultism to orderly common sense" and tolerated no "magic spells, incantations, mystical mummeries, cabalistic jargon, occult signs and figures, and unadulterated bosh."[55] Why, asked Samuel B. Brittan, did one have to master "the wild vagaries" of Hermetic philosophy in order to test the actual presence of tangible objects and describe, in a simple narrative way, the visible phenomena that one saw. Using these and similar arguments, spiritualist publications in the last quarter of the nineteenth century systematically repudiated black magic, white magic, Rosicrucianism, and Cabalism. They further attacked the "musty tomes" of such individuals as Paracelsus, Cornelius Agrippa, Raymond Tully, Nostradamus, Albertus Magnus, Eugenius Philalithes, Girolamo Cardano, Robert Fludd, and Éliphas Lévi.[56]

In many ways these disclaimers made perfect sense, and no student of comparative religious ideas can ignore them. But the argument that nineteenth-century spiritualism and nineteenth-century occultism were absolutely distinct does suppress important considerations. In the first place, the rhetoric of denial, of the sort that has been quoted, itself indicates that spiritualist leaders were conscious of occult traditions. In their repeated assaults on Theosophy, spiritualists in effect conceded the common appeal that enemies of both movements, in the bluntness of their attacks, had managed to lay open. When spiritualist publications had to warn readers against "current idealisms, transcendentalisms, and fanciful conceits, born of crude speculations and nurtured by spurious philosophies and pseudo-science," they were admitting that, without alertness to distinctions, one could easily confuse spiritualism with ostensibly opposite things.[57]

In fact, with respect to a few particulars, spiritualism did share ideas with the occult traditions it repudiated. One link can be traced through Andrew Jackson Davis, who emerged, because of his prolific writings and longevity, as one of the most prominent nineteenth-century spiritualist leaders. As noted before, Davis's version of Swedenborgian philosophy promoted a pantheistically tending idealism that was later to find its way into the metaphysics of Christian Science. Davis's early followers were in rapid retreat from a Protestant orthodoxy based on Scripture. In somewhat the same fashion as the transcendentalists, they looked upon nature as "a dispensation of types foreshadowing the eternal world."[58] In believing that lower natural phenomena were linked harmoniously to a cosmic whole, they necessarily stressed the inadequacies of ordinary sense perception in unlocking nature's system of symbols. To discover the laws of universal correspondence, they had to call on help from the inward eye. Learning to see with the inward eye did not come naturally to most people. It required instruction and encouragement.

Davis himself placed no special emphasis on secret or esoteric wisdom. However, the title of one of his autobiographies, *The Magic Staff,* did suggest the portrait of a magus. Davis, in imitation of Swedenborg, regarded himself as a special seer, a person whose cosmic connections were somehow more developed than those of other professional mediums. His philosophy then bore a close relationship to an intellectual world that was slightly more exotic than ordinary romanticism and that did owe something to magical lore. Davis resembled Madame Blavatsky in one important particular: both tried to find truth in some other way than in the procedures of ordinary empirical science. Both, of course, praised science and insisted that discoverable uniform laws of nature existed. But their means of discovery were meant to posit a "third way" between the alternatives posed on the one hand by a faith in religious scriptures and on the other by a commitment to naturalistic science.

Despite the widespread cultural appeal of Davis's Harmonial Philosophy, one cannot hold it responsible for all the connections that critics of spiritualism made between it and occultism. Davis was not a typical spiritualist. That is, he never spoke authoritatively for spiritualism in the same way that Joseph Smith and Brigham Young spoke for Mormonism. Moreover, the early publications of the spiritualist movement that Davis's philosophy influenced, the *Univercoelum* and the *Shekinah,* had little to do with growing American interest in spiritualism in the mid-nineteenth century. Without question spiritualism interested most Americans because of its fairly straightforward promise to provide empirical proof of life after death.[59] Only a handful of the movement's leaders showed any concern for what some writers at the end of the century called "speculative occultism."

However, if "speculative occultism" was anathema to most American spiritualist writers, a few of them in the last quarter of the nineteenth century expressed a tentative approval of something called "practical occultism."[60] The appearance of the phrase in some spiritualist publications served to renew some long-standing controversies. Critics of spiritualism claimed that the phrase confirmed what they had always said: spiritualist mediumship was just another version of necromancy. Spiritualists responded with old arguments. Mediums, they said, were passive agents who had no formulas to control the appearance and activities of their spirit controls. Rather than fitting the image of sorcerers, they were suffering victims who had not chosen their roles. Although many Americans did carry out amateur experiments to test their mediumistic powers, spiritualist publications had fairly consistently discouraged systematic attempts to develop a mediumistic potential that had not appeared spontaneously.

The common disclaimers of magical intentions in nineteenth-century spiritualist literature were seriously intended. However, with respect to associations drawn between spiritualism and "practical occultism," they did not erase the fact that developed mediums claimed to do things well beyond the resources of most other religious leaders. Mediums made predictions. They passed along useful information from the spirit world. And, in a significant link to nineteenth-century Mormonism and Christian Science, they often claimed the power to heal.[61] Their professional services may or may not have been magical in some strict sense of that word, but they certainly went beyond ordinary Protestant pastoral care. Because they did, critics of the movement were able to make the charge of necromancy seem plausible. Those critics were not surprised when the prominent spiritualist medium Cora Tappan wrote that occultism and spiritualism both sought to open "to the comprehension and mind of man the existence of a world of magic, of spiritual powers and gifts, or an underlying spiritual science which belongs to human life."[62] She published that observation in the *Banner of Light,* which was the most widely circulated spiritualist newspaper and the one that insisted most sharply on the distinction betwen spiritualism and Theosophy.

Therefore, while not forgetting why many sincere spiritualists thought it unfair for critics to dismiss them as occultist (and to refer at the same time to such scandalously hidden forces as gravity and electricity), we must recognize that any movement as widespread and as loosely organized as spiritualism was bound to contain dominant and submerged tendencies. Since even the dominant tendency sought to expand the realm of the visible beyond what many exponents of empiricism thought reasonable, the kind of science heralded by spiritualism inevitably came into question.

Nineteenth-century spiritualists are, of course, not responsible for what happened later, but the context of their activities prepared ways in which their successors could grow more comfortable with occultist associations. Many twentieth-century spiritualist publications regularly advertise books on occultism (a practice that in fact began in the nineteenth century) and show a strong interest in how "our spiritual unfoldment" might be aided by Eastern religions and pre-Christian rites. While spiritualists continue to insist that their facts "are as demonstrable and as susceptible of proof and duplications as the miracles of the test tube and retort," they are more inclined to add that "science is helpless to know of spiritual phenomena until it accepts the spiritual path of life." Science in short must learn the "language of occultism."[63] The rhetoric of denial, shaped by nineteenth-century spiritualists to disclaim any association with Theosophy, has in recent years become the property of psychical researchers and parapsychologists. But the latter know, just as nineteenth-century spiritualist leaders knew, that the burden of carrying unwanted associations does not result entirely from the malicious misrepresentation of their critics.

What, then, may we conclude? We must first return to a question raised at the outset. Why did religious groups whose public rhetoric disclaimed occult associations nonetheless adopt practices that allowed their enemies plausibly to pin those associations on them? Why, for example, did Mormons and Christian Scientists conduct so much business in secret? As noted before, secrecy was undoubtedly for them one means of self-protection. In a classic article on secret societies, Georg Simmel demonstrated how secrecy can offer protection for newly born ideas.[64] On the other hand, the strategy of shrouding behavior in mystery has obvious drawbacks. Once people suspect that a group's teachings and practices are being screened from public view, secrecy can produce more persecution than protection. That result certainly was confirmed in the experience of nineteenth-century religious groups who discovered that their secret rites and meetings deeply offended the Protestant and republican values of many Americans.[65]

A puzzle then develops in understanding a religious group's continued insistence on secrecy once it provoked serious problems between the group and the rest of the world. Secrecy often led to internal turmoil as well. Group members who were left out of the secret, which only the inner circle knew about, often became bitter apostates at the moment the secret was revealed to them. One thinks especially of the rupture that the disclosure of polygamy caused within the Mormon church. Moreover, in a hierarchical group that posits levels of spiritual consciousness and certain but not easily communicated knowledge, secrecy greatly increases the potential for schism. Quarrels easily developed among Eddy's ambitious students over which one of them understood Christian Science best, that is, which one of them had really understood the hidden messages.

Secrecy is, of course, one way a group under fire can hide fundamentally deceitful practices, and historians cannot ignore questions of fraud that haunt the reputations of Smith, Eddy, and scores of spiritualist mediums. Nonetheless, in thinking about the reasons for secret practices that proved disfunctional, they should not neglect other possibilities. For example, they should not forget the saving paradox of the sociologist: anything that is disfunctional is also functional. Any practice suggesting occultism aroused opposition. Hence, plenty of reason existed to avoid it. Still, the practice might have an irresistible utility. Without doubt, a shared secret, or the promise of sharing a secret, is a bonding agent; keeping the secret is an expression of allegiance, of loyalty, to the group.[66] The solidarity of a group is then only strengthened by any persecution caused by its secret practices. I am not arguing that the leaders of Mormonism, Christian Science, and spiritualism adopted secretive ways in a deliberate attempt to invite attacks. But they all developed ritual procedures that boasted to the outside world their claim: "We know more." The aggressiveness in the message about an unorthodox "third way" was intentional.

The practices, then, which hostile critics of these movements called with some correctness occult, operated in simple and obvious ways to create and maintain a sense of separate and special identity. In many ways the practices created a sense of difference between the groups and their enemies that was altogether artificial. These nineteenth-century Americans were implicated far more in the "ordinary" culture than either they or their critics recognized. Nonetheless, a rhetoric of militant distinction, however exaggerated, provided these groups the psychological space in which they could maintain a belief in their dramatic intellectual innovations. It provided them with the mental stamina to resist what they regarded as strong conformist pressures. In these matters the perceived realities control behavior. The claim to know a unique, higher set of truths, which was protected or gathered by an inner circle of special seers, provoked persecution but also played a decisive role in turning Mormonism, Christian Science, and spiritualism, against what might seem to have been overwhelming odds, into important social realities.

I don't want to leave readers thinking that the occult features of Mormonism, Christian Science, and spiritualism were only handy strategies that signified nothing about what people inside and outside the movements believed. I do, in fact, think that the belief structures implied by occultism have considerable relevance for understanding American culture in the nineteenth century, and for that matter in the twentieth century. Granted, these three religious movements we are not dealing with elaborate occult systems. The occultist associations were not, however, trivial. The men and women in these movements developed rituals and practices that promised to turn people into gods, summon spirits into home parlors, and heal humankind from the claims of sickness and death. Judged against the aspirations of some ancient esoteric philosophies, those claims are perhaps modest. But they look exceedingly bold when placed against the things many American scientists and Protestant leaders were saying during the latter part of the nineteenth century.

Of course, if the bold claims interested or seemed plausible to only the people who enlisted in the three movements, we would be dealing with a relatively minor cultural phenomenon—perhaps even a disappearing impulse. However, the game of denominational counting, a game kept lively by the politics of American sectarianism, may in this case be especially misleading. To understand the enormous publicity that attended Mormonism, Christian Science, and spiritualism, one has to appreciate the degree to which they developed a vocabulary that fascinated many Americans who had no formal connections to them or even opposed them. The fact that the movements focused national debate does not mean that all the Americans who followed the debate had the same ideas about what issues were at stake. It does, however, suggest that many Americans did not view everything which naturalistic science failed to countenance as superstitious. From time to time in the past one hundred years the American press has heralded the advent of an occult revival. A closer historical look may suggest a more continuous public interest in ideas tinged with occult associations. Those ideas are better understood as part of a dominant popular outlook than as inexplicable and irrational outbursts in an uncomplicatedly secular age.

NOTES

1. An encyclopedic though somewhat superficial treatment of nineteenth-century occultism in America and England is James Webb, *The Flight from Reason* (London: Macdonald, 1971). For another approach to some of the problems raised by this essay, see Robert S. Ellwood, Jr., *Alternative Altars:*

Unconventional and Eastern Spirituality in America (Chicago: University of Chicago Press, 1979).

2.   George Marsden, *Fundamentalism and American Culture: The Shaping of Twentieth Century Evangelicalism, 1870–1925* (New York: Oxford University Press, 1980).

3.   The blanket terms "occultism" and "occultists," which in contemporary usage cover all these phenomena, were apparently coined by A. P. Sinnett in *The Occult World* (London: Trubner, 1883). Older uses of the word "occult" were not limited to activities suggestive of alchemy, magic, or mysticism, but by the mid-nineteenth century these were the most common associations.

4.   See Bronislaw Malinowski, *Magic, Science and Religion and Other Essays* (Garden City, N.Y.: Doubleday, 1954), and Émile Durkheim, *The Elementary Forms of the Religious Life* (London: George Allen and Unwin, 1915), esp. pp. 23–47.

5.   Further clarifications of occultist intentions and practices can be found in Edward A. Tiryakian, *On the Margin of the Visible: Sociology, the Esoteric, and the Occult* (New York: John Wiley, 1974).

6.   Sinnett, *Occult World*, p. 1.

7.   William James McKendrick McCormick, *Occultism: The True Origin of Mormonism* (Belfast: Raven, 1967). For connections between Mormonism and "ordinary" American culture, see Leonard Arrington and Davis Bitton, *The Mormon Experience: A History of the Latter-Day Saints* (New York: Knopf, 1979); James B. Allen and Marvin S. Hill, *Mormonism and American Culture* (New York: Harper and Row, 1972); Klaus J. Hansen, *Mormonism and the American Experience* (Chicago: University of Chicago Press, 1981).

8.   The first stories that circulated about Joseph Smith stressed his early role as a fortune teller and the incantations he used to search for buried gold and silver (drawing circles in the earth, muttering to himself, propitiating spirits that protected the treasure). See, for example, Eber Howe, *Mormonism Unvailed: or A Faithful Account of That Singular Imposition and Delusion, from Its Rise to the Present Time* (Painesville, Ohio: Howe, 1834), pp. 238, 242, 249, 259, and *passim*.

9.   Fawn Brodie, *No Man Knows My History: The Life of Joseph Smith, the Mormon Prophet* (1945; New York: Knopf, 1971), pp. 168–75. A more recent biography, that challenges Brodie on many points, is Donna Hill, *Joseph Smith, the First Mormon* (Garden City, N.Y.: Doubleday, 1977).

10.   Howe, *Mormonism Unvailed*, frontispiece and p. 37.

11.   B. H. Roberts, *History of the Church of Jesus Christ of Latter Day Saints* (Salt Lake City: Deseret, 1961), 4:464.

12.   Daniel Kidder, *Mormonism and the Mormons: A Historical View of the Rise and Progress of the Sect Self-Styled Latter-Day Saints* (New York: G. Lane and P. P. Sandford, 1842), p. 311.

13.   Benjamin Ferris, *Utah and the Mormons: The History, Government, Doctrines, Customs and Prospects of the Latter-day Saints* (New York: Harper and Bros., 1854), p. 190. The durability of these charges is quite impressive. In 1900 the Reverend Thomas W. Young said of the Mormons:

"Their proselyting missionaries are instructed to withold 'the choicest morsels of the doctrines from the crass multitude.' These esoteric truths are only for those who are brought into the conferences of the priesthood, and their secret gatherings in the temple." *Mormonism: Its Origin, Doctrines, and Dangers* (Ann Arbor, Mich.: George Wahr, 1900).

14. Roberts, *History of the Church*, 1:43.

15. Ibid., 6:289.

16. For Mormon denunciations of Avard, see Roberts, *History of the Church*, 3:179, and Smith's letter in *Times and Seasons*, July, 1840. See also Leland Gentry, "The Danite Band of 1838," *Brigham Young University Studies*, 14 (1974):421–50, and Arrington and Bitton, *Mormon Experience*.

17. Roberts, *History of the Church*, 5:xxix. As it turned out, he had good reason. The leaking of news about Smith's other wives prompted apostacies and set off a chain of events that resulted, among other things, in the murder of Smith and the formation of the Reorganized Church of Jesus Christ of Latter Day Saints. The latter group rejected secret ritual.

18. Roberts, *History of the Church*, 6:290–91; 5:2. Robert B. Flanders has discussed aspects of Smith's secret policies in *Nauvoo: Kingdom on the Mississippi* (Urbana: University of Illinois Press, 1965).

19. John Hyde, Jr., *Mormonism: Its Leaders and Designs* (New York: W. P. Fetridge, 1857), p. 89. The most popular exposé of the temple rituals was Increase McGee Van Dusen and Maria Van Dusen, *Startling Disclosures of the Wonderful Ceremonies of the Mormon Spiritual Wife System.* First published in 1847, it went through a number of increasingly elaborate editions during the 1850s. The extent to which Mormons did hatch plots against the U.S. government has remained a controversial question. See Klaus J. Hansen, *Quest for Empire: The Political Kingdom of God and the Council of Fifty in Mormon History* (East Lansing: Michigan State University Press, 1967).

20. John C. Bennett, the mayor of Nauvoo who became Smith's bitter enemy, is credited with introducing Smith to Masonry. But other leading Mormons, including Heber Kimball, Brigham Young, and Smith's brother Hyrum, had earlier been Masons. For a defense of Smith's motives in forming the lodge, see Anthony W. Ivins, *The Relationship of "Mormonism" and Freemasonry* (Salt Lake City: Deseret News Press, 1934), p. 177. One Mormon did demand that Governor Ford protect the Smith brothers at Carthage because they were Master Masons. Roberts, *History of the Church*, 6:603.

21. Brodie, *No Man Knows My History*, p. 282,

22. For a historical account of Masonry, see J. M. Roberts, *The Mythology of the Secret Societies* (New York: Scribner's, 1972).

23. Howe, *Mormonism Unvailed*, p. 176.

24. In addition to Ivins, see E. Cecil McGavin, *Mormonism and Masonry* (Salt Lake City: Stevens and Wallis, 1947). For a Masonic polemic against Joseph Smith, see S. H. Goodwin, *Mormonism and Masonry* (Washington, D.C.: Masonic Service Association of the United States, 1924).

25. The most ambitious account of the philosophy of Christian Science is Stephen Gottschalk, *The Emergence of Christian Science in American*

Religious Life (Berkeley: University of California Press, 1973). Also see Robert Peel's three-volume biography, *Mary Baker Eddy* (New York: Holt Rinehart, Winston, 1966–77).

26. Francis Edward Marsten, *The Mask of Christian Science* (New York: American Tract Society, 1909), p. 6 and *passim*.

27. Swami Abhedananda, *Christian Science and Vedanta* (New York: Vedanta Society, 1902), p. 1. Also see Wendell Thomas, *Hinduism Invades America* (New York: Beacon Press, 1930), and Raymond J. Cunningham, "The Impact of Christian Science on the American Churches, 1880–1910," *American Historical Review,* 72 (1967):885–905.

28. Mary Baker Eddy, *Retrospection and Introspection* (Boston: W. G. Nixon, 1891), pp. 47, 77.

29. The influence can best be examined in Horatio W. Dresser, ed., *The Quimby Manuscripts Showing the Discovery of Spiritual Healing and the Origin of Christian Science* (New York: Thomas Crowell, 1921). Even Robert Peel, Eddy's "official" biographer, concedes that Eddy owed more to Quimby than she acknowledged.

30. Hermann S. Ficke, "The Source of Science and Health," *Bibliotheca Sacra,* 85 (1928):417–23.

31. The best examination of these intellectual connections is J. Stillson Judah, *The History and Philosophy of the Metaphysical Movements in America* (Philadelphia: Westminster Press, 1967). For material on the Harmonial Philosophy of Andrew Jackson Davis, see William Leach, *True Love and Perfect Union: The Feminist Reform of Sex and Society* (New York: Basic Books, 1980); Robert W. Delp, "Andrew Jackson Davis: Prophet of American Spiritualism," *Journal of American History,* 54 (1967):43–56.

32. Judah, *Metaphysical Movements,* p. 273; Mary Baker Eddy, *Science and Health,* 6th ed. (Boston: Eddy, 1883); *Christian Science Journal,* June, 1885.

33. Eddy, *Science and Health* (Lynn: Asa G. Eddy, 1878), p. 156.

34. Tiryakian, *On the Margin of the Visible,* p. 267.

35. *Christian Science Journal,* Mar., 1886.

36. Tiryakian, *On the Margin of the Visible,* pp. 19, 24.

37. This charge, made by Richard Kennedy, was printed in the series of muckraking attacks written for *McClures Magazine* by Georgine Milmine. They appeared between Jan., 1907, and June, 1908.

38. Eddy gave this reason when she temporarily withdrew from circulation her controversial *Christ and Christmas;* "Hear, O Israel," *Christian Science Journal,* 11 (1894):11, 472.

39. Arthur Corey, who resigned from the church in 1945, tried unconvincingly to disassociate Eddy from the policy of secrecy that affected Christian Science instruction. See the introduction to his *Christian Science Class Instruction* (Los Gatos, Calif.: Farrallon Press, 1950).

40. Mircea Eliade, *Occultism, Witchcraft, and Cultural Fashions: Essays in Comparative Religions* (Chicago: University of Chicago Press, 1976), p. 56.

41. Eddy, *Science and Health,* 3d ed. (Lynn: Asa G. Eddy, 1881), 2:42.

42. Eddy, *Science and Health* (Lynn: Asa G. Eddy, 1878), 2:47.

43. Eddy, *Science and Health with Key to the Scriptures,* 190th ed. (Boston: Joseph Armstrong, 1900), p. 282.

44. Milmine, *McClures Magazine,* 29 (Sept., 1907):579; 29 (July, 1907):346.

45. Adam H. Dickey, *Memoirs of Mary Baker Eddy* (Brookline, Mass.: Lillian Dickey, 1927). A church-approved version of Eddy's last years, also written by a member of the household, makes no mention of malicious animal magnetism; see Rev. Irving C. Tomlinson, *Twelve Years with Mary Baker Eddy: Recollections and Experiences* (Boston: Christian Science Publication Society, 1945).

46. Dickey, *Memoirs,* pp. 44–45, 47–49, 123.

47. Eddy, *Retrospection and Introspection,* pp. 27–28.

48. Eddy, *Science and Health* (1878), 2:143–44.

49. *Christian Science Journal,* Aug., 1886, pp. 77–89.

50. Eddy was not very different from A. P. Sinnett, who wrote (*The Occult World,* p. 1): "My present wish is to sketch the outlines of this knowledge (unknown to modern culture), to record with exactitude the experimental proofs I have obtained that occult science invests its adepts with a control of natural forces superior to that enjoyed by physicists of the ordinary type."

51. R. Laurence Moore, *In Search of White Crows: Spiritualism, Parapsychology, and American Culture* (New York: Oxford University Press, 1977), esp. chs. 1 and 9.

52. Other self-proclaimed occultists made the same criticism of spiritualism. Éliphas Lévi, for example, criticized spiritualists for performing "ceremonial magic" without adequate attention to an underlying philosophy.

53. "Lecture of Mary F. Davis," *Religio-Philosophical Journal,* Oct. 23, 1875; "Review of Sinnett's Occult World," *Banner of Light,* June 3, 1882; A. E. Newton, "Oriental vs. Occidental Spiritualism," *Banner of Light,* Apr. 23, 1887.

54. William Emmette Coleman, "Lecture on Spiritualism," *Religio-Philosophical Journal,* Jan. 27, 1877.

55. J. J. Morse, "Luxoriant Tomfoolery," *Religio-Philosophical Journal,* Oct. 23, 1875; Coleman, "Lecture on Spiritualism."

56. "Letter from S. B. Brittan," *Religio-Philosophical Journal,* Nov. 6, 1875.

57. "Preface" to William Emmette Coleman, *Practical Occultism: A Course of Lectures through the Trance Mediumship of James Johnson Morse* (San Francisco: Carrier Dove, 1888).

58. H. T. Cheever, "Our Tutor Is Nature," *Spirit Messenger and Harmonial Advocate,* vol. 1 (Dec. 25, 1852); Moore, *In Search of White Crows,* pp. 11–12, 52–53.

59. Moore, *In Search of White Crows,* pp. 10, 17, 66–67.

60. See, for example, Oliver Bland, *The Adventures of a Modern Occultist* (New York: Dodd, Mead, 1920); Coleman, *Practical Occultism.*

61. Critics also said that the special spiritual claims made by leaders of these movements were used as a justification for ignoring common moral principles, especially sexual ones.

62. Cora Tappan, "The History of Occultism and Its Relation to Spiritualism," *Banner of Light*, Aug. 26, 1876.

63. *Progressive Thinker*, Oct. 15, 1938, Apr. 3, 1937.

64. Georg Simmel, "The Sociology of Secrecy and of Secret Societies," *American Journal of Sociology*, 11 (1906):441–98.

65. David B. Davis, "Some Themes of Counter-Subversion: An Analysis of Anti-Masonic, Anti-Catholic, and Anti-Mormon Literature," *Mississippi Valley Historical Review*, 47 (1960): 209.

66. Simmel, "Sociology of Secrecy," pp. 470, 473, 475, 477, and *passim*.

7

Vivekananda and American Occultism

STEVEN F. WALKER

"By 1880," writes Donald Meyer, "the divisive sectarianism of an earlier generation had given way to a spirit of cooperation and good will. . . . Americans had successfully compensated for their religious diversity by cultivating a kind of generalized religious consciousness in both their institutional and their personal lives." One consequence of this shift away from dogmatic sectarianism was the liberal and intellectually tolerant interest in what Thomas Wentworth Higginson called "The Sympathy of Religions," and the most notable "institutional" event of this new frame of mind must now be seen as the Parliament of Religions held as part of the Chicago World's Fair.[1]

When the Parliament of Religions opened on September 11, 1893, few visitors to the World's Columbian Exposition in Chicago were prepared for the enthusiastic reception an unknown monk from India was to be greeted with by a surprised and delighted audience assembled in the Art Institute's Hall of Columbus. Professor John Henry Wright of the Harvard Classics Department had written ahead to the officials of the Parliament of Religions giving his warm assurances of support to the participation of Vivekananda (the monastic name of the foreign visitor who had arrived in America barely a month before), but only he and a few others had had the chance to gauge the brilliance of mind and depth of soul that were to make such an immediate impression on the assembled listeners in Chicago. Today the name of Vivekananda is widely known throughout India, where he is remembered as one of the foremost figures of the Hindu renaissance of the nineteenth century. However, it is fair to say that nearly a century later it is not widely known in America that in this country, from July, 1893, to April, 1895, and again from August, 1899, to July, 1900, one of the most distinguished figures in India's recent history began his career as a writer, lecturer, and religious teacher.

The initial impact of Vivekananda on his American audience is perhaps best documented by the enthusiastic appraisal of his thought by William James, who quoted from his writings not only in *The Varieties of Religious Experience* (1902)[2] but also in his widely read *Pragmatism* (1907), where he wrote that "the paragon of all monistic systems is the Vedânta philosophy of Hindostan, and the paragon of Vedântist missionaries was the late Swami Vivekananda who visited our land some years ago." If James's enthusiasm for the man was tempered by a good deal of skepticism for his system, which, he stated with some irony, "imparts a perfect sumptuosity of security" ("we all have some ear for this monistic music: it elevates and reassures," he added later), he nevertheless was willing to grant the system "a high pragmatic value."[3] The reaction of the popular audience to the lectures and charismatic appeal of Vivekananda is to be sought in the numerous newspaper accounts that Marie Louise Burke has presented, along with other hitherto unpublished material, in two recent and invaluable studies published by the Vedanta Society of Northern California,[4] one of the active centers for the teaching of Vedanta philosophy founded at the request of his American admirers either by Vivekananda or by the fellow monks of the same order (the Ramakrishna Mission).

Since Vivekananda came to America as a religious teacher, as a representative of the universalizing tendencies of Vedanta philosophy, itself a product of centuries of orthodox commentary on the *Upanishads* and other sacred texts of Hinduism, it is only fair to state at the outset that Vivekananda's views on turn-of-the-century occultism in America developed only as a response to circumstances. He himself had no interest in promoting the "mystic East" view of Indian philosophy that the Theosophy movement, founded by Madame Blavatsky in 1875 and led by Annie Besant at the time Vivekananda began his active career as a religious teacher, encouraged among its followers. As a recent article by Rakhahari Chatterji, a political scientist from Calcutta University, puts it, "Simply on religious grounds the Swami had to fight Theosophy; for his Vedantism could by no means compromise with the occultism and supernaturalism of Theosophy. For, in the opinion of Vivekananda, one could not be a Hindu and a believer in such third-rate magical powers of religion at the same time."[5] Although Vivekananda respected the character of Annie Besant ("that she is one of the most sincere of women, her greatest enemy will concede"),[6] and generally avoided

Lithographic poster of Swami Vivekananda, Chicago, 1893. Courtesy of Vedanta Society of Northern California.

public condemnation of the movement, his private opinion of Theosophy is adequately revealed in interviews and private papers. He castigated "this Indian grafting of American Spiritualism—with only a few Sanskrit words taking the place of spiritualistic jargon—Mahâtmâ missiles taking the place of ghostly raps and taps, and Mahatmic inspiration that of obsession by ghosts." He wrote scornfully that "the Hindus have enough of religious teaching and teachers amidst themselves . . . and they do not stand in need of dead ghosts of Russians and Americans" (*CW*, 4:318).

The widespread public interest in occult phenomena in the America of the 1890s, and "the mode of the day to trace mysterious and psychical powers to India" (Burke, p. 617), elicited some acute remarks and sometimes humorous jibes from Vivekananda. From what is in this context perhaps a unique and certainly an unusual perspective, these barbs shed light on one aspect of American life at the end of the nineteenth century. His scattered reflections on the occultist fads and ideas of the time demonstrated the truth of the proposition, for an audience prepared for a demonstration of the opposite, that occultism was *not* the best of what India had to offer America.

One of Vivekananda's first American students, Leon Landsberg, penned a satirical portrait of the American occultist scene in 1896:

> We Americans are a very receptive nation; and that is why our country has become the hot-bed of all kinds of religious and irreligious monstrosities that ever sprang from a human brain. There is no theory so absurd, no doctrine so irrational, no claim so extravagant, no fraud so transparent that it cannot find here numerous believers and—a ready market. . . . Hundreds of societies and sects have been given birth to, to feed the credulity of the people and, in turn, draw support therefrom. The whole atmosphere is here in some places filled with hobgloblins, spooks, and Mahatmas . . . ; and new prophets are rising every day in Israel, sent from some great hierophant of the "Brotherhood of the Motherhood of the Golden Candelabra" and similar known and unknowable Gobi and Himalaya dwellers to start some new sect for the salvation of the world, and pocket from $25 to $100 initiation fee from fools ready to pay it. (Burke, pp. 616–17)

It was this atmosphere that Vivekananda had to contend with—an atmosphere particularly trying to someone who was initially treated by credulous Americans (and by newspaper reporters in search of a good story) as an expert on the occult all the more qualified since he came from exotic India. In fact, as he wrote an English friend, he "had never

had anything to do with these phases of religion, in India or elsewhere."
On the contrary, he believed that "only the Advaita philosophy [the
nondualist school of Vedanta] can save mankind, whether in East or
West, from 'devil worship' and kindred superstitions, giving tone and
strength to the very nature of man" (*CW*, 8:335).

Vivekananda's condemnation of occultism was not, however, accompanied by a disbelief in the actual occurrence of occult phenomena. He
had come to America already prepared to accept the scientific validity
of at least some strange events, as the following anecdote concerning
his early years of wandering in India illustrates, in the humorous tone
he often adopted in describing such apparently inexplicable occurrences. Asked by some Himalayan villagers to examine and, if possible,
to exorcize a man who was possessed by a spirit and who was able to
touch a red-hot axe without being burned or experiencing any pain,
Vivekananda had a chance to see for himself if the event was no more
than a clever fraud:

> Once there, I felt a strong impulse to examine the axe rather
> closely, but the instant I touched it, I burnt my fingers, although
> the thing had been cooled down to blackness. The smarting made
> me restless and all my theories about the axe phenomenon were
> spirited away from my mind! However, smarting with the burn, I
> placed my hand on the head of the man and repeated for a short
> while the Japa. It was a matter of surprise to find that the man
> came round in ten or twelve minutes. Then oh, the gushing rever-
> ence the villagers showed to me! I was taken to be some wonderful
> man! But, all the same, I couldn't make any head or tail of the
> whole business. So without a word one way or the other, I re-
> turned with my host to his hut. It was about midnight, and I went
> to bed. But what with the smarting burn in the hand and the im-
> penetrable puzzle of the whole affair, I couldn't have any sleep that
> night. Thinking of the burning axe failing to harm living human
> flesh, it occurred again and again to my mind, "There are more
> things in heaven and earth, Horatio, than are dreamt of in your
> philosophy." (*CW*, 6:516)

On another occasion a newspaper reporter asked Vivekananda
questions concerning the "fakirs" of India who obsessed the American
public's imagination (such stories were always felt to make good copy).
In reply Vivekananda described how he tested a fakir for fraud:

> Five months ago, . . . or just one month before I left India to come
> to this country, I happened in company in a caravan or party of 25
> to sojourn for a space in a city in the interior. While there we

learned of the marvelous work of one of these itinerant magicians and had him brought before us. He told us he would produce for us any article we desired. We stripped him, at his request, until he was quite naked and placed him in the corner of the room. I threw my travelling blanket about him and then we called upon him to do as he had promised. He asked what we should like, and I asked for a bunch of . . . grapes, and straightway the fellow brought them forth from under his blanket. Oranges and other fruits were produced, and finally great dishes of steaming rice. (*CW*, 7:285)

The same strange event was later discussed in one of Vivekananda's lectures in California, where he commented on the general conclusions to which his experience had brought him. He recognized that there was a great deal of fraud involved in such occult performances, but "whenever you see fraud, you have also to say that fraud is an imitation. There must be some truth somewhere, that is being imitated." He then turned to the traditional studies of occult phenomena and powers preserved in the various yoga scriptures of India:

These facts, the Hindus, being analytically minded, took up and investigated. And they came to certain remarkable conclusions; that is, they made a science of it. They found out that all these, though extraordinary, are also natural; there is nothing supernatural. They are under laws just the same as any other physical phenomenon. It is not a freak of nature that a man is born with such powers. They can be systematically studied, practised, and acquired. . . . All these extraordinary powers are in the mind of man. . . . And each mind, wherever it is located, is in actual communication with the whole world. (*CW*, 2:12–13)

Nevertheless, as a religious teacher Vivekananda denied any specific religious value to occult phenomena. In so doing, he ran counter not only to the emotional prejudices of the spiritualistically inclined members of his audience but also to a more widespread acceptance among Christian sects that "miracles" constituted some form of proof for theological assertions. A reporter for the *Washington Post* quoted him as saying, "I am not a believer in miracles—they are repugnant to me in matters of religion. You might bring the world tumbling down about my ears, but that would be no proof to me that there was a God, or that you worked by his agency, if there was one" (*CW*, 2:498).[7] When a Memphis lady asked him if he could perform any magic tricks of the sort that Indian fakirs were supposed to be adept at, Vivekananda replied immediately, "What have those things to do with religion? Do they make a man purer? The Satan of your Bible is powerful, but differs from God in not being pure" (Burke, p. 617). His advice to Americans on matters occult was succinct: "If you want your nation to live, keep away from all these things" (*CW*, 8:185). He gave much the same advice to his fellow Indians, but in even stronger terms, adding that "we have become weak, and that is why occultism and mysticism come to us—these creepy things; there may be great truths in them, but they have nearly destroyed us" (*CW*, 3:224). In both cases it was the religious teacher, speaking to East and West alike, who insisted that "we are fools indeed to give up God for legends of ghosts or flying hobgoblins" (*CW*, 4:59).

Vivekananda's general dislike of American occultism was accompanied by a critique of some of its specific practices. He contrasted the healthy-minded approach of Vedanta, with its call for spiritual self-reliance and strength, and what he considered to be the morbid and weak-minded fascination with strange events on the part of the occultists. In his New York talks on raja yoga, for example, he appealed to the Vedantic concept of freedom in order to discredit the very notion of a beneficial use of hypnosis:

> The so-called hypnotic suggestion can only act upon a weak mind. And until the operator, by means of fixed gaze or otherwise, has succeeded in putting the mind of the subject in a sort of passive, morbid condition, his suggestions never work. . . . Every attempt at control which is not voluntary, not with the controller's own mind, is not only disastrous, but it defeats the end. The goal of each soul is freedom, mastery—freedom from the slavery of matter and thought, mastery of external and internal nature. Instead of leading towards that, every will-current from another, in whatever form it comes, . . . only rivets one link more to the already existing heavy chain of bondage of past thoughts, past superstitions.[8] (*CW*, 1:172)

Vivekananda attributed most of the occultist practices to sheer materialistic opportunism. He wrote from New York to one of his brother monks in India that "this is a thoroughly materialistic country. The people of this Christian land will recognise religion only if you can cure diseases, work miracles, and open up avenues to money; and they understand little of anything else" (*CW*, 6:271). This did not prevent him, however, from placing himself under the care of an illiterate "magnetic healing woman" in Los Angeles, a certain Mrs. Melton.[9] Mrs. Melton's treatment seems to have consisted of vigorous massage charged with "magnetism." Apparently Vivekananda felt the therapy did him some good. Humor and open-mindedness join in his appraisal

of the value of Mrs. Melton's treatment: "Whether it is magnetic healing, California ozone, or the end of the present spell of bad karma, I am
improving" (*CW*, 8:486).

The notion of a bodily survival after death was totally alien to Vivekananda's Vedantic aspiration toward freedom from material constraints. His experience of spiritualist meetings or seances aroused only
feelings of dismay, as can be seen from the following passage from a
lecture given in San Francisco in April, 1900, near the end of his American stay.

> People like to think that even after death their relatives continue
> to exist in the same bodies, and the spiritualists play on their super-
> stitions. I would be very sorry to know that my dead father is still
> wearing his filthy body. People get consolation from this, that their
> fathers are all encased in matter. In another place they brought me
> Jesus Christ. I said, "Lord, how do you do?" It makes me feel
> hopeless. If that great saintly man is still wearing the body, what
> is to become of us poor creatures? (*CW*, 8:133)

Exactly what Vivekananda thought about death and the fate of the
"departed" may be gathered from a letter he wrote to Mrs. Ole Bull,
wife of the famous Norwegian violinist, whose house in Cambridge,
Massachusetts, was a meeting place for the intellectual community.
Vivekananda stayed there in October, 1894, when perhaps he met
William James for the first time. Mrs. Ole Bull's father died a few
months later, and his letter of consolation to her indicates why the stage
machinery of spiritualistic seances offended his sense of the dignity of
death:

> Coming and going is all pure delusion. The soul never comes nor
> goes. Where is the place to which it shall go when all space is *in
> the soul*? When shall be the time for entering and departing when
> all time is *in the soul*? . . . All souls that ever have been, are, or
> shall be, are all in the present tense and—to use a material simile
> —are all standing at one geometrical point. . . . The whole secret
> is, then, that your father has given up the old garment he was wear-
> ing and is standing where he was through all eternity. (*CW*, 5:
> 68–69)

In a lighter mood, Vivekananda enjoyed telling the story of a couple
of spiritualist mediums who shared kitchen facilities with him in a New
York rooming house. Although they worked as a team and were married, the two did not get along well together. After one of their tiffs, the
wife would turn to their fellow boarder from far-off India and com-

plain: "Is it fair of him to treat me like this, when I make all the ghosts?"[10]

When questioned by American reporters on matters of the occult, as he often was, Vivekananda never denied the possibility of occult phenomena actually occurring, and on occasion gave credence to certain types. The following account of an interview appeared in the *Memphis Commercial* for January 15, 1894, during the period when Vivekananda was touring the country with engagements arranged for the most part by a lecture bureau:

> The subject of suspended animation was broached and the Hindu monk told the *Commercial* reporter that he himself had known a man who went into a sealed cave, which was then closed up with a trap door, and remained there for many years without food. There was a decided stir of interest among those who heard this assertion. Vive Kananda [*sic*] entertained not the slightest doubt of the genuineness of this case. He says that in the case of suspended animation, growth is for the time being arrested. . . . He thinks the studies which enabled persons to accomplish that feat were suggested by hibernating animals.[11]

It is to be noted that Vivekananda avoided the sensational aspect of the phenomenon, which he treated cautiously via the analogy of a known natural phenomenon, that of hibernation.

The period of Vivekananda's stay in America coincided with the flourishing of societies for psychical research in the Western nations. Although he was often billed as one who possessed "deep penetration into things occult," to quote the *Memphis Appeal-Avalanche* (Burke, p. 164), Vivekananda was reluctant to indulge his audience's appetite for stories of strange events, given the unfavorable conclusions he had come to regarding the religious value of occult phenomena. Nevertheless, his attitude toward the scientific investigation of psychical or occult phenomena cannot be said to have been completely negative, especially since the ancient writings on yoga in India dealt analytically with such material. While in London he took part in a debate on the question, "Can psychic phenomena be proved from a scientific basis?" After insisting that "in order to have scientific explanation of psychical phenomena, we require not only perfect evidence on the part of the phenomena themselves, but a good deal of training on the part of those who want to see," Vivekananda indicated clearly that the training of the *seer*, in the religious sense of the term, was the major concern for him:

In my opinion, therefore, I go really one step further than the lecturer, and advance the opinion that most of the psychical phenomena—not only little things like spirit-rappings or table-rappings which are mere child's play, not merely little things like telepathy which I have seen boys do even—most of the psychical phenomena which the last speaker calls the higher clairvoyance, but which I would rather beg to call the experiences of the super-conscious state of the mind, are the very stepping-stones to real psychological investigation. (*CW*, 4:194–95)

To the extent, then, that occult or psychical phenomena pointed toward the attainment of a higher state of consciousness, Vivekananda found something of value in their investigation. Otherwise, he was quick to ridicule the exercise of psychical powers: "Reading other men's thoughts! If I must read everyone else's thoughts for five minutes at a time I shall go crazy" (*CW*, 4:60). In his talks on raja yoga in New York, during which he commented on a classic text (Patanjali's *Yoga Sutras*), Vivekananda warned his students that "the possession of what are called occult powers is only intensifying the world, and in the end, intensifying suffering. Though as a scientist Patanjali is bound to point out the possibilities of this science, he never misses an opportunity to warn us against these powers" (*CW*, 1:211).

Even if Vivekananda's views on turn-of-the-century American occultism were generally critical, he still saw some value in the American fascination with weird happenings and outlandish doctrines. On occasion he pointed out the possibility of "great truths" being found in "these creepy things" (*CW*, 3:224). At a discussion following his lecture on Vedanta philosophy at the Graduate Philosophical Society of Harvard University (March 25, 1896), he was asked whether he had "made any study of the principles of self-hypnotism." Rather than replying directly to the question, Vivekananda directed his answer toward the issue of religious values, appealing to the Vedantic idea of an ultimate truth whose realization releases a person from ignorance, and quoting from the *Upanishads*: "What you call hypnotism in the West is only a part of the real thing. The Hindus call it self-hypnotisation. They say you are hypnotised already, and that you should get out of it and de-hypnotise yourself. 'There the sun cannot illumine, nor the moon, nor the stars; the flash of lightning cannot illumine that; what to speak of this mortal fire! That shining, everything else shines.' That is not hypnotisation, but de-hypnotisation." (*CW*, 5:303).[12]

In the course of the same discussion someone asked Vivekananda

about the "manifestations" a yogi could demonstrate. Again Vivekananda quickly sidestepped a discussion of psychical phenomena in
order to indicate that yogic powers might be viewed as evidence that
total freedom of the mind could be attained: "I have seen the lower
things that can be done by the power of the mind, and therefore I have
no right to disbelieve that the highest things can be done. The ideal of
the Yogi is eternal peace and love through omniscience and omnipo-
tence" (*CW*, 5:305).[13]

Since the idea behind the notion of "self-hypnosis" appealed to his
religious sense, his reaction to the first question did not result in a satirical retort, as would have been expected. In the second case, one sus-
pects that the serious and scholarly atmosphere of a Harvard gathering
encouraged him to present psychical powers in a more favorable light,
since the sensational aspect of the question did not run the risk of wind-
ing up as good copy for a newspaper story, and also since the idea behind the notion of psychical powers—the potentially unlimited powers
of the mind—was for him one of the "great truths."

Although Vivekananda did not attempt to claim scientific validity for
one of the most traditionally held of Hindu beliefs, reincarnation, it too
appealed to him because the idea of a potentially infinite development
of the mind lay hidden in it. According to the idea of reincarnation or
metempsychosis, the soul perfects itself over innumerable lifetimes, and
ultimately attains perfect freedom. This conviction was clearly incompatible with the idea of a heaven or a hell where all progress comes to
an eternal halt after one lifetime alone, and even more incompatible
with the Calvinist doctrine of predestination with its radical denial of
the soul's freedom to work out its own salvation. The following anecdote reveals the American public's interest in the theory of reincarnation, about which Vivekananda was often asked to speak. It also constitutes a sketch of a highly picturesque and amusing Socratic dialogue on
a matter of occult interest between a Hindu monk and a Presbyterian
cowboy, as reported by the *Memphis Appeal-Avalanche*:

> I met with a peculiar incident while on a train leaving the city of
> Minneapolis. There was a cowboy on the train. He was a rough
> sort of fellow and a Presbyterian of the blue nose type. He walked
> up and asked me where I was from. I told him India. "What are
> you?" he said. "Hindu," I replied. "Then you must go to hell," he
> remarked. I told him of this theory, and after [my] explaining it,
> he said he had always believed in it, because he said that one day
> when he was chopping a log, his little sister came out in her clothes

and said that she used to be a man. That is why he believed in the transmigration of souls.[14] (*CW,* 7:422–23)

But Vivekananda had gone on to explain to his Memphis audience that what appealed to him in the theory of metempsychosis (in spite of its logical implausibility: "according to logic, hypothesis and theory must not be believed") was its moral depth and the idea of justice that it contained, which allowed the soul to correct its own mistakes and to become more perfect through its own actions.

Vivekananda's reactions to the spectacle of the American occultist scene of the 1890s are epitomized by his comments on the Greenacre Conference, a summer retreat on the banks of the Piscataqua River near Eliot, Maine, which had been organized by Sarah Farmer as an open forum for the free expression of religious views.[15] Vivekananda was invited by Miss Farmer to attend the conference in the summer of 1894. He found himself to be in great sympathy with the aims of its founder, in spite of the occultist fads in which she and the others indulged. He wrote to Mrs. Ole Bull, "I will be only too glad to take Miss Farmer's advice, in spite of ghosts and spooks. Behind the spooks I *see* a heart of immense love, only covered with a thin film of laudable ambition—even that is bound to vanish in a few years" (Burke, p. 476). But, writing to two of his Chicago students from the Greenacre Conference, he underscored the essential difference between the tendency of occultist thought and genuine religious thought as he understood it: "Instead of materialising the spirit, that is, dragging the spiritual to the material plane as these folks do, convert the matter into spirit. . . . Seek not, touch not with your toes even, anything that is uncanny" (*CW,* 6:261–62). Nevertheless, he wrote to one of the same students a year later, urging her to go to Greenacre with all its "spiritualists, table turnings, palmists, astrologers etc. etc." (*CW,* 8:340). Of the people gathered there, especially the younger people who camped out during the conference, he said: "You will be astounded with the liberty they enjoy in the camps, but they are very good and pure people there—a little erratic and that is all" (*CW,* 6:260).

Although he had come to think well of many *occultists,* Vivekananda did not change his views on *occultism,* as can be seen from a letter written to a friend in 1895: "I am perfectly aware that although some truth underlies the mass of mystical thought which has burst upon the Western world of late, it is for the most part full of motives, unworthy, or insane" (*CW,* 8:335).[16]

Swami Vivekananda at Greenacre, near Eliot, Maine. Courtesy of
Vedanta Society of Northern California.

NOTES

1. Donald H. Meyer, "The Victorian Crisis of Faith," in Daniel Walker Howe, ed., *Victorian America* (Philadelphia: University of Philadelphia Press, 1976), pp. 66–67; Paul A. Carter, *The Spiritual Crisis of the Gilded Age* (De Kalb, Ill.: Northern Illinois University Press, 1971), p. 217.

2. William James, *The Varieties of Religious Experience* (New York: New American Library, 1958), p. 387, n. 28.

3. William James, *Pragmatism* (New York: New American Library, 1974), pp. 102, 104.

4. Marie Louise Burke, *Swami Vivekananda in America: New Discoveries* (Calcutta: Advaita Ashrama, 1978), hereafter cited in the text as Burke; Burke, *Swami Vivekananda: His Second Visit to the West* (Calcutta: Advaita Ashrama, 1973).

5. Rakhahari Chatterji, "Vivekananda and Contemporary India," *Prabuddha Bharata,* 84 (1979):192.

6. Vivekananda, *The Complete Works of Vivekananda,* 8 vols. (Calcutta: Advaita Ashrama, 1970–71), 5:224, hereafter cited in the text as *CW.*

7. *Washington Post,* Oct. 29, 1894.

8. The submission of Sophia Peabody, Nathaniel Hawthorne's fiancee, to hypnosis elicited a similar protest from Hawthorne. See C. E. Schorer, "Hawthorne and Hypnosis," *Nathaniel Hawthorne Journal 1972,* pp. 239–44. Paul A. Carter remarks quite rightly that Vivekananda "carefully and consistently disentangled his message from the faddish occultism which it superficially resembled" (*Spiritual Crisis of the Gilded Age,* p. 216, n. 55).

9. Burke, *Swami Vivekananda: His Second Visit to the West,* pp. 175–77.

10. *Reminiscences of Swami Vivekananda* (Calcutta: Advaita Ashrama, 1964), p. 187.

11. *CW,* 5:184. This may be an allusion to Pavhari Baba, a saintly man for whom Vivekananda had great respect and whose life he once evoked in a biographical sketch (see *CW,* 4:283–95).

12. The quotation is from the *Katha Upanishad.*

13. The lecture as well as the discussion notes were published the same year. See Vivekananda, *The Vedanta Philosophy: An Address before the Graduate Philosophical Society of Harvard University, March 25, 1896* (Cambridge, Mass.: Printed for the Society, 1896). A second edition came out the following year.

14. *Memphis Appeal-Avalanche,* Jan. 20, 1894.

15. See Burke, pp. 472–82, for an account of the Greenacre Conference.

16. For a brief discussion of Vivekananda's life and thought, see Christopher Isherwood, *Ramakrishna and His Disciples* (New York: Simon and Schuster, 1970), pp. 186–216, 316–28. For a full biography and discussion, see Swami Nikhilananda, *Vivekananda* (New York: Ramakrishna-Vivekananda Center, 1953), and Romain Rolland, *The Life of Vivekananda and the Universal Gospel* (Calcutta: Advaita Ashrama, 1931). More succinct accounts of Vivekananda in America can be found in the brief bio-

graphical sketch by C. B. Tripathi in Marc Pachter and Frances Wein, eds., *Abroad in America: Visitors to the New Nation* (Washington, D.C.: National Portrait Gallery, Smithsonian Institution, 1976), pp. 239–46, and in the last chapter, "The Meeting of East and West," of Carter, *Spiritual Crisis of the Gilded Age,* pp. 210–21.

8

Women in Occult America

MARY FARRELL BEDNAROWSKI

EVEN A CURSORY SURVEY of American religious history reveals that while women rarely had acknowledged authority in mainstream Judaism and Christianity, they have been prominent in a number of movements with occult characteristics, such as spiritualism, Theosophy, and feminist witchcraft. This chapter, a comparative study of these three movements—two with origins in the nineteenth century and one a product of the twentieth—has two purposes: first, to demonstrate the abiding concern for women's rights that has been part of a number of occult movements in America; and, second, to explicate the variety of forms of the occult in which this concern has been expressed, from the spirit messages of spiritualism to the Eastern esotericism of Theosophy, to the psychologically oriented occultism of feminist witchcraft.

A contemporary analysis provides some of the themes that become apparent in an investigation of occult movements which have taken up the causes of women. In the spring of 1975 *Quest: A Feminist Quarterly* published an edition on women and spirituality. One of the articles, "Spiritual Explorations Cross-Country," charted a summer tour by Susan Rennie and Kirsten Grimstad during which they found a "widespread and surging interest in . . . the spiritual aspects of life. . . . We found that wherever there are feminist communities, women are studying psychic and non-material phenomena. . . ." Grimstad and Rennie confessed an initial "indifference bordering on uneasiness and apprehension," later attributed to their culturally induced antagonism to anything that could not be validated "scientifically" and their "association of things spiritual with reactionary politics."[1] By the end of the tour they felt they had come to understand the feminist implications of this interest in an occult kind of spirituality:

Women, feminists, are becoming sensitized and receptive to the psychic potential inherent in human nature—and they are realizing that women in particular are the repository of powers and capabilities that have been suppressed, that have been casualties of western *man's* drive to technological control over nature. It is as if feminists have recognized an even deeper source of female alienation and fragmentation than the sex role polarization which has so effectively limited women's lives—the mind/body dualism progressively fostered by patriarchal culture. In acknowledging this side of our being, women are in effect striving for a total integration and wholeness. Accepting the wholeness that includes psychic awareness and exploration takes feminist consciousness into an entirely new dimension—it amounts to a new definition of reality.[2]

Although expressed in the language of contemporary feminism, this short article points to at least three prominent themes in all the movements under consideration, regardless of historical context and irrespective of different understandings of the meaning of "occult." These themes are seen in embryo form in spiritualism and are more fully articulated in Theosophy and feminist witchcraft. First, there is an indictment of male-dominated Western society as both "unnatural" and as antagonistic to woman's very nature. Second, there is an insistence on the need to heal the Cartesian split in the universe, to reintegrate spirit and matter, mind or soul and body, experience and reason. Third, there is an affirmation of woman's nature as defined by the particular movement as especially suited for the enterprise of restoring wholeness and balance to all the institutions of society. Interwoven with these themes is the implication that women must seek the development of their own spirituality outside the framework of institutionalized religion—that the mere reform of existing institutions is not enough. To repeat Grimstad and Rennie, they are talking about a "new definition of reality."

Before beginning an analysis of the distinct ways in which spiritualism, Theosophy, and feminist witchcraft have expressed concern for women through their particular understandings of the occult, it is useful both from a historical and a rhetorical point of view to note the strikingly similar assessments on the part of these movements as to how the male-centeredness of organized religion has produced a society which oppresses and denigrates women. W. J. Colville, a spiritualist, claimed that "people cannot entertain an exclusively masculine idea of Deity and at the same time believe that motherhood is as divine as fatherhood. The degradation of women is always supported most strongly where the belief is regnant that only males are fit to officiate at sacred altars."[3] A Theosophist, Helen Knothe, spoke of the need to "look for and find the divine aspect of woman," and "at the same time ... prove the essential woman aspect of Divinity. ... When women realize their own inherent Divinity, then shall they occupy the place which is rightfully theirs in the full light of Her love."[4] According to Z. Budapest, a feminist witch, "What people believe (faith—religions) is political because it influences their actions and because it is a vehicle by which a religion perpetuates a social system." Budapest interprets society as patriarchal in nature, stripped of woman's power, because "male energy pretends to power by disclaiming the female force."[5]

As for the particularities of these movements, there is no mistaking the vehemence of the feminism of nineteenth-century American spiritualism, although the movement never produced a very coherent theoretical basis for it, nor, as R. Laurence Moore points out, did the pro-feminist views of spiritualism have much influence outside the movement itself.[6] In fact, on the surface, it is difficult to ascertain exactly what accounts for the spiritualists' concern with women's rights. They had no interest in emphasizing the intuitive or mystical or emotional aspects of religion associated, rightly or wrongly, with feminine spirituality. Just the reverse, in fact: the spiritualists' intent was to demystify the universe and the supernatural in order to replace religious beliefs with scientific facts based on the physical manifestations of the spirits: "Religion indeed," said one spiritualist, "may quicken the aspirations of men after union with the Divine; but it is Science, earnest, deep-fathoming science, alone, that can determine the nature of that holy and wondrous Essence. ..."[7] Spiritualism preached the kind of scientific evaluation of the spiritual with its emphasis on the sensory and the rational that twentieth-century feminists would come to see as particularly antagonistic to feminine spirituality. Further, the spiritualist pro-feminist stance did not emerge from an occult world view that sought to balance the cosmic principles of male and female, because the spiritualists did not consider themselves occultists—that label, they said, was imposed upon them from outside the movement. According to R. Laurence Moore, "People kept equating their interest in spirit voices with mysticism, or occultism or magic (or all three), whereas they insisted that it had nothing to do with any of these."[8]

From what bases, then, did the feminism of nineteenth-century American spiritualism arise? And how was it manifested within the movement? On the very simplest level, spiritualists saw themselves as champions not only of liberal religion but of liberal politics and social conventions as well. Henry James portrays graphically, if not sym-

pathetically, the intertwining of both feminist and occult concerns in
The Bostonians.[9] Robert Riegel cites the numerous feminists who were
interested in both spiritualism and Theosophy, although he expresses
puzzlement over the connection.[10] R. Laurence Moore mentions that
when people's most important ideas have been rejected, as has certainly been the case with feminism and occultism most of the time in
American society, "the temptation arose for them to make common
cause with champions of other rejected ideas."[11] A short notice in the
May 13, 1876, *Banner of Light,* a spiritualist weekly, underscores this
thesis of the interconnectedness of liberal causes: the item publicized a
"Mass Convention" of the spiritualists of Minnesota, promising a "feast
of reason and a flow of soul," and inviting "all Spiritualists, together
with Liberals of every name and kind. . . ."[12]

Spiritualists affirmed their pro-feminist bias with scatter-shot attacks
aimed at a variety of institutions, the most frequent target being organized religion, which they believed had foundered because it had
fallen into the hands of a powerful and degenerate elite—the ordained
male clergy.[13] Male-dominated medicine also came in for accusations.
During its more than fifty-year history the *Banner of Light* carried a
substantial number of ads for alternate sources of medical aid, aimed
against the "Medical Institution made up of a combination of specu-
lating individuals, having no higher objective than money-making."
One nontraditional clinic offered the services of "Mrs. R. E. Dilling-
ham, Assistant, who will be present at all times, for the reception of
ladies and will prescribe for them when more consistent and desirable."[14] There were also occasional ads for books on birth control techniques, whose chapter titles betray a pro-feminist bias. One such was
Henry C. Wright's *The Unwelcome Child; or, The Crime of an Un-
desired Maternity.* One chapter, "A Protest of Humanity against Legal-
ized Sensualism," was directed against the total sexual rights afforded
husbands by the legal right of marriage.[15] That the spiritualists saw
themselves pitted against the ministerial and medical professions is also
evident from other sources. The biographer of Cora L. V. Scott, a healing and trance medium who began her career as a child in Wisconsin,
mentions that she "aroused the antagonism of the regular physicians
and clergymen in the neighborhood. The former were without patients
and the latter lacked audiences."[16] The spiritualists were also concerned
with politics and urged that women actively seek the vote to improve
their lot. An article in the *Spiritualist,* a Wisconsin monthly of short
duration, advised women, "Voting would make you more independent.
Your feeling of dependence on men is proverbial. You are legally help-

less, and men know it, and are apt to take advantage of it. Your relief is in the vote."[17]

Protests like those above give a good sense of the variety of areas in which spiritualist feminism expressed itself, but they fail to provide clues as to any underlying framework that would support a feminist stance other than general liberal, anti-institutional tendencies. Indeed, the movement never moved beyond the "attack" stage in its theory of feminism. That is not to say that spiritualism had only a superficial appeal for women—it provided them with access to mediumship, which was a legitimate form of spiritual leadership within the movement; it denied the truth of the doctrine of original sin and human depravity and woman as the "first transgressor" in Eden; and it expended a great deal of rhetoric on the need for equal rights for women in religion, politics, and marriage.[18]

Even if spiritualism did not provide a coherent underpinning for its feminism, it did make an attempt at pulling the universe together, at reintegrating spirit and matter in its search for "natural" laws that would prevail in both the material and the spiritual worlds. The spiritualists saw themselves as leaders in the search for such laws and proclaimed that *"the Spirit World* is after all, but a finer material world, as real, as substantial; and as directly within the province of universal law as that which we now inhabit."[19] The concern with universal laws had its significance for women in at least one area, that of marriage and the relationship between the sexes.

The spiritualists' preoccupation with the laws governing sexuality certainly stems in part from frequent accusations that they advocated free love and divorce. They denied these charges bitterly and attempted to make known what they considered their highly rational and moral views by an explanation of the "marriage law," which Lizzie Doten described as "a law of nature, which existed from the beginning. When God created the male and female, the very fact that he did create them male and female implanted the marriage law in their nature."[20] While this description does not in itself sound very revolutionary, the spiritualists believed that the marriage law operated on both the physical and the spiritual planes and that it drew together persons of like nature destined to be "spiritual affinities." Unfortunately, the legal and social conditions of marriage in nineteenth-century America operated to prevent the union of spiritual affinities who discovered each other after an unhappy marriage. As a result, spiritualists expressed their antagonism to conventional morality, which prevented particularly the woman from seeking a divorce without irreparable harm to her reputation. The spiritualists insisted that the "marriage law" is "the divine law of reciprocal love" and "is above all legal or ecclesiastical statutes." To them it was inevitable that "the latter must in time pass away in order that the former may be left to free itself, before the highest ideal of the human species will appear on earth."[21] According to William H. Dixon, author of *Spiritual Wives,* "If a woman is free to make her own terms with God, why should she not be able to make her own terms with man?"[22]

Quite apart from any consideration of how much spiritualists put the rhetoric of free love into practice, it is interesting to see their attempt to get beyond what they considered the artificially imposed conventions of society and to seek out the "natural" and the cosmically rooted. That they sought to do so totally under the aegis of science is a measure of the intensity of appeal of the empirical method in mid-nineteenth-century America. Whether they realized it or not, the spiritualists were invoking the occult doctrine that like is attracted to like in their theory of spiritual affinities, and they made use of their understanding of universal law to try to free women from a double standard of morality.

The reality they posited other than the obviously physical was that of the spirits and the spheres they inhabited. Even though the women mediums in particular stressed that they had no control over the spirits, that they passively received and passed on the messages, the spiritualists nonetheless hoped to acquire the power that would proceed from a knowledge of the universal laws governing spirit and matter. Women had as much opportunity to seek this power as men, a power that would free them from the conventions of society and from helplessness in the face of the unfathomable.

No matter how unconventional their religious and social attitudes may have been in regard to women, the spiritualists never moved beyond the stereotype of nineteenth-century womanhood as more spiritual, sensitive, and passive than the male, and in need of protection. In fact, the typical female medium fits this description perfectly.[23] While they affirmed women's rights to religious, political, and social authority, there is almost no evidence that the spiritualists recognized that the very dependencies woman were expected to cultivate as part of their nature prevented them from attaining the equality they sought. Lizzie Doten, for example, traveled all over America as a trance medium; she spoke in public on many controversial subjects including free love and the theology of Ralph Waldo Emerson, and she defended the lot of the workingwoman. But even as she defended the right of women—and men—to love freely (although not lustfully, as she pointed out), she still spoke of "the pure young girl," and the "yearning sympathy of her nature, pure as the water of a gushing rill," attracted to the "strong manly form . . . the arms stretched out with such tender and loving support."[24] Spiritualism questioned with great energy the fact that women were excluded from so many avenues to power, but never went so far as to question society's description of what a woman should be and what that description might have to do with her exclusion.

In contrast with spiritualism, Theosophy was from the beginning a movement admittedly and intentionally occult in nature. The doctrines of Theosophy proceeded from Helena Blavatsky's amalgam of Eastern religious doctrines and occult principles. Evident from the beginning and expressed in the first goal of the Theosophical Society—"to form a Universal Brotherhood of Humanity without distinction or race, colour, or creed"—the feminism of Theosophy had as its basis a belief in the need for the balance of the masculine and feminine principles in the cosmos and an adulation of the Mother Goddess. According to the Theosophists, in societies where women were deprived of their rights, the cosmic balance was upset and the disequilibrium brought with it all the ills that were so obvious in turn-of-the-century America—war, political corruption, economic inequity, and unhappiness between the sexes with its consequences in deteriorating family life. For the Theosophists who believed in spiritual evolution, the coming age must certainly bring with it an improvement in woman's lot in all aspects of society: "And now the Great Teachers will affirm the rights of woman. . . . Woman will have to be armed with courage, and, first of all, she will have to restrain her heart from unwise giving, for there must be the Golden Balance in everything."[25]

Theosophists' criticisms of society are often expressed in more abstract terms than those of spiritualism, reflecting their more cosmic concern with balance. In 1913 Charlotte Despard, a British Theosophist with an American audience, claimed that "the falsity of the present relations between man and woman lies at the base of many of the worst evils with which Humanity has had to struggle." Despard saw both the woman's movement as it existed just before World War I and the growth of Theosophy as evidence that society was in the grips of a spiritual awakening that would ensure the rights of women, and she outlined the essential changes that must occur before such developments could proceed: "(a) the recognition of a uniform moral standard, (b) not uniformity which is a foolish perversion of our demand, but unity, (c) that in the rebuilding of national and international life, women shall stand side by side with their brothers, and (d) that Public Opinion . . . be kept alive, instructed and active, until it takes the place in the community of conscience in the individual."[26]

The same general tenor of the Theosophical argument for women's rights appears in a more contemporary source, the spring, 1976, issue of the *American Theosophist,* dedicated to a discussion of the "Feminine Principle." Editor William Quinn stresses, like Despard, that "co-equality of the feminine and the masculine principles is a fact—not a hypothesis. The fact is apparent not only in grandiose perceptions of the cosmos and in the interplay of the tremendous forces governing the universe, it is quite apparent at a more mundane level: that of the sexes."[27] Quinn attributes women's inequality to a predominance of the male principle over the female in American culture. The remedy is a reorientation toward wholeness and unity: "If the dual aspects are truly co-equal, then the idea of 'predominance of one' must be mutually exclusive of co-equality, for co-equality precludes imbalance."[28]

These rather abstractly phrased and sometimes implicit indictments of society that are typical of Theosophical feminism did not obviate the need for criticism directed at specific institutions, however, and the Theosophists made attacks as scathing as anything launched by the spiritualists, directed particularly at organized religion. In the May, 1925, issue of the *Theosophist,* a "Member of the League of the Church Militant" accused the male priesthood of the world's religions of keeping women from spiritual equality: "The priesthood of the *Churches* of all religions has looked on all womanhood as Magdalen, the creature of sin, the polluted, unclean, the temptress, the unworthy. Why? Because of her sex current, because of a function of the physical body, because of a quality of the rājasic body, because of an attractive quality of the desire body. The masculine priesthood was afraid of these."[29] This excerpt reveals all the bitterness found in the contemporary feminist movement that women's bodies have been used and reviled—that woman's sexuality has been used against her to keep her from positions of authority, not through any fault of her own but because the priests "recognized their own weakness, and instead of facing their foe—their own lower nature—fair and square in the face and conquering it, they acknowledged and acquiesced in their moral weakness but maintained the innocence and purity necessary to their office . . . by arrogating to themselves occult spiritual power and banishing from their environment possible excitements of sex."[30]

The Theosophists were not naive, then, about many of the causes of women's oppressions, but they were more likely to express them in broader terms than is the case above and to express in the same general way their optimism that women's rights would triumph over a corrupt society. The "remarkable coincidence" that Charlotte Despard saw "between the uprising of woman . . . all over the world and the rise and growth of Theosophy" convinced her that "the Woman's Cause is bound to triumph, because there is an irresistible force behind it."[31] In the occult world view of the Theosophists it was not only desirable that the feminine principle assert itself by an increase in women's rights, it was a cosmic necessity.

Theosophy's understanding of the essence of the feminine nature was founded on another aspect of its occult world view: the importance of the Mother Goddess in the Theosophical system. Helen Knothe quotes from Blavatsky's *Secret Doctrine* in support of her contention that the Mother in ancient religions predates the Father: "The higher gods of antiquity are all 'Sons of the Mother' before they become 'Sons of the Father.' . . . All these, the upper and the lower Hierarchies included, emanate from the Heavenly or Celestial Virgin, the Great Mother in all religions, the Androgyne, the Sephira Adam Kadmon."[32] Knothe uses the *Secret Doctrine* to argue the need for recognition of the feminine manifestation of the divine, which will in turn assure the acceptance of the divine aspect of woman. Knothe sees "maternity" as the essential quality of the feminine principle and as necessary for the spiritual fulfillment of women. This maternity may be figurative rather than literal: "Whether child-bearing or not, woman is essentially maternal, and only fully enters her kingdom when she becomes a mother." Knothe speaks of motherhood in occult terms as "an initiation into a divine experience, generating and giving birth to form."[33]

But the maternal aspect of the feminine has implications beyond the experience of the individual. Writing just before Knothe, W. K. Heyting laments that women in politics seem merely to imitate men and predicts for women that "their supposed freedom in being able to hold these positions will be nothing but a burden."[34] Heyting asks whether women have "nothing to give to the body politic which is peculiarly and undeniably theirs by right of their womanhood, something that men cannot contribute so effectively?" He suggests that the answer lies in woman's capacity to "mother," to be "guided by that personal love for humanity which men lack. . . ."[35]

Another spokesperson for what appears to be a traditional interpretation of women's roles coming out of a radical religious stance was Katherine Tingley, leader of the Point Loma Theosophical community in California until her death in 1929. In a series of lectures on Woman's

Katherine Tingley. Courtesy of Point Loma Publications.

Mission by women leaders at Point Loma in 1915, Tingley said, "I believe in the equality of the sexes, but I hold that man has a mission and that woman has also a mission, and that these missions are not the same; the difference is due in part to lines of evolution." Tingley urges that the balance of the sexes must prevail: "If a woman is to understand the duties of real wifehood and motherhood, and to reach the dignity of ideal womanhood, she must cultivate her femininity. She was born a woman and she must *be* a woman in the truest sense; and the contrast between men and women exists in life."[36] These are interesting words from a strong woman leader of a large group of people (500 at its maximum), who lived in a community in the company of other strong women, among them Gertrude Van Pelt, a physician, and Grace Knoche, mother of the present head of the Theosophical Society International. Tingley does echo the general cultural perception of woman's nature as more "spiritual" than man's: "Woman is more mystical than man; she lives more in the heart. Her emotional nature, however, becomes a source of weakness if not governed understandingly."[37] While that sounds very traditional, Tingley cautions women that they must live out their nature within the framework of the "higher life" of Theosophy, that unless they do they will always "be imposed upon. They are forever sacrificing their lives to no beneficial result, forever bearing children in disharmony, who must later suffer just as they have done. For there is no balance in their lives, no justice."[38] If the balance of male and female is maintained in a society, then woman finds fulfillment rather than exploitation in her role as mother and nurturer, for she mirrors the Mother Goddess.

Reality for the woman—and the man—Theosophist was composed not only of matter but of a mystic center in nature, of forces and principles, of higher levels of being and knowing than those apparent in the earthly sphere. The woman's power over that reality arose from her cultivated understanding that she participated in divinity and that since "sin does not consist in fulfilling any of the functions of nature,"[39] the incidence of her gender would not keep her from exercising that power.

By contrast with both spiritualism and Theosophy, whose memberships were both male and female and whose feminism was one among other concerns, feminist witchcraft is a separatist movement, drawing its energy from women alone and seeing itself in opposition to male society and male values. Feminist witchcraft considers itself as practicing the Dianic tradition and, in fact, sets itself apart from the Craft, the contemporary, neo-pagan witchcraft described by Margot Adler in *Drawing Down the Moon.* Adler says that "a number of feminists have stated that women are Witches by right of the fact that they are women, that nothing else is needed, and feminist Witch Z. Budapest has at times declared the Craft to be 'Wimmins Religion,' a religion not open to men."[40]

As a product of the counterculture revolution of the 1960s and the contemporary feminist movement, feminist witchcraft rejects both technocracy and the revelations of traditional Christianity and Judaism. It seeks truth in the depths of the female psyche and finds its energy in the worship of "the goddess." Any hint of the supernatural is missing from feminist witchcraft, but neither does the movement accept the "merely" natural universe of the materialist. Like the Theosophist, the feminist witch articulates an understanding of the feminine principle, but, as will become evident, it takes a different twist from the cosmic to the personal. Z. Budapest says that "feminist witches are wimmin who search within themselves for the female principle of the universe and who relate as daughters to the Creatrix. We believe that just as it is time to fight for the right to control our bodies, it is also time to fight for our sweet womon souls."[41]

The breadth of the criticisms against contemporary society by feminist witches in some ways resembles that of the nineteenth-century spiritualists. In fact, Z. Budapest's *The Holy Book of Women's Mysteries* has sections on alternative medicine and astrological birth control that echo the ads in the nineteenth-century *Banner of Light*. But the basis for the criticisms is different. Spiritualist feminism embraced the scientific and insisted that traditional religion was not rational enough. Feminist witchcraft criticizes society because its institutions, particularly religion, are too rational, too falsely coherent. According to one feminist witch, the basis for a new woman's spirituality will arise out of a variety of struggles: "Feminist spirituality has taken form in Sisterhood—in our solidarity based on a vision of personal freedom, self-definition, and in our struggle together for social and political change. The contemporary women's movement has created space for women to begin to perceive reality with a clarity that seeks to encompass many complexities. This perception has been trivialized by male dominated cultures that present the world in primarily rational terms."[42] The feminist witch seeks not just reform of social institutions but, rather, "fundamental change in cultural beliefs, society's institutions, and human relationships—beginning with the rejoining of woman to woman."[43]

For feminist witches, criticism of society implies an interdependence of spirituality and politics, which, as Margot Adler points out, is a distinguishing mark setting them apart from other practitioners of the

Craft. This does not necessarily mean that feminist witches advocate violent revolution; for most of them the combining of spirituality and politics has meant the redefining of "politics." "Traditionally," says Dorothy Riddle, "spirituality has had to do with loving, and politics has had to do with power. We have seen them as unrelated because we have experienced our personal lives and relationships as separate from our work and institutional involvements."[44] For the feminist witch who advocates a holistic view of life over a compartmentalized view, every aspect of a woman's being has political import: "One important contribution of feminism is our dawning recognition that our lives are a whole, that the personal is political and the political is personal, that how we are with ourselves and each other *is* the revolution."[45]

This understanding of the interconnectedness of the political and the personal stems from an occult view that is natural rather than supernatural in its underpinnings. Starhawk, a feminist witch, speaks of her belief as "earth religion. . . . There is no dichotomy between spirit and flesh. . . . The Goddess is manifest in the world; she brings life into being, *is* nature, *is* flesh. . . . Spiritual union is found in life, with nature, passion, sensuality—through being fully human, fully one's self."[46] In *Changing of the Gods,* Naomi Goldenberg sees feminist witchcraft as creating a "powerful new religion" that is earth-bound in its worship of the goddess. Their understanding of the occult doctrine, "as above, so below," leads feminist witches to reject a male God in a faraway heaven so that women will have the strength to reject male rule on earth. This creation is an indictment of "a civilization in which males in high places imitate a male god in heaven—both think themselves above the petty concerns of simple nurture and delight in generative life."[47]

Feminist witches make use of ritual worship of the goddess in order to strengthen woman's identification with the divine feminine in herself, and they make use of the "occult sciences," such as astrology and the reading of Tarot cards, as ways of practicing what they call a prepatriarchal understanding of the self and its connections with the cycles of the universe. Carol Christ suggests further that women, not only feminist witches, find in the Tarot cards "a prepatriarchal set of images that can be more useful in charting their spiritual journeys than Biblical symbolism."[48] While many of the rituals and practices are communal in nature and designed to stress not only cosmic rootedness but also sisterhood, others are performed by the individual. One of them is a "Self-Blessing Ritual," which Z. Budapest describes as a way "of exorcising the patriarchal policeman, cleansing the deep mind, and filling it with positive images of the strength and beauty of women."[49] Another is a kind of "Morning Offering," with a poignant earth-bound theme said each morning by a Minneapolis witch, Carol Wisewomoon: "I get up and thank the night, give blessing to creatures who live at night and are going to bed, look at the sun and say good morning to her; ring my bell which gives new dimensions to the air, breathe the sound the bell sends across the room, light the candle and feel the heat of the flame. I ask 'the women' for strength, wisdom and serenity and surrender the results of that day."[50]

Feminist witchcraft sees woman's nature as inherently divine, as not merely reflecting the goddess but, as Mary Daly says, be-ing the Goddess.[51] Like spiritualism and Theosophy, feminist witchcraft denies human depravity and affirms the essential goodness of the human person, but because of its separatist tendencies, feminist witchcraft elevates woman's nature above man's in its life-giving abilities. Z. Budapest claims that men cannot be considered equal to women in divinity.[52] Whereas spiritualism stressed woman's passive nature as particularly conducive to spirit communication and Theosophy considered woman's maternal nature as essential to balance and wholeness in the cosmos and society, feminist witches speak of the necessity of women's ascendency over men: "We believe that female control of the death (male) principle yields human evolution."[53] Feminist witches do not deny the reality, or even the importance, of the male principle, but they claim that balance of the male and female principles can be cultivated within the individual. Margot Adler sees in feminist witchcraft a tendency toward dogmatism, a "substituting 'Big Mama' for 'Big Daddy,' " but many feminist witches see themselves as trying to overcome the dualism inherent in Western culture that has so distinguished the characteristics of male and female from each other that it is impossible for one person to achieve any kind of balance of both. Feminist witches describe themselves as committing a "political act" when they replace the Father with the Mother: "The image of the Mother does not lose its old connotations of earth, intuition, nature, the body, the emotions, the unconscious, etc. But it also lays claim to many of the connotations previously attributed to the father symbol: beauty, light, goodness, authority, activity, etc."[54] The feminist witch claims both sun and moon, both heaven and earth, and she invokes the goddess in herself and in other women in her efforts to make it possible.

For the feminist witch the only reality is the physical universe, but it is a reality that is inherently sacred, full of psychic energy that she can tap as she understands her own nature as participating in that of the goddess. For the feminist witch this power is not manipulative but, rather, "the psychic power with which our spiritual awareness brings us in touch . . . the power to generate new visions and the power to end or shield ourselves from old habits or old ways of being."[55]

In contrast with the women who have sought religious fulfillment in marginal religious groups such as spiritualism, Theosophy, and feminist witchcraft, many thousands of women have been content to participate in mainstream Christianity and Judaism. As historians like Nancy Cott have pointed out, their functions—centered around charitable and missionary societies, nonclerical teaching, and the safeguarding of home and family—provided a source of strength and identity as well as the feeling of sisterhood.[56] But for those women who felt, perhaps with a different intensity, their deprivation of the kind of spiritual equality that could lead to ordination, religious fulfillment and the development of a feminine spirituality would have to come from without the system. For within the system, both the affirmation of the churches as well as their negative judgments bespoke the relegation of women to a lower spiritual order.

In 1853, when Antoinette Brown was ordained as the first Congregational minister in America, the male minister who preached at her ordination ceremony defended women ministers in a way that was enlightened for the time, but exemplified the kind of tortured exegesis that has accompanied much theological reflection on whether there is scriptural basis for the ordination of women. The Reverend Luther Lee contended that Paul's admonition that women keep silent in church extended only to married women; further, if a married woman's husband gave his permission, she, too, might be ordained.[57] In 1976, when the Sacred Congregation for the Doctrine of the Faith of the Roman Catholic Church made its pronouncement on the question of women's ordination, Franjo Cardinal Seper, speaking for the congregation and with the approval of Paul VI, explained that "the problems of sacramental theology, especially when they concern the ministerial priesthood . . . cannot be solved except in the light of Revelation." According to the Church, revelation had made clear that the maleness of Jesus must be reflected in the priesthood: "When Christ's role in the Eucharist is to be expressed sacramentally, there would not be this 'natural resemblance' which must exist between Christ and his minister if the role of Christ were not taken by a man."[58] According to Sister Elizabeth Carroll, this statement says that "woman . . . has no 'imaging' power of Christ in this world or the next."[59]

While the examples above deal specifically with women's ordination, the questions they raise are broader and deal with the effect of a "closed" revelation on women's position in the churches, the churches' attitude toward woman's gender and sexuality, her relationship to the numinous, and her subjection to male authority.

At least three occult movements in American history have provided an arena where women have addressed these issues, protested against the prevailing structures, and worked to create an alternate reality based on a new revelation that would be more affirming both of woman's sexuality and her spirituality.[60] For the spiritualists and the Theosophists the new revelation had exterior bases, that of the spirits and the Mahatmas. For feminist witches it has been an interior phenomenon: "I am constantly being revealed to myself, I am constantly reaching new understandings of how to be myself-Source on Earth."[61] The power of participation in the divine that came with the new revelation and the new reality was a power that adhered within and could be developed by the individual, leaving her free to define and create her own kind of spirituality beyond what she considered to be the strictures of church and society.

NOTES

1. Kirsten Grimstad and Susan Rennie, "Spiritual Explorations Cross-Country," *Quest*, 1 (1975):50.

2. Ibid., pp. 50–51.

3. W. J. Colville, *Ancient Mysteries and Modern Revelations* (New York: R. F. Fenno, 1910), p. 342. The spiritualists were by no means the first to articulate the connection between a male-dominated religion and woman's oppression. Shaker Elder Frederick Evans held the "lost and fallen world" responsible for the "*degradation* and *oppression* of WOMAN": "Thus it appears that those who reject their Heavenly Mother, do thereby reject *true wisdom*. And this accounts for self evident want of *wisdom* in all human governments and societies, civil and religious." See *A Short Treatise on the Second Appearing of Christ in and through the Order of the Female* (Boston: Bazin and Chandler, 1853), p. 14. Nor is the connection perceived only by those in occult groups. Carol Christ, a feminist theologian who has done a great deal of work on "the goddess," says that "religions centered on the worship of a male God create 'moods' and 'motivations' that keep women in a state of psychological dependence on men and male authority, while at the same time legitimating the *political* and *social* authority of fathers and sons in the institutions of society." See "Why Women Need the Goddess," in Carol P. Christ and Judith Plaskow, eds., *Womanspirit Rising: A Feminist Reader in Religion* (San Francisco: Harper and Row, 1979), p. 275.

4. Helen Knothe, "The Woman-Aspect of Divinity," *Theosophist*, 49 (1928):454.

5. Z. Budapest, *The Holy Book of Women's Mysteries, Part I* (Los Angeles: Susan B. Anthony Coven no. 1, 1979), pp. 10–11.

6. R. Laurence Moore, *In Search of White Crows: Spiritualism, Parapsychology, and American Culture* (New York: Oxford University Press, 1977), p. 83.

7. R, "Review—'Reichenbach's Dynamics,' " *Shekinah*, 1 (1852):197–99.

8. Moore, *In Search of White Crows*, p. 224.

9. See Howard Kerr's analysis of *The Bostonians* in *Mediums, and Spirit-Rappers, and Roaring Radicals: Spiritualism in American Literature, 1850–1900* (Urbana: University of Illinois Press, 1972).

10. Robert Riegel, *American Feminists* (Lawrence: University of Kansas Press, 1963), p. 191.

11. Moore, *In Search of White Crows*, p. 226.

12. *Banner of Light*, May 13, 1876.

13. A typical accusation against the clergy appears in a list of resolutions passed by the Northern Wisconsin Association of Spiritualists in 1874: "Resolved, that the 50,000 ministers of the United States furnish a greater ration of criminals in our prisons than do the 5,000,000 Spiritualists, particularly in their infidelity to marriage and terrible record of adultery in every community around us. . . ." See *Milwaukee Journal*, Jan. 13, 1874.

14. *Banner of Light*, July 16, 1857.

15. Ibid., May 13, 1876.

16. Harrison D. Barrett, *Life Work of Mrs. Cora L. V. Richmond* (Chicago: Hack & Anderson, 1895), pp. 8–9.

17. *Spiritualist*, July, 1868.

18. See Mary Farrell Bednarowski, "Outside the Mainstream: Women's Religion and Women Religious Leaders in Nineteenth Century America," *Journal of the American Academy of Religion*, 48 (1980):207–31, for a discussion of the characteristics of Shakerism, spiritualism, Christian Science, and Theosophy that made them particularly attractive to women.

19. Lizzie Doten, *Poems of Progress* (Boston: Colby and Rich, 1870), pp. 7–8.

20. Lizzie Doten, *Free Love and Affinity: A Discourse Delivered under Spirit Influence at the Melodean, Boston* (Boston, 1867), p. 5.

21. *Milwaukee Journal*, May 13, 1874, a further excerpt from the proceedings of the Northern Wisconsin Association of Spiritualists.

22. William Hepworth Dixon, *Spiritual Wives*, 2d ed. (Philadelphia: Lippincott, 1868), p. 385.

23. See ch. 4, "The Medium and Her Message: A Case of Female Professionalism," in Moore, *In Search of White Crows*, pp. 102–32.

24. Doten, "Free Love and Affinity," p. 6.

25. *Woman* (New York: Agni Yoga Society, 1958). The quotation is taken from the Foreword, which is an excerpt from the *Letters of Helena Roerich*, 1:409. Other publication information not given.

26. Charlotte Despard, *Theosophy and the Woman's Movement* (London: Theosophical Publishing Society, 1913), p. 27.

27. Bill Quinn, "The Feminine Principle," *American Theosophist*, 64 (1976):102–3.

28. Ibid.

29. "Woman and Holy Orders by a Member of the League of the Church Militant," *Theosophist,* 46–2 (1925):203–4.

30. Ibid., p. 204.

31. Despard, *Theosophy and the Woman's Movement,* pp. 43–44.

32. Helen Knothe, "Woman-Aspect of Divinity," p. 452. Knothe does not mention the possibility of "Daughters" of the Mother.

33. Ibid., pp. 453–54.

34. W. J. Heyting, "Woman's Place in Politics," *Theosophist,* 47 (1926): 403–4. The tone of the article strikes an ominous note with the contemporary reader, since it seems to be advocating a kind of selective breeding.

35. Ibid., p. 409.

36. Katherine Tingley et al., *Woman's Mission: Short Addresses by Katherine Tingley and Other Officials of the Woman's International Theosophical League,* . . . February 7, 1915 (Point Loma, Calif.: Woman's Theosophical League, 1915), pp. 24–25. Emmett Greenwalt mentions, in *California Utopia: Point Loma, 1892–1942,* 2d rev. ed. (San Diego: Point Loma Publications, 1978), p. 168n, that Tingley was opposed to the suffragette movement. But John and Kirby Van Mater, of the Theosophical University Library in Pasadena, both of whom lived at Point Loma, told me in Apr., 1980, that they find that allegation very puzzling. John Van Mater was particularly gracious in helping me find material related to women in the Theosophical Society International, as were Mary Jo Schneider and Wayne Montgomery with their assistance at the Olcott Library of the Theosophical Society in America, Wheaton, Ill.

37. Katherine Tingley, *Theosophy the Path of the Mystic,* comp. Grace Knoche (Point Loma, Calif.: Woman's International Theosophical League, 1922), p. 130.

38. Ibid., p. 125. This excerpt is taken from sec. IV, "Woman and the Theosophic Home."

39. "Woman and Holy Orders, etc.," p. 204.

40. Margot Adler, *Drawing Down the Moon* (New York: Viking, 1979), p. 173. Z. Budapest states very directly in *The Holy Book of Women's Mysteries, Part I,* "We are opposed to teaching our magic and our craft to men until equality of the sexes is reality" (p. 10). Morgan McFarland, on the other hand, says that there may be men at a coven if they do not outnumber the women, but her Dianic tradition "condones and even encourages all-female circles and covens." See "Witchcraft: The Art of Remembering," *Quest,* 1 (1975):46.

41. Budapest, *Holy Book of Women's Mysteries, Part I,* p. 9. The spelling of "womon" indicates an avoidance of "man."

42. Judy Davis and Juanita Weaver, "Dimensions of Spirituality," *Quest,* 1 (1975):2.

43. Ibid., p. 3.

44. Dorothy Riddle, "New Visions of Spiritual Power," *Quest,* 1 (1975): 7.

45. Ibid.

46. Starhawk, "Witchcraft and Women's Culture," in Christ and Plaskow, eds., *Womanspirit Rising,* p. 263.

47. Naomi Goldenberg, *Changing of the Gods: Feminism and the End of Traditional Religions* (Boston: Beacon Press, 1979), p. 90.

48. Carol P. Christ, *Diving Deep and Surfacing: Women Writers on Spiritual Quest* (Boston: Beacon Press, 1980), p. 94.

49. Z. Budapest, "Self-Blessing Ritual," in Christ and Plaskow, eds., *Womanspirit Rising*, p. 272.

50. Carol Wisewomoon, "I'm a lesbian, I'm a witch," *Minneapolis Tribune*, May 10, 1980, interview by Ruth Hammond.

51. Mary Daly, *Gyn/Ecology: The Metaethics of Radical Feminism* (Boston: Beacon Press, 1978). Daly makes use of words like "hag" and "crone" in what she calls a transvaluated sense to denote women of strength, courage, and wisdom.

52. Goldenberg, *Changing of the Gods*, p. 103.

53. Budapest, *Holy Book of Women's Mysteries, Part I*, p. 9.

54. Barbara Starret, "I Dream in Female: The Metaphysics of Evolution," *Amazon Quarterly*, 3 (1974):24–25, quoted in Adler, *Drawing Down the Moon*, p. 214.

55. Riddle, "New Visions of Spiritual Power," p. 8.

56. Nancy Cott, *The Bonds of Womanhood: "Woman's Sphere" in New England, 1780–1835* (New Haven, Conn.: Yale University Press, 1977).

57. Luther Lee, *Woman's Right to Preach the Gospel: A Sermon Preached at the Ordination of the Rev. Miss Antoinette L. Brown at South Butler, Wayne County, N.Y., Sept. 15, 1853* (Syracuse, N.Y.: Lee, 1853), p. 21.

58. Franjo Cardinal Seper, *Declaration on the Question of the Admission of Women to the Ministerial Priesthood* (Rome: Sacred Congregation for the Doctrine of the Faith, 1976), p. 6.

59. Sister Elizabeth Carroll, RSM, *Women's Ordination and the Catholic Church* (Washington, D.C.: Center of Concern—Focus: Toward a World That Is Human, 1977), p. 4.

60. Of course, an occult movement is not without its own traps for women. Carol Christ was speaking of contemporary goddess worship when she stated optimistically, "This view will not be a new monism in which differences between the body and mind and nature are denied, but it will be a more integrated view in which the differences are not viewed in hierarchical and oppositional ways." *Diving Deep and Surfacing*, p. 129. Nineteenth-century spiritualists might have heeded that description as they imposed a kind of tyranny of the scientific method on the universe. The Theosophists could have benefited from an admonition to keep the understanding of the male and female principles from reifying into a description of the sex roles that already prevailed in the dominant culture. Finally, as mentioned above, some feminist witches have begun to perceive that "Big Mama" can be just as restricting as "Big Daddy."

61. Riddle, "New Visions of Spiritual Power," p. 11.

9

Paranormal Memorates in the American Vernacular

LARRY DANIELSON

GHOST STORIES. The term conjures up Scout campfires, Halloween parties, and cars parked in night-time cemeteries. For those of us more than casually interested in the supernatural, it suggests Algernon Blackwood, Henry James, the Society for Psychical Research, and *National Enquirer* headlines. Narratives about paranormal visitations are numerous and represent a wide range of literature, printed and oral, that has persisted over thousands of years in spite of skeptics and materialists. It is seldom emphasized, however, that the apparitions which populate the literature are transmuted spirits, revitalized from many sources, for example, oral hearsay, traditional legend, and personal experience. In each account they are re-created to form new variations on ancient themes through the vigorous play of the human imagination and the manipulation of artistic convention. Even when the narrative purports to describe actual paranormal experience, the art of the storyteller is at work. In such cases the processes of transmutation involve a complex interaction between personal experience, traditional lore about the supernatural, and canons of narrative aesthetics. The following pages explore these processes that affect the first-person paranormal testimonial.

Personal experience stories have often been used as data sources by students of psychic phenomena. Authoritative analyses, of course, have relied on those accounts that can be characterized as evidential—descriptions of experience which contain details that can be objectively documented and which concern unusual events that cannot be readily explained as "natural" phenomena.[1] Cautious studies eliminate narratives of little or no evidential value and are careful to distinguish "more reliable" from "less reliable" accounts. The latter sources, most psychic researchers attest, rely on folk belief and oral hearsay and are subject to elaboration and exaggeration. Paranormal personal experience stories that appear in the mass media and circulate in oral tradition therefore carry little weight in official parapsychological investigations. In my opinion, however, they deserve serious attention because they illustrate the same processes of recall and performance that affect the pristine evidential account accepted by the parapsychologist.

Vernacular first-person narratives, those stories common to popular print and conversation, can reveal dramatically the complicated interrelations among the recall of experience, the influence of traditional belief and concept on the account, and the aesthetic decisions made in the performance of the story for the narrator's audience. If we can observe these processes at work in popular materials, we will learn to be aware of them in other kinds of personal experience accounts, even those accepted as reliable and evidential. Thereby the evaluation of narrative sources by parapsychologists will be better informed and more judicious. At the same time the general reader interested in psychic phenomena will be sensitized to the complex ways a story about a ghostly encounter comes to be told. The supernatural "true experience" story is an art form shaped by tradition, convention, and the narrator's performance skills, regardless of its evidential strengths or weaknesses.

I have limited the narratives examined here to American English-language texts that deal with the same subject matter, the spontaneous paranormal visitation to individuals with whom the apparition shares some kind of relationship, e.g., familial, occupational, or social. This restriction of subject matter eliminates apparitions summoned by occult specialists as well as encounters with unrecognized phantasms in public places and reportedly haunted locations, i.e., stories closely related to the conventional local legend. The narratives in question are also confined to first-person accounts that have appeared in vernacular contexts of the past few decades. Such personal experience stories are usually classified as "memorates" in folklore scholarship.[2] Limiting the corpus of texts to the memorate genre helps control the influence of serial transmission on the stories under study. As first-person narratives they are affected primarily by the narrator's repeated accounts of a singular experience rather than by the more numerous and complicated serial chains of story transmission common to legendry and rumor. A particular individual's narrative skills and exposure to supernatural accounts by others are complex enough topics without the addition of a hypothesized story chain involving many narrators.

My primary sources comprise sixty-nine vernacular American memorates and include archived transcriptions of oral texts; narratives collected, edited, and published in academic folklore collections; popular paperback accounts; and letters to specialized periodicals like *Fate* magazine.[3] The texts are a miscellany of stories actively pursued by folklorists from a wide range of informants, located in popular occult journals that solicit such contributions, and on occasion encountered by chance in tabloid newspapers. Therefore they have been shaped by different contexts, communication media, and narrator intent. They do, however, adequately represent the kinds of supernatural memorate common to American vernacular culture of the past fifty years.

The following text, collected as an oral reminiscence in Illinois, is a good example of a paranormal folk memorate recounted in conversation rather than in print. It illustrates a number of content and stylistic elements frequently found in the corpus.

Text A

Years ago I was kneeling down to say my prayers. Chancing to look up, I saw a man staring at me, then he vanished. Several days later I received a letter stating that my uncle had just died in the East. My aunt soon came to Quincy. Among her effects was a photograph of my deceased uncle. When I saw the picture I was startled to find that it was the very likeness of the man whom I had seen a few weeks before standing by my bed. I had never seen my uncle nor had I ever seen a photograph of him.[4]

Like many of the paranormal memorates collected from oral tradition, the account is brief and to the point. Apparently the visitation occurs at night in the percipient's home, and the apparition is a relative of the narrator, both traits typical of the texts in question. The percipient at the time of the experience is not in a critical condition, psychologically or physically, although this content element is found in about two-thirds of the memorates analyzed. The time elapsed between the occurrence and its description to the collector is only generally indicated in the phrase "years ago," probably when the informant was a child. In contrast, a little over three-fourth of the vernacular texts deal with paranormal experiences in the adult years. Because of the discrepancy between "days" and "weeks" it is not clear whether the visitant is an apparition of the recently deceased uncle or of the relative while still alive. Well over a third of the texts concern death coincidences, a com-

THE WORLD'S MYSTERIES EXPLORED

FATE ®

FEBRUARY 1977 75¢

56350-3PDC

ARE UFOs TINKERING WITH OUR SATELLITES? 62

THERE IS LIFE AFTER DEATH 67

Paul Solomon, ANOTHER CAYCE? 56

GIBEON –
where the sun stood still 42

. . .Plus Many Other
Intriguing Features

Fate Magazine is a popular contemporary source of personal experience narratives of ghostly visitation and articles on other "occult" matters. Reproduced courtesy of Fate Magazine.

mon form of crisis apparition in which the percipient is unaware of the
visitant's death at the time of the spirit's appearance. The storyteller
uses a number of artistic conventions often found in folk literature and
in many of the transcribed oral texts in the collection. For example, no
more than two characters interact at a time, external action rather than
internal subjective condition is emphasized, and narrative development
is chronological and direct.[5] The memorate concludes with a startling
identification of the visitant through a material object, a frequent structural element in popular supernatural narrative. Over half of the texts
include this feature, although in most cases its objective evidential value
is slight.

The next narrative is from a *Fate* magazine column, "My Proof of
Survival." It exemplifies the conventional popular print account of
bereavement and subsequent comfort offered by the deceased, a common occurrence in spiritualist literature and related publications. Paranormal narratives of this type, unlike the oral accounts, tend to be more
detailed and explicit. In fact, the editors of the column often request the
writer to specify names, dates, and places for the publication.[6]

Text B

When my sister Louise and her husband Jim Hendrix were
killed in a plane crash on June 3, 1958, I felt as if I had nothing
left to live for. Perhaps I was inordinately disturbed by their
deaths but they had been a wonderful couple and it meant a lot
to me to see my sister happy. I think the fact they had been married only two short months grieved me most. No one could know
how deeply depressed I became when they were killed.

As the weeks passed my unhappiness did not abate. The world
turned black and the air crash haunted my dreams and waking
thoughts. I sought relief from my nightmare life from my church,
my family, my doctor and my friends but these attempts were
futile.

Two months after the tragedy I left my home in Beverly Hills,
Calif., to go to my Malibu Beach cottage for a rest. On August 7
I was sitting near the fireplace reading when I felt a presence behind me. I turned to see Louise and Jim standing in the center of
my living room holding hands. I felt no fear and for the first time
in weeks I smiled.

Louise spoke softly, "Please don't grieve for us. We never have
been happier. Our love is stronger than ever. One day you will
join us and we once again will be together but until then, be
happy."

> Jim and Louise both smiled and suddenly vanished.
>
> Everyone remarked my swift recovery from grief, but I could not tell my story. Now that I knew Louise and Jim were happy, I could be happy too.[7]

This account also concerns familial relation, but in this case the supernatural visitors appear to aid the living. Over 40 percent of the apparitions described in the accounts are purposeful, most of them involved in helpful missions to the living. The interval between the experience and its public narration is about a decade. Usually lengthier time periods separate the occurrence from the story that describes it. The emphasis on emotional state, very important in this text, is characteristic of popular print stories, in contrast to oral memorates, as is the tendency toward a more literary diction. However, the typical patterns of two-to-a-scene (the brother-in-law does not participate in the interaction between the sisters) and straightforward chronological plot development are present here. The percipient does not use the conventional citation of evidence after the action is described, but, as in over half the stories investigated, concludes the account with an interpretation of the experience and its personal value.

It is tempting to compare this corpus of texts with bodies of similar narratives assembled by other researchers. Several shared traits emerge. Well over half the percipients in these popular accounts are women, when the sex of the percipient is indicated. The same pattern is found in other surveys, for example, in the well-known Census of Hallucinations by the British Society for Psychical Research, published in 1890, and in D. J. West's Mass Observation survey fifty-eight years later.[8] A cooperative analysis of 165 evidential cases in 1956, directed by Hornell Hart, indicates that over three-fourths of the apparitions in question "appear to some person with whom the appearer has some strong emotional bond."[9] Eighty-six percent of the spirits described in our American vernacular collection can be similarly categorized. The Institute of Psychophysical Research returns, collected by questionnaire between 1968 and 1974, indicate that most apparitional experiences transpire in familiar surroundings, in 83 percent of the cases indoors.[10] Almost all the narratives used in the present study place the percipient in similar settings.

More comparisons could be made and more percentages quoted, but the surveys available differ so much in their sophistication and classification of traits that correlations become inconclusive. However, one feature noted in several analyses is particularly relevant to the present study. The 1890 Census of Hallucinations proposes that "hallucinations of the most impressive class will not only be better remembered than others, but will . . . be more often mentioned by the percipients to their friends. There is some interest therefore in trying to ascertain what kinds are most talked about and seeing how far these are also shown by the tables to be the best remembered."[11] D. J. West, in reference to the 1890 census, points out that the most dramatic instances of supernatural encounters are usually placed in a time period long past and that this fact bears on the evaluation of paranormal narrative: "With the passing of time, helped perhaps by frequent retelling, coincidences that were not originally remarkable become exaggerated and elaborated out of all recognition. Indeed, it amounts to an almost invariable law in spontaneous cases that the more remarkable the alleged coincidence the worse the supporting evidence, and conversely, the better the evidence the weaker is the coincidence."[12]

Most of our vernacular texts refer to the length of time between experience and narration. Over 71 percent of the accounts that provide information concerning this time interval describe supernatural events that occurred ten years earlier or more. Only two of the memorates deal with a paranormal experience of the preceding year. The collection is admittedly small, but its weight toward description of long past rather than recent experience is striking. Intervening time periods have provided many opportunities for sharing a particular memorate. Since such stories are told in many different contexts, the same narrative is influenced by canons of both collective and personal taste in storytelling aesthetics. In addition, narrative materials and popular conventions familiar to the raconteur can influence narrations of the incident. The processes of exaggeration and elaboration hypothesized by West may be important in shaping the vernacular memorate because it is subject to the influences of social interaction and audience expectation.

The personal experience stories used here often involve striking coincidences that as a rule cannot be verified. In Text A, for example, the resemblance between apparition and photograph cannot be authenticated and the concurrence of death and paranormal visit is unclear. Text B reports a completely subjective experience and our response to it must rely on trust in the narrator's verity. West's suspicions about such accounts are not shared by all students of psychic phenomena. Hornell Hart finds that two sets of narratives, 165 in all, when separated into more reliable and less reliable accounts, share most content traits. Therefore we should not assume, as West does, that the absence of evidential detail invalidates the supernatural experience story.[13]

Furthermore, Hart argues, elaboration and magnification of striking detail do not characterize paranormal stories as they circulate over time. Instead, the accounts tend to drop details that strengthen the evidential value of the story.[14] For Hart, then, the present corpus of texts might lack evidential detail, but its absence would not necessarily invalidate the accounts as sources useful in the study of apparitional experience.

Hart's argument is controversial and has been criticized by other parapsychologists.[15] Studies in the maintenance of narrative in oral tradition and story recall can be used to support Hart's position, but they also corroborate West's contention. The evaluation of continuity and change in the recounting of personal experience is not as simple as the two researchers suggest. Frederic C. Bartlett's experiments with human memory, for example, conclude that although literal duplication is rare in instances of repeated reproduction, "the general form, or outline, is remarkably persistent." In cases of frequent reproduction, details and form change little because of stereotyping that takes place early in the series. In contrast, when the story is seldom re-told, "omission of detail, simplification of events and structure, and transformation of items into more familiar detail may go on almost indefinitely." "Long-distance remembering" appears to function somewhat differently, for it is more often characterized by elaboration, importation, and invention which rely on visual images. Bartlett finds that the subject's "interests and tendencies," preformed before the reproduction series, influence and often transform striking details in the narrative.[16]

Rumor studies are also relevant to the evaluation of paranormal materials. Gordon W. Allport and Leo Postman have found that, in rumor, irrelevancies are leveled, certain features sharpened, and the whole assimilated to cultural and individual standards of judgment.[17] They point out that although certain details are accented, the rumor often becomes simplified as it circulates. The exception to this generalization occurs in stories that arise in crisis situations, but only as the participants emotionally involved in the crisis describe the event. Subsequent narrators level and sharpen the rumor and the more normal condensation process reasserts itself as the rumor becomes further removed from those emotionally affected by the event.[18] This developmental pattern may be pertinent to the genesis and evolution of the supernatural memorate. If so, crisis apparition stories in the first person would tend toward elaboration. Subsequent re-tellings by the participant as time passes and emotional involvement cools would be characterized by a less complex and elaborately detailed narrative, and certain elements would be stressed at the expense of others. Once more the theory that simple accounts rapidly transform into yarns as they are circulated and retold over time must be re-examined.

The assertion that most narrators of personal experience stories are trustworthy historians is similarly naive. The contrary positions of West and Hart fail to acknowledge the complex factors that affect the narrative act: differing social contexts, the influence of other stories on the account, the artistic concerns of the narrator, and the attitudes of both raconteur and audience toward the story content. The memorates analyzed here fail to provide information that would illuminate the comparative importance of these components in the evolution of paranormal personal experience story. Only two note that the initial experience has been described in other situations. Detailed "life histories" of specific narratives are a necessity if arguments about continuity and change in their development over time are to be substantiated. Folklore studies will be especially pertinent when the matters of narrative performance and the influence of folk belief and literature on the paranormal account are assessed.

Two major surveys of hallucinatory experience in Britain, the 1890 Census and the 1948 Mass Observation project, find that apparitions of the living are more common than apparitions of the dead.[19] The American vernacular data, in contrast, describe apparitions of the known dead in 55 percent of the cases and supernatural appearances of the living in only 6 percent. The remaining texts concern paranormal encounters with persons unknown to be dead or dying. This discrepancy may be explained by the fact that the American narratives are more closely related to collective supernatural traditions than the British sources, which include solicited responses from a diverse population of respondents. The present texts either have been collected by folklorists, who often seek out the active tradition-bearer, or have appeared in occult publications and popular ghost narrative collections. These print sources usually encourage uncritical interest in paranormal phenomena of all kinds and serve a readership committed to or tolerant of apparitional accounts. The American vernacular narratives are probably more indebted to traditional supernatural themes and conventions than the cases collected in more official surveys. Self-motivated exposure to supernatural traditions of many kinds—oral reminiscence, local legend, tabloid newspaper story, and television drama—may be an important factor in explaining the American narrator's keen interest in the return of the recognizable dead.

A traditional motif, as defined in folklore studies, is "the smallest element in a tale having a power to persist in tradition." It may be an actor, an item "in the background of the action—magic objects, unusual actions, strange beliefs, and the like," or a single incident, the most common class of motif.[20] Although the term is now readily criticized because of its ambiguous and ethnocentric conceptualization,[21] it is still employed to designate minimal content elements in folk narrative that have circulated in oral tradition. Stith Thompson's six-volume *Motif-Index of Folk Literature* is a catalogue of traditional elements found in folk narrative throughout the world and is still used for classification purposes in comparative research. All the memorates used in the present study include traditional motifs cited in Thompson or its counterpart, Ernest W. Baughman's *Type and Motif Index of the Folktales of England and North America*.[22] These conventional elements have circulated for centuries, perhaps millennia, and have found their way into many genres, including the legend, ballad, epic, myth, and magic tale. They also often appear in belletristic fiction concerning the supernatural and even popular song.[23] As traditional motifs they are familiar to most of us because of their ubiquity and dramatic character. It is possible that their presence in personal experience narrative may be interpreted as the internalization of fictive motif.[24]

D. J. West deals with several possible explanations of the supernatural experience story that must be considered before the case can be accepted as "clear-cut independent evidence for the paranormal," for instance, fraud, mistaken identity, deceptive memory and false testimony, expectancy and suggestion, chance coincidence, and insanity. Most relevant to the present study is his discussion of conformity to type and the role that collective tradition may play in effecting striking similarities between apparently independent cases. Conformity to type, in West's opinion, is no more evidence of actual occurrence than are cases of witchcraft and black magic that resemble one another.[25]

There are only a few investigations of the ways traditional concept and popular narrative might shape the supernatural experience testimonial. West describes in detail the most convincing instance of nonconscious fabrication that relies on a traditional motif, E723.6, "Appearance of his wraith as announcement of person's death." In 1876 an apparition appeared to the chief judge of the Supreme Consular Court of China and Japan, a supernatural encounter that coincided with the visitant's death. The percipient's testimony was published eight years later in the *Proceedings of the Society for Psychical Research*. Further inquiries proved the narrative to contain several important inconsistencies and to lack any type of convincing corroboration. The distinguished, and embarrassed, narrator was forced to admit that his memory of the event had deceived him. He had unconsciously incorporated many unfounded coincidences into the story during the interval between the vision and its published record.[26]

All our American vernacular accounts are variations on traditional motifs and appear to be unsophisticated testimonials narrated by people unaccustomed to using the kind of rhetoric valued by the formally educated. The following two texts are typical oral memorates that elaborate motifs commonly found in Western folk tradition.

Text C

We lived down here in the Bottom with nothing but willows and water all around our house. One night I went over to the neighbor's house and their house was just like ours, nothing but water and willows. No one could get near the window. And I saw my sister looking in the window. I tried every way to make the rest see her but they didn't. And my sister died just when I seen her looking in at the window.[27]

Text D

About a year ago I had been ironing, was a little tired out, so went and laid down on the bed. While I was there I saw something pass the window. I didn't see the head, but I saw a orange and blue checked coat go by the window. I jump up and ran to the door, thinking my cousin would be there, for she had a orange and blue coat just like the one I saw go by the window. When I didn't see her at the door, I was so sure, I went out and looked around the stove wood ranked up, thinking she was hiding from me. Didn't see anything. It was a token, for she died the next night.[28]

Both texts can be classified as versions of E723.6.1*(b), "Wraith passes window of house," a more specific form of E723.6, "Appearance of his wraith as announcement of person's death." Narratives, mostly in the third person, that incorporate these motifs have been collected throughout the Western world and occasionally in the United States. (It is likely that stories based on these motifs are widely distributed in North America, but they are not officially cited in the Baughman index.) Do these two Illinois memorates record actual paranormal experiences or, because of psychological factors, do they assimilate traditional belief narrative elements into the narrators' memorate repertoires? The same motifs, although supported by evidential detail, appear in nonvernacular paranormal experience stories that are fully accredited in psychic studies.

Such oral narratives are easily dismissed by academic parapsychologists as first-person fantasies, influenced by folk tradition and popular convention. They can as easily be categorized by the folklorist, together with related evidential data acceptable to the parapsychologist, as elaborations on ancient, widely diffused ideas that humankind continues to find compelling even though they are untenable to the rational mind. For the committed spiritualist, the same body of memorates, evidential and nonevidential, provides narrative proof of supernatural realities. For this audience the international motifs upon which the accounts are based merely reflect those realities. Only after painstaking inquiries into case after case will we approach a solution to this dilemma of interpretation. Such investigations must acknowledge that the transformation of fictive experience into personal testimonial may take place in unexpected ways in all kinds of narrative acts, whether evidential history or informal reminiscence.

Perhaps researchers in psychic phenomena have failed to explore the role of traditional lore in paranormal accounts because they have rarely paid attention to the manner in which narrative performance influences audience response. George Owen, for example, discusses the purposeful, corporeal return of the dead in Scots-English folk balladry and confines it to "exercises in popular literature" indebted to peasant folk belief.[29] The fact that such supernatural figures are presented in a form of folk poetry characterized by artistic stylization and commonplace certainly must affect the contemporary audience response to the events described. Owen's evaluation of the same content presented as a realistic first-person account might not be so abrupt. Victor Sims critiques two detailed versions of a popular supernatural legend, "The Vanishing Hitchhiker," Baughman motif E332.3.3.1, and comments on their complicated action, lack of narrative logic, and failure to provide evidential detail.[30] Aniela Jaffe, in her Jungian analysis of apparition and precognition, evaluates another version of the legend from a similar point of view and dismisses it as an improbable experience.[31]

These evaluations of folk literature texts as incredible are misinformed interpretations of oral tradition. The "Vanishing Hitchhiker" legend is widely distributed, and its appearance throughout North America has been investigated by several folklorists. Three variant texts of the legend are the subject of a rhetorical analysis that finds the versions to differ significantly in terms of narrative coherence and stylistic features.[32] The legend sometimes appears in the form of a personal experience story, and as a memorate it is told in a much less literary and more convincing fashion than the versions discussed by Sims and Jaffe.[33] A single traditional motif can be dealt with in many different ways, both orally and in print, and can move from genre to genre with chameleon ease. Perhaps if Sims and Jaffe had studied the same story transformed into memorate, they would have found it to be an acceptable evidential account. The distinction between the content of legend and first-person testimonial is sometimes not so striking as parapsychologists have suggested.

The following memorate "by Francie Smith as told to Bess Eyres" is more closely related to the short story than the personal reminiscence in style as well as structure.

Text E

"Francie, Francie, wake up. This is father."

I roused from an early nap that June evening in 1935 to feel a light touch on my shoulder.

"Why, Father, is that you?" How could it be? I was at home in Akron, Ohio, and Amon Smith, my beloved father-in-law, lived in Central City, Nebr.

The voice had been a soft whisper and I felt his presence but I couldn't see his figure. Amon Smith said, "I've come to say good-bye, Francie. I have to go now."

I sprang from the porch lounge and peered into the fast-deepening evening gloom.

"Father, where did you go? Are you in the house?"

The only reply was the chirping of busy crickets and sleepy nesting sounds from a robin's nest in the thick vine that climbed over the porch.

A feeling of unreality gripped me. "What's wrong with me? Where can he have gone?"

Sounds of the clock chiming eight were followed by rapid footsteps coming up the front walk. A wave of relief swept over me. My husband Walt slammed the screen door shut and strode into the house. I glanced beyond him, expecting to see his father.

At that moment the telephone shrilled its sharp command. The bitter acrid taste of fear rose in my throat.

"Don't answer it, Walt!"

"Don't answer it? Fran, what's wrong with you? You look like you've seen a ghost."

Some of my fear communicated to Walt, for he lifted the receiver hesitatingly.

"Yes, this is Walter Smith. Oh, no! It can't be. What time?
Yes, we'll come."

He turned from the phone. "Fran, Father. . . ."

"Yes, I know, Walt. He died about five minutes before eight.
He came and said good-bye to me."[34]

The use of direct quotation, the literary diction, and the dramatic presentation of the phone-call confirmation separate this account from most of the other vernacular narratives. Perhaps Francie Smith, the percipient, would have described the event less self-consciously and, as a result, in a more convincing fashion than Bess Eyres, the interpreter of the oral memorate. In this case the narrative performance inspires more suspicion about the verity of the account than interest in its authenticity. Whether a letter to a magazine column, an oral testimonial, or a story written to an interested specialist in the paranormal, the narrator's skills in rhetoric filter the experience as the narrative is told and re-told. The performance dimensions of the paranormal memorate cannot be disregarded simply because the story deals with past experience and is intended to convey information.

The vernacular American texts referred to in this study are performances, expressive acts in which "a person assumes responsibility to an audience," as Dell Hymes puts it.[35] According to Hymes, there is a "difference between knowing tradition and presenting it, between knowing what and knowing how, between knowledge, on the one hand, and motivation and identification, on the other, as components of competence in the use of language." Even when the ostensible purpose of the narrative is primarily to share information about a past experience, a "breakthrough" into authoritative performance may take place.[36]

Folklorists and sociolinguists often concern themselves with oral performance *in situ,* paying close attention to participant transactions, tone, kinesics, and linguistic and paralinguistic manipulation of sound, among other components of the performance event.[37] It is also possible to examine printed vernacular texts in terms of their aesthetic competence, just as belletristic literature is analyzed as effective or ineffective artistic expression. The following two oral memorates, collected and transcribed from different informants by the same folklore student, deal with purposeful apparitions who warn the percipient of impending difficulties.[38] Text F is a version of motif E336, "Return from dead to give counsel," and Text G, a version of E545.2, "Dead predict death." Although contextual and metatextual elements in the performances cannot be considered here—this information is not provided by the collector—a straightforward textual analysis will illustrate the artistic choices made by the narrator in describing personal supernatural experience.

Text F

You know I use to laugh when people talked about ghosts when I was a kid, but I had an experience that really changed my mind.

When I was young, I lived with my grandfather and grandmother. Well, my grandmother died when I was in my teens. One night after running around with the guys in town, I came home and went to bed. I looked up and there was my grandmother standing at the foot of my bed. She told me to quit running around with the guys that I messed with because they were going to get in big trouble.

I still can't get over this because there was big trouble a little later that year and all the guys were involved. I told my grandfather about grandmother coming to me, but he just laughed and said that I must have been dreaming.

I know to this day that she walked in my room and stood at the foot of my bed just as if she were alive. She wasn't surrounded by any glowing light or anything like that, but just normal as can be.

Text G

One morning I woke and saw my father standing at the foot of my bed. [The informant's father died in 1942, twenty-six years before the interview.] He told me to beware that my brother was going to have a heart attack.

I told my brother that I was worried about him and asked him to see a doctor as soon as possible. He thought I was nuts, but he promised me he would.

He went to the doctor's that afternoon and the doctor said that he was in the best possible physical shape.

That night he was driving to Indianapolis to pick up mother at the airport. He stopped for a traffic light by the big brick church on Meridian. When the light turned green, he slumped over in the seat and died of a heart attack.

The core action of the two memorates is obviously the same: the percipient is in bed, suddenly sees a deceased family member at the foot of the bed who warns the person about a future event, and the prognosticated event transpires. The literary dimensions of the stories vary a good deal, however. Contrast, for example, the different ways the subject matter is framed. Text F introduces the account with a statement that functions as a validation of the experience, essentially "I was also a skeptic about spirits until. . . ." The narrator thereby escapes the charge of gullibility and indicates the historicity of the ghostly occurrence. The story action is followed by a forceful statement of belief in its reality, even in the face of the grandfather's skepticism. The narrative concludes with an observation that tends to separate the informant from others whose supernatural tales follow more predictable patterns of spirit description, for example, figures that glow.

Text G plunges immediately into the action. The audience/collector receives no indication of the narrator's attitude toward the experience and the possible ways it has affected her own ideas about the supernatural. Since this is an oral memorate, told in a face-to-face context, this information may have been supplied in conversational exchanges before the narration or may have been previously known to the collector. The story concludes abruptly, a structural device that is often found in a legend subtype, the urban horror legend. The alarming confirmation of the spirit's warning is a shock technique facilitated by the nature of the preceding story content. The brother's death needs no explication and can be simply, directly described. Narrator G's dramatic conclusion allows her audience to draw their own conclusions. She does not resort to an affirmation of belief as found in Text F.

Narrator F provides more circumstantial detail than narrator G, perhaps because the audience/collector was unfamiliar with the informant's family background. This information about social milieu is important in implying a strong grandmother-grandson relationship. Text G gives us no parallel information—it may have been known to the audience/collector—but its conclusion contains several vivid details. The narrator could have ended the story quite prosaically after noting her brother's physical examination: "And he had a heart attack that night." Instead, we find out exactly where the death took place, what the man was doing at the time, and how the victim might have appeared to an onlooker as he experienced the heart attack. Even if the audience is unfamiliar with the locale, concrete details selected by the narrator efficiently and dramatically re-create the death scene. The placement of the corroborative incident in the "real" world of Indianapolis, airports, and traffic lights is characteristic of the legend genre.[39] Like the sudden conclusion, typical of the urban horror legend, the use of contemporary, concrete detail in Text G may reflect the influence of the legend genre on the rendering of personal experience into interesting, direct story.

Narrator F resorts to other means in order to satisfy his audience. He transforms personal experience into an account that persuades through the juxtaposition of belief and disbelief at key points in the narrative: skeptical "kid" versus "people [who] talked about ghosts," credulous grandson versus incredulous grandfather, rational observer versus other percipients with overactive imaginations. These juxtapositions, together with the informant's vagueness about the group's "big trouble," make Text F more ambiguous than Text G and defuse a possible climactic conclusion. At the same time Text F affirms in careful ways the reality of a paranormal experience in a world that often rejects it.

The collector indicates in a short annotation to Text F that the experience described took place about thirty years before its recounting at the time of the interview. No such specific information is provided concerning Text G, although we can surmise from the age of the narrator and the date of collection that, at the most, a twenty-six-year time interval separates the experience and its narrative description. How often have the percipients shared these paranormal stories? Have the memorates changed in content, structure, and style over time? Have other supernatural legends and first-person reminiscences affected the stories? What accounts for the earnest, somewhat cautious tone of Text F and the swift but sure presentation in Text G?

Most of these questions cannot be answered without further interviews with the informants and extensive observation of their narrative acts. Fortunately, a few remarks by the collector appended to the texts suggest an explanation for the dissimilar narrative techniques used by informants F and G. She notes that narrator F "is an educated man and . . . seemed a little reserved" in recounting the experience. Did the informant suspect that his listener might discount the memorate as evidence of a superstitious imagination? Such an attitude would help explain the contrasts between belief and skepticism throughout the story. Narrator G, on the other hand, "firmly believes everything she tells, and at a family gathering she can talk all night of experiences." For informant G it is unnecessary to address the skeptic's questions. Her explicit belief in the reality of the supernatural experience apparently demands no explanation or apology. She can allow the narrative events to speak for themselves without cautious introductions and conclusions. It may be, too, that narrator G is an active tradition-bearer, since she is described as an enthusiastic storyteller and therefore probably alert to the vernacular narrative arts about her, especially those that deal with supernatural beliefs. As noted above, her account follows the traditional legend format more closely than Text F. In both cases the explanation for the contrasting types of narrative performance is not to be found in the experiences upon which the stories are based, but can be ascribed to the nature of their narrators' predispositions and aesthetic sensibilities.

The texts discussed here have been limited to brief stories that represent a wide range of narrative artistry and dependence on popular conventions about the supernatural. Although they are not the type of accounts respected as data sources in parapsychological research, they do illustrate the important role of *homo narrans* in the description of personal experience and the manipulation of traditional motifs and literary conventions. It is probable that these processes play a significant role in maintaining a given story in both oral and print media. Just as a badly told joke dies in transmission, a memorate that fails to intrigue, to cohere, to satisfy, meets a similar fate. An authoritative performance, whether in oral tradition or popular print, will gratify its audience, which in turn will encourage the repeated performance of the narrative. Similarly, sensitivity to and appreciation for familiar story elements and popular conventions, on the part of both raconteur and audience, may affect the act of narration as the memorate is recounted again and again.

At present, the vernacular texts available for further study of the paranormal memorate constitute a miscellany of narratives supplemented by little or no context data. It is difficult, if not impossible, to locate versions of the same memorate collected in different situations from the same informant over a period of time without an extensive collection of field data focused on a single narrator. Such a time-consuming microstudy would have to include careful attention to the informant's full narrative repertoire and his/her exposure to and participation in various art forms that concern the supernatural—fictive accounts in the mass media as well as experience stories shared by others in print and oral tradition. An extended project of this kind, requiring both a patient investigator and an unusually cooperative subject, would help answer some of the questions I have proposed. Phantasms, however they are explained, shape-shift between experience and its treatment in narrative. An awareness of the complex interaction among tradition, canons of narrative art, and the different contexts in which the memorate is shared in its life history is crucial in understanding the relation between paranormal experience and its verbal description.

The vernacular memorates discussed here suggest the complicated interplay between the storytelling act and traditional lore about the supernatural visitation. Similar interactions, in varying degrees, must govern other kinds of paranormal accounts, even those accepted as authentic, evidential testimonials in psychic studies. Regardless of our educational and cultural backgrounds, the external influences of popular tradition and artistic convention affect all of us who describe past occurrences, although we may recognize them only on occasion. The present exploration of vernacular testimonial deals with stories told by others, but it is equally pertinent to stories that we tell one another. An informed sensitivity to the ways that narrative transforms experience, actual or putative, will ultimately clarify the truths that the paranormal memorate seeks to express.

NOTES

1. See G. N. M. Tyrrell's discussion of evidence in the evaluation of paranormal narrative in *Apparitions* (London: Gerald Duckworth, 1953), pp. 25–29.

2. Linda Dégh and Andrew Vázsonyi, "The Memorate and the Proto-Memorate," *Journal of American Folklore,* 87 (1974):225–39, discuss the genre in detail, including problems of definition.

3. The memorate sources include Fred W. Allsopp, *Folklore of Romantic Arkansas* (New York: Grolier Society, 1931), pp. 259–61; Henry Benford, *Living with Ghosts* (Broderick, Calif.: Hearthstone, 1969), pp. 32–34; Dennis Bardens, *Ghosts and Hauntings* (New York: Taplinger Publishing Co., 1968), pp. 65–66; "Case of the Will of Mr. James L. Chaffin," *Proceedings of the Society for Psychical Research,* 36 (1926–28):519–20; Richard M. Dorson, *American Negro Folktales* (Greenwich, Conn.: Fawcett, 1967), pp. 225–27; *Fate,* Jan., 1969, pp. 102–6, 108; Feb., 1969, pp. 99–100, 106, 108; Mar., 1969, pp. 99–100, 102, 108; May, 1969, pp. 101–2, 106, 108; June, 1969, p. 99; July, 1970, pp. 64, 99–100, 104–6; Sept., 1970, pp. 105–6; Nov., 1970, pp. 118, 120; Dec., 1970, pp. 114–18, 120; Hans Holzer, *Ghosts I've Met* (London: Herbert Jenkins, 1966), pp. 60–61; Harry Middleton Hyatt, *Folk-Lore from Adams County Illinois* (Hannibal, Mo.: Western Printing and Lithographing Co., 1965), pp. 769, 779–83, 786, 788; Louis C. Jones, *Things That Go Bump in the Night* (New York: Hill and Wang, 1959), pp. 2–4; Ruth Ann Musick, *The Telltale Lilac Bush and Other West Virginia Ghost Tales* (Lexington: University of Kentucky Press, 1964), pp. 112–14; Claire Noall, "Superstitions, Customs, and Prescriptions of Mormon Midwives," *California Folklore Quarterly,* 3 (1944): 105; *Occult,* July, 1938, p. 18; Dec., 1938, p. 18; Jan., 1939, pp. 15, 20; Mar., 1939, p. 19; Apr., 1939, p. 18; June, 1939, pp. 14–15, 25; Danton Walker, *I Believe in Ghosts* (New York: Taplinger Publishing Co., 1969), pp. 32–34. The archive texts used can be located at the Indiana University Folklore Institute Archives, Bloomington, under the following accession numbers: 1, 521, 578, 1875 (69/72), and 1877 (69/72).

4. Hyatt, *Folk-Lore,* text 15804, p. 780.

5. See Axel Olrik, "Epic Laws of Folk Narrative," in Alan Dundes, ed., *The Study of Folklore* (Englewood Cliffs, N.J.: Prentice-Hall, 1965), pp. 129–41.

6. Wayne Karplus, "The Framework of Oral Supernatural Tales" (manuscript, Folklore Archive, English Department, University of Illinois, Urbana), pp. 34–35.

7. *Fate,* Jan., 1969, pp. 102–3.

8. "Report on the Census of Hallucinations," *Proceedings of the Society for Psychical Research,* 10 (1894):152–54, and D. J. West, *Psychical Research Today* (Harmondsworth, Middlesex: Penguin Books, 1962), p. 37.

9. "Six Theories about Apparitions," *Proceedings of the Society for Psychical Research,* 50 (1956):159.

10. Celia Green and Charles McCreery, *Apparitions* (London: Hamish Hamilton, 1975), p. 123.

11. "Report on the Census of Hallucinations," p. 68.

12. West, *Psychical Research Today,* p. 39.

13. "Six Theories about Apparitions," p. 171.

14. Ibid., p. 170. See also G. W. Lambert's comparison of two versions of the same haunting separated by nearly eighty years: "Beavor Lodge: An Old Ghost Story Retold," *Journal of the Society for Psychical Research,* 42 (1964):273–82. Lambert concurs with Hart on the matter of narrative transmission.

15. Writes Gardner Murphy: "I think there may be some confusion about what happens to apparition stories as they are retold. Surely they may lose authenticating detail, and yet at the same time grow more marvellous and impressive.... What is terribly impressive may owe its quality to the very elaborations which make it unconvincing to the careful critic." See "Six Theories about Apparitions," p. 170.

16. Frederic C. Bartlett, *Remembering: A Study in Experimental and Social Psychology* (Cambridge: Cambridge University Press, 1967), p. 93.

17. Gordon W. Allport and Leo Postman, *The Psychology of Rumor* (New York: Henry Holt, 1947), p. 147.

18. Ibid., pp. 153–54.

19. D. J. West, "A Mass-Observation Questionnaire on Hallucinations," *Journal of the Society for Psychical Research,* 34 (1948):190.

20. Stith Thompson, *The Folktale* (New York: Holt, Rinehart and Winston, 1967), pp. 415–16.

21. See, e.g., Alan Dundes, "From Etic to Emic Units in the Structural Study of Folktales," in Dundes, *Analytic Essays in Folklore* (The Hague: Mouton, 1975), pp. 62–64.

22. The following motifs from Stith Thompson, *Motif-Index of Folk Literature,* vol. 2, D-E (Bloomington: Indiana University Press, 1966), and Ernest W. Baughman, *Type and Motif Index of the Folktales of England and North America* (Indiana University Folklore Series, no. 20; The Hague: Mouton, 1966), are found in the texts used in this study: E221 "Dead spouse's malevolent return," E221.2 "Dead wife returns to reprove husband's second wife," E222.01 "Mother haunts daughter," E300 "Friendly return of the dead," E320 "Dead relative's friendly return," E323 "Dead mother's friendly return," E323.1 "Dead mother returns to see baby," E323.6 "Mother returns to encourage daughter in great difficulties," E325 "Dead sister's friendly return," E326 "Dead brother's friendly return," E327 "Dead father's friendly return," E327.4 "Ghost of father returns to

rebuke child," E361 "Return from the dead to stop weeping," E361.2 "Return from dead to give consoling message," E363.2 "Ghost returns to protect the living," E363.3 "Ghost warns the living," E363.4 "Ghost reassures living," E364 "Dead returns to say farewell," E366 "Return from dead to give counsel," E419.10 "Concern of ghost about belongings of its lifetime," E544 "Ghost leaves evidence of his appearance," E545 "The dead speak," E545.2 "Dead predict death," E545.3 "Dead announces own death," E545.13 "Man converses with dead," E574 "Appearance of ghost serves as death omen," E586 "Dead returns soon after burial," E586.0.1 "Ghost returns before burial," E723 "Wraiths of persons separate from body," E723.1 "Person sees his own wraith," E723.2 "Seeing one's wraith a sign that person is to die shortly," E723.4.5 "Wraith gives information of death in family," E723.6 "Appearance of his wraith as announcement of person's death," E723.6.1*(b) "Wraith passes window of house," E723.6.1*(h) "Wraith enters outbuilding," E723.6.2* "Wraith appears out-of-doors," E723.6.2*(b) "Wraith appears in house yard."

23. "Laurie," a popular ballad recorded by Dickie Lee (Eric Records, 45 rpm, no. 120), is based on Baughman, E332.3.3.1, "The Vanishing Hitchhiker"; a Red Sovine song, "Phantom 309," on *Red Sovine: Classic Narrations* (Starday, SLP 436), is an interesting inversion of the legend.

24. See my discussion of this phenomenon in oral history accounts: "The Folklorist, the Oral Historian, and Local History," *Oral History Review 1980,* pp. 69–70.

25. D. J. West, "The Investigation of Spontaneous Cases," *Proceedings of the Society for Psychical Research,* 48 (1946–49):294, 274–95 passim.

26. West, *Psychical Research Today,* pp. 40–41. Another detailed examination of a series of mysterious experiences with apparent spirits follows. In it a careful psychological investigation provides a convincing explanation of the apparitions in terms of the percipient's neurosis. See ibid., pp. 43–47. Other relevant discussions include D. J. West, "The 'Haunted' Dance Hall," *Journal of the Society for Psychical Research,* 34 (1947–48): 294–300; George Owen in George Owen and Victor Sims, *Science and the Spook* (New York: Garrett Publications, 1971), p. 59; and Frank Smyth, *Ghosts and Poltergeists* (New York: Doubleday, 1976), p. 16.

27. Hyatt, *Folk-Lore,* text 15809, p. 781.

28. Ibid., text 15812, p. 781.

29. Owen and Sims, *Science and the Spook,* pp. 47–48.

30. Ibid., pp. 103–8.

31. Aniela Jaffe, *Apparitions and Precognition* (New Hyde Park, N.Y.: University Books, 1963), pp. 181–83.

32. Baughman cites many American versions for E332.3.3.1, "The Vanishing Hitchhiker." The rhetorical analysis appears in E. C. Barksdale and Daniel Popp, "The Teller and the Tale," *Fabula,* 18 (1977):249–52.

33. See "The Baffling Case of the Hitchhiking Ghost," *National Enquirer,* July 4, 1978, p. 4.

34. *Fate,* Nov., 1970, pp. 118, 120.

35. Dell Hymes, "Breakthrough into Performance," in Dan Ben-Amos and Kenneth S. Goldstein, eds., *Folklore: Performance and Communication* (The Hague: Mouton, 1975), p. 18.

36. Ibid.

37. See, e.g., the variety of excellent articles in sec. I, "Performance," and sec. II, "Performance and Communication," in Ben-Amos and Goldstein, eds., *Folklore: Performance and Communication*. See also Barre Toelken, "The 'Pretty Languages' of Yellowman: Genre, Mode, and Texture in Navaho Coyote Narratives," and V. Hrdlickova, "Japanese Professional Storytellers," in Dan Ben-Amos, ed., *Folklore Genres* (Austin: University of Texas Press, 1976), pp. 145–70 and 171–90 respectively.

38. Texts F and G were collected in 1968 and archived in the Indiana University Folklore Institute Archives, Bloomington, under accession numbers 1875 (69/72) and 1877 (69/72) respectively.

39. See Linda Dégh, "Folk Narrative," in Richard M. Dorson, ed., *Folklore and Folklife: An Introduction* (Chicago: University of Chicago Press, 1972), pp. 72–77.

10

UFOs and the Search for Scientific Legitimacy

DAVID M. JACOBS

ON JUNE 24, 1947, Kenneth Arnold, a businessman from Boise, Idaho, was flying in his private plane over the state of Washington when he saw nine oddly shaped objects moving like "saucers skipping over water." Since that day, tens of thousands of people around the world have reported seeing unidentified flying objects (UFOs). Most reports have had "conventional" explanations. About 10 percent of the reports have defied analysis and conventional explanation; the objects in these reports remain unidentified and have been the subject of a major scientific controversy.

The scientific community and the U.S. Air Force, for the most part, have maintained that the UFO phenomenon is not anomalous and that UFOs have mundane origins. Lay UFO researchers—mostly average citizens but including some scientists—have claimed that the unidentified reports represent a truly anomalous phenomenon whose origins are completely unconventional. These UFO proponents set out in the late 1940s to turn the study of UFOs into a legitimate area of scientific inquiry. Yet in the three decades since Kenneth Arnold's sighting, scientific legitimacy has been elusive, and the changing character of UFO reports has forced UFO proponents to modify their mission.

The first UFO reports in the late 1940s described "silvery" or "metallic" unconventionally shaped objects high in the sky that performed maneuvers apparently beyond the known technological capabilities of the time. Witnesses reported seeing UFOs singly or in groups hovering, zig-zagging, making seemingly impossible right-angle turns, swooping low, "dancing" about, and flying away at tremendous speeds. Pilots reported seeing UFOs "pace" their planes or fly circles around them.

Some witnesses claimed to have seen objects land at a distance, but no confirmation could be obtained. Although no one saw an object land nearby or met the occupants of a UFO, the objects' maneuvers suggested that they were under intelligent control and that landings and even "contact" were possible.[1]

Concerned that people were sighting "real" objects that might be truly unknown or, in the cold-war environment of the times, Soviet secret weapons, the Air Force took on the role of official UFO investigating body. It collected UFO reports, classified them as sensitive data, and claimed to study each one thoroughly. By 1949 the Air Force had concluded that the objects were not secret weapons from the Soviet Union or any other country. That left three explanations: the objects came from outer space and could threaten the national security; they were unknown natural phenomena; or they were misidentifications of conventional phenomena, which suggested the possibility of a "mass hallucination." By 1953 the Air Force had determined that the objects did not display characteristics suggesting that they had extraterrestrial origins, that they did not threaten the national security, and that they were not unknown natural phenomena.[2]

Only one explanation remained: the objects probably represented misidentifications of conventional phenomena, with some reports having psychological origins. Thus UFO reports became a public relations problem for the Air Force, which concentrated on downplaying them—rather than analyzing them—for fear that the Soviet Union could use "flying saucer hysteria" as a weapon of psychological warfare.

Dissatisfied with the Air Force's investigation, civilian "ufologists" formed UFO organizations (e.g. the Aerial Phenomenon Research Organization, Civilian Saucer Investigations) to collect and investigate UFO reports. Most UFO proponents became adherents of the only available "nonconventional" theory about the origins of UFOs, the "nuts-and-bolts" extraterrestrial hypothesis: structured craft were flying to earth from other planets by traversing time and space. UFO advocates argued that the phenomenon obviously warranted immediate and complete scientific study. They criticized the Air Force for preventing such study by restricting access to the data and by assuring the public that Air Force scientists were investigating the subject. Such secrecy and tight security fueled speculation of an Air Force cover-up.

The extraterrestrial hypothesis—the ufologists' belief structure, or paradigm—was based on data from UFO reports, which supported the idea that UFOs came from "outer space." After all, credible, reputable people reported seeing strangely shaped metallic objects in the sky, which performed bizarre maneuvers in a technologically "impossible" manner. The sightings seemed to happen at random, with no particular educational or cultural group especially likely to see them. The sightings took place all over the world and conformed to neither the geographical boundaries nor the technological level of the country in which they were seen. UFO reports appeared to occur independently of societal events. A growing number of radar reports, photographs, and motion pictures of alleged UFOs suggested that UFOs could be divorced from the vagaries of human perception.

Despite the mounting evidence for the extraterrestrial hypothesis, UFO proponents found themselves constantly on the defensive. Proving that UFOs had an objective reality and were of extraterrestrial origin turned out to be difficult. The evidence for the existence—to say nothing of the origin—of the phenomenon was largely anecdotal. A UFO had not yet "crashed," no one had produced artifacts, and no one had yet collected objective scientific data on the objects. If "nuts-and-bolts" hardware were involved, then why had there been no mechanical failures and why had a UFO occupant not made official contact? Although UFO proponents reasoned that the occupants did not want to cause panic among humans, the basic question remained: if UFOs were intelligently controlled craft from an advanced society somewhere in outer space, why did "they" not reveal themselves for all to see? Extraordinary claims required extraordinary evidence, and UFO proponents did not have it.

During the early 1950s numerous local flying saucer "clubs" came into being. Fueled by sensationalistic pulp articles, these faddists speculated that UFOs were "time travelers," "space animals," agents of God or Satan, or occult emanations. Most UFO proponents found these theories ridiculous and dangerous—ridiculous because they had no basis in evidence from the reports, and dangerous because they gave the field of UFO research a "fringy" aura and invited ridicule. Indeed, ridicule became an extremely important factor because of the efforts of the infamous "contactees" of the 1950s.[3]

Led by "Professor" George Adamski, "Dr." Daniel Fry, Truman Bethurum, Howard Menger, and others, the contactees claimed that they had ongoing contact with "space people" who had come to earth for benevolent reasons, usually to prevent atomic war and bring about world peace. According to the contactees, the space people lived in utopian worlds that were technologically, morally, culturally, and intellectually superior. The contactees claimed to have paranormal contact with aliens, through telepathy and other extrasensory means. Their stories suggested that contact with the "space brothers" would not take place officially but would involve selected private citizens. Claiming to be the chosen ones, the contactees embarked on money-making ventures to spread the space people's message to earthlings.[4]

The contactees presented a serious challenge to the extraterrestrial hypothesis and to UFO research. If UFOs were intelligently controlled hardware, it was possible that someone might have had contact with the "occupants" of the vehicle. Did contact have to come "officially"? How could one define alien intelligence or motivation? If space people were indeed so advanced that they had solved the problems of space travel, then they might very well be able to select humans for contact. And if space people had such powers and abilities, it might be impossible to study them because they might have the means to prevent their own detection.

Furthermore, the contactees created a crisis in credibility. Their sensational and unsupportable claims about trips in flying saucers and visits to other planets encouraged ridicule and made the quest for scientific legitimacy all the more difficult. Eventually, with their claims either disproven or thrown seriously into question, the contactees lost their followers, and the media attention they received dwindled.[5]

Although the contactees faded from popularity, they had had a major effect on the style of thought about the UFO phenomenon. Their claims frightened UFO proponents and forced them to set limits on the paradigm of the extraterrestrial hypothesis in order to maintain its aura of legitimacy. For example, the National Investigations Committee on Aerial Phenomena (NICAP) decreed that it would not accept reports of contact with UFO occupants—regardless of the claimant's reputation. Other UFO organizations instituted similar policies. By limiting study to "rational" UFO reports, proponents tried to reduce the potential public ridicule and enhance the "reasonableness" of the witnesses. Moreover, as long as the reports suggested rationally acting, "hard" objects that did not display occult or paranormal qualities, the study of the phenomenon could remain within the realm of established scientific disciplines. The extraterrestrial hypothesis need not be tainted by "crackpot" aspects, and the paradigm could be maintained without having to deal with potential anomalies.[6]

The extraterrestrial hypothesis gained favor throughout the 1950s. Nearly all the books about UFOs published in that decade espoused the extraterrestrial hypothesis.[7] Moreover, in the major wave of sightings in 1952 the data collected supported the idea of a "rational" phenomenon: UFOs were reported near military bases, atomic installations, and other sensitive areas, suggesting that "they" were interested in our military capabilities; UFOs were seen more frequently in rural than in urban areas, suggesting that the UFOs were trying to "hide" their identity—perhaps "they" were learning about earth in preparation for an eventual landing, perhaps "they" were interested in earth's resources for possible exploitation. Whatever the reasons, the UFOs were, as one ufologist later said, certainly "cautious and curious," and the phenomenon exhibited an apparent rationality that most UFO proponents readily claimed was evidence of interplanetary visitation.[8]

Yet within the logical framework of the extraterrestrial hypothesis lurked some only vaguely realized illogicalities. For example, by 1957 —after nearly ten years of continual reports—UFOs had still not made "official" contact; not one UFO had crashed; and although stories and rumors had circulated to the contrary, no one had captured UFO occupants or had collected pieces of a UFO. The space ships were quite passive and evidently made no mistakes, even though a margin of error of zero for any artificially manufactured object seemed impossible.

A significant change in the character of UFO reports came about in the 1957 wave. Increasing numbers of people began to report electrical and/or mechanical interference with automobiles or appliances when in close proximity to a UFO. Also, more people reported seeing UFOs on or near the ground. It seemed as if UFOs were coming closer to earth. For UFO proponents, this change made it all the more imperative that the public and the scientific community understand the enormity of the problem.[9]

Scientists who had cursorily surveyed the phenomenon found the evidence for its existence wanting. Its lack of verifiability, lack of predictability, and the poor quality of anecdotal data suggested to scientists that UFOs had no objective reality as an anomalous phenomenon. They argued that anecdotal data were inappropriate for scientific scrutiny, that the possibility of hoaxes and fabrications would always make conclusions questionable, and that the Air Force had mounted a major scientific analysis and found the extraterrestrial hypothesis to be unsupportable. These scientific arguments against the feasibility of that hypothesis were extremely persuasive. The problem of overcoming the incomprehensible distances, even at the speed of light, seemed insurmountable. Along with the scientific gaps came the problem of ridicule: because of the contactees, occasional hoaxes, and lack of any kind of physical evidence, scientists did not select UFOs as a subject of research for fear that it might reflect adversely on their judgment and hinder their careers.[10]

For the UFO proponents, their best chance for scientific respectability rested in stressing the patterns of evidence, the reliability of witnesses, the increasing number of reports, the global pervasiveness of the sightings, and the logical "visitation from outer space" quality of the phenomenon. To this end, Coral Lorenzen of the Aerial Phenomena Research Organization (APRO) wrote *The Great Flying Saucer Hoax* (1962), which detailed UFO sightings around the world and even included some low-level and bizarre cases from South America. This was the most complete description of the UFO phenomenon to date.[11] In 1964 NICAP published *The UFO Evidence,* a carefully compiled compendium of NICAP's UFO reports. The book categorized the phenomenon by color, shape, location, noise, and other characteristics and strongly emphasized the seemingly intelligent behavior of the UFOs. Its main thrust was that reliable, reputable witnesses—including professional people, scientists, engineers, ministers, judges, and the like—saw a variety of unconventional, apparently artificially constructed objects in the sky that appeared to be under intelligent control; it made as strong a case for the "nuts-and-bolts" extraterrestrial origin of UFOs as had yet been made. NICAP sent the book free to every congressman and to every scientist who wanted it.[12]

In the late 1960s, however, UFO reports began to take on a different character. New data seemed to militate against the clear-cut rationality of the phenomenon. Although most witnesses still reported high-level objects, many more than before said they saw UFOs close to or on the ground. UFOs were said to follow cars for blocks or miles. Sometimes investigators found mysterious marks on the grass or soil where witnesses claimed an object had landed. Reports more frequently indicated interference with automobile engines, radios, television sets, and other electrical devices. Some witnesses reported feeling physical effects (such as heat, "prickly sensations") while near a UFO; others alleged that they had a feeling of euphoria when they sighted a UFO. Some claimed an overpowering experience of panic and fear when a UFO was overhead; others reported feeling physically paralyzed or unable to take their eyes off the object even though they wanted to. A few witnesses claimed that they were being "watched" or that somehow the unseen UFO occupants "knew" all about them. Often a component of the new reports was the profoundly incomprehensible allegation that objects simply "materialized" in front of witnesses and then disappeared or "de-materialized." Witnesses steadfastly contended that the objects had neither flown into the area nor flown away. Some reports suggested that several objects "blended" together into one UFO and, conversely, that one object could "separate" into two distinct entities. These reports fundamentally contradicted the notion of "hard" UFOs; at the same time there were numerous reports of landed UFOs leaving markings in the ground, which indicated that some of them were indeed "hard."[13]

In addition, reports of UFO occupants increased. These gained the immediate attention of UFO proponents because the witnesses were not contactees who basked in media publicity and monetary gain. Rather, they were ordinary people whose subsequent behavior was not suspicious, and their assertions could not be correlated with behavior suggesting hoax or hallucination. Witnesses typically reported seeing "people" collecting flora samples near a landed UFO; when the beings realized someone was watching, they quickly entered the object, which just as quickly departed. Other witnesses claimed to have seen occupants through windows in UFOs as the object hovered at a low level.[14] Some seemingly reliable witnesses claimed to have seen UFO occupants from a short distance and even tried to communicate with them.

These reports threw the extraterrestrial hypothesis into doubt and again opened the door to claims of contact with space people. UFO investigators were afraid that scientists would consider the entire UFO phenomenon unworthy of attention if these new cases were presented seriously. Inevitably, however, the more bizarre reports forced their way into the ufologists' conservative belief structure because of witness reliability and the number of such reports. By the end of the 1960s much of the prosaic quality of the earlier UFO reports had disappeared, replaced by accounts of a phenomenon more bizarre, less comprehensible, less rational, and less amenable to control or study than the reports of the 1940s and 1950s.

It seemed that as time went on, as more data became available, and as one learned more about the subject, the less susceptible to rational inquiry it became and hence the less one knew about it. The accumulation of knowledge about UFOs did not necessarily support firmly held theories about their origins. Indeed, the accumulation of knowledge seemed to lead to more questions, not to answers. As a result UFO researchers slowly began to lose whatever intellectual control they thought they had over the subject.

At the same time in the late 1960s when UFO researchers were beginning to feel less sure about the nature of UFOs, established political and scientific institutions began to take a closer look at the UFO phenomenon. In 1966, after years of intensive pressure from UFO proponents, the House Committee on Armed Services held hearings on the subject of UFOs and the Air Force's handling of the problem. As an outcome of the hearings, the Air Force contracted with the University of Colorado to study the phenomenon and decide whether it was extra-terrestrial. Physicist Dr. Edward U. Condon was named head of the project. The eighteen-month study, which was completed in late 1968, found no evidence of extraterrestrial visitation, and Condon concluded that further study was unwarranted.[15] On the basis of this recommenda-tion, the Air Force closed down its UFO investigating unit, and after a great amount of publicity about the Condon committee's negative find-ings, scientific interest began to wane. But the existence of the Condon committee and the general public interest in UFOs had prompted many individual scientists to look into the UFO enigma on their own. Now these scientists and UFO proponents bitterly attacked the Condon com-mittee's conclusions. They charged that the committee had used biased, inexperienced, and untrained scientists, and that its methodology and assumptions were faulty. They felt that by searching for a simple solu-tion to the UFO problem (deciding whether they came from outer space), the Condon committee members had shared an assumption about UFOs that was based on superficial knowledge of the subject.[16]

Although general scientific interest in UFOs was decreasing, so much criticism had been mounted against the Condon committee that the American Association for the Advancement of Science scheduled a symposium on UFOs for its December, 1969, meeting. The symposium was the last manifestation of organized scientific interest. Fifteen papers about UFOs were presented with the majority taking a negative posi-tion. No ongoing scientific studies resulted from the symposium, and the scientific community remained wary of the subject.[17]

By the early 1970s it became clear that neither established science nor the government would consider the study of UFOs to be an area of legitimate research. However, by this time UFO proponents had quietly begun to alter their mission. The search for scientific legitimacy was losing its position as the primary goal. Instead, UFO proponents were coming together with interested scientists and other academics to form their own research community. This shift in focus was due not only to the Condon committee's effect and the closing down of the Air Force unit, but also to the impact that the new UFO reports were having, espe-cially the "abduction" cases.

The most well-known and important abduction case was that of Barney and Betty Hill, which occurred in 1961 but came to public attention in 1966. It seemed to provide evidence both for and against the extraterrestrial paradigm.

The Hills, an interracial couple and upstanding members of the community, claimed that while returning to New Hampshire from Montreal, they were telepathically forced to drive onto a deserted road where occupants took them aboard a landed "spacecraft," physically examined them, and then released them. The Hills could "hear" the occupants talking to them through their heads but not through their ears. The occupants gave them a "posthypnotic" suggestion not to remember the incident. A number of years later a psychiatrist brought the event to the Hills' consciousness through regression hypnosis.[18]

The Hills were the antithesis of the 1950s-style contactee. As an interracial couple in their late thirties, they did not seem like the type who desired "lunatic fringe" attention. They did not have ongoing experiences with the space brothers; they had no message imparted to them and no "mission" to accomplish. Betty Hill was a social worker, and Barney Hill worked for the Postal Service. Barney was black and active in the U.S. Civil Rights Commission and in the local chapter of the National Association for the Advancement of Colored People. Moreover, the Hill case was extremely mundane and apparently comprehensible. It had a beginning, middle, and end. The occupants seemed to be searching for information about human anatomy; they were apparently moral (they did not kill or kidnap the Hills), inquisitive, reasonable, and kind—at one point a "doctor" stopped Betty Hill's pain by putting his hand on her head. The Hill case held out the possibility of an extraterrestrial technology not unlike that found on earth, but it also contained paranormal elements in that the Hills were forced to act and think against their will, and they communicated telepathically with the alleged extraterrestrials.

The impact of the Hill case on the study of UFOs was enormous. It opened the door for further acceptance of qualitatively stranger cases that might have been rejected as spurious in the past. It also moved the UFO phenomenon more into the realm of the occult while retaining the extraterrestrial hypothesis as a basis. Once UFO proponents accepted the credibility of the Hill case, they began more readily to accept other cases of abduction and occupant sightings. For instance, a unique 1957 case from Brazil, in which sexual contact between a "space woman" and a farmer was reported, became the object of debate, and many serious researchers in the 1960s categorized the case as legitimate, a judgment unthinkable just a few years before.[19]

The Dr. "X" case in France in 1968 seemed to offer more evidence that UFOs might have a nonmaterial component. Dr. X, a physician in a small town, claimed that one night he saw two UFOs over the valley below his hilltop house. The two objects "blended" into one, and this object came to within a few feet of his house and beamed a light on him as he stared at it. Then the object disappeared with an explosive sound. The entire incident took no more than one minute. The next day a rash appeared in the form of an isosceles triangle centered over his navel. He was amazed to discover that the same was true of his young son, who had seen the incident from another window. A wound that Dr. X had received in the Algerian war twelve years before was completely healed, as was a gash on his leg. Within the next year Dr. X claimed episodes of levitation and an increased awareness of and interest in the cosmos. The physician steadfastly refused publicity and would not have his name used or his photograph taken for fear of attracting ridicule to himself and his child.[20]

The Dr. X case raised fundamental issues about the nature of reality that could not fit into any previous system of thought. Whatever the explanation, it was clear that the nuts-and-bolts idea of the phenomenon had to be revised.

The process of revision proved difficult. Nothing seemed as commonsensical as the extraterrestrial hypothesis, but it did not explain all the observations. As a result, some UFO researchers began to posit ideas that UFOs were "ultraterrestrials," existing on an ill-defined level of reality called the "astral plane," or coming from a "parallel universe," "fourth dimension," "fifth dimension," or "alternate reality." One idea tentatively placed the phenomenon in both reality and the human psyche, explaining that in the twentieth century stories about UFOs and their occupants had taken the place of fairy tales. Another theory suggested that UFOs had both a hard nuts-and-bolts component as well as a psychic component, and that the shapes of UFOs and the behavior of the occupants were determined by the technological and cultural level of the society in which they were sighted.[21]

These ultraterrestrial theories led the person interested in systematic inquiry away from the idea that the phenomenon could be measured, quantified, and studied in the normal course of scientific inquiry. Such theories resulted, in part, from widespread frustration. UFO proponents had failed to solve the mystery; they had failed to achieve scientific legitimacy; they had failed to prove any contention that they had made about the subject since the 1940s. The phenomenon had become so strange in the 1970s that it had moved beyond intellectual control. The new theories gave UFO proponents a renewed sense of intellectual achievement, allowing them to feel that they were working on a solution.

Not all UFO proponents adopted the new ideas, of course. Many argued that the extraterrestrial hypothesis accounted for most of the

reports and that it was premature to discard it. They stressed that abandoning the nuts-and-bolts theory meant developing a new methodology
for studying the paranormal and giving the UFO phenomenon up to the
occult, which would spell the doom for any future chance at scientific
legitimacy. But the new theories had immediate and widespread influence. At a conference sponsored by the Center for UFO Studies in
1976, a poll of fifty leading UFO researchers attending showed that the
group was evenly split between those who advocated the new ultraterrestrial theories and those who subscribed to the increasingly disfavored
extraterrestrial theory.[22]

One point of resistance to the new theories was the methodology used
in many of the abduction cases. Once the Hill case was published, UFO
investigators used regression hypnosis to uncover hidden data from the
minds of alleged abductees and UFO witnesses. Almost immediately a
new body of abduction cases had emerged. UFO researchers questioned
whether they were dealing with a real and perhaps sinister aspect of the
phenomenon or merely with something that was a function of hypnosis
and had no basis in external objective reality.

As UFO proponents agonized over this problem, Alvin Lawson, a
professor of English at California State University at Long Beach and
a UFO researcher, mounted an experiment that threw the entire notion
of using hypnosis into deeper dispute. He selected student volunteers
who knew nothing about UFOs. He put them into a hypnotic trance,
told them that they would be abducted by a UFO, and asked them to
describe the events that transpired during the "abduction." Lawson
found some similarities between these hypnotically induced abduction
cases and the "real" abduction reports, thus shrouding all the "real"
abduction cases derived from hypnosis in a cloud of suspicion.[23]

As the ultraterrestrial theories found more and more of their bases in
the occult, the UFO phenomenon had come full circle. In a Kuhnian
sense, although the original paradigm of flying saucers coming from
outer space had given way to more bizarre theories, both kinds of hypotheses suggested a nonterrestrial origin.

In many ways the approach of UFO researchers in the early 1950s
was similar to that of nineteenth-century spiritualists. In trying to make
spirit communication credible, says R. Laurence Moore, the spiritualists maintained four principles: "a rejection of supernaturalism, a firm
belief in the inviolability of natural law, a reliance on external facts
rather than on an inward state of mind, and a faith in the progressive
development of knowledge."[24] The same was true of the early UFO
proponents: they rejected occult explanations of UFOs, believed in the

laws of physics, relied on external facts rather than on inward states of mind, and thought that increased knowledge would lead to more evidence to support their contentions. As long as the reports of the phenomenon remained rational, logical, and understandable, ufologists could continue to press for scientific inquiry on the basis that the phenomenon could be studied within the confines of "normal" science.

Yet each of the four principles was subject to the capriciousness of the phenomenon. By the 1970s UFO proponents were forced to accept the possibility of a paranormal explanation, to admit that some UFOs seemed to break the laws of physics, to rely on internal perception of an altered state of mind for information about the phenomenon, and to acknowledge that increased data about UFOs had thrown their original contentions into doubt. Like the nineteenth-century spiritualists described by Moore, so the UFO proponents had failed in their quest for scientific acceptance.

An important difference between the efforts of the spiritualists and twentieth-century UFO proponents was the phenomenon itself. Whereas the "spirits" could not exist without being called forth by humans or without human mediums, the UFO phenomenon seemed to exist outside human perception. In the 1950s and 1960s UFO proponents tried to prove the existence of the phenomenon through the use of photographs, spectral analysis, and other machine verifications. These nonanecdotal forms of verification would, they hoped, fulfill the requirements for scientific analysis. When such proofs turned out to be impossible to attain or inconclusive, UFO researchers had to return to human perception and anecdotal "evidence" as the basis on which the phenomenon could be verified and knowledge expanded. This increasingly greater reliance on human perception led UFO proponents away from the objective reality of UFOs and toward subjective impressions elicited from witnesses by the new "mediums," the hypnotists. Thus, as the evidence became increasingly anecdotal, it also became less susceptible to scientific verification.

By the end of the 1970s the UFO phenomenon had changed dramatically and yet remained as enigmatic as ever. UFO proponents confronted a phenomenon that had become more heterogeneous, more mysterious, more occult, and less amenable to traditional scientific inquiry. They had spent years building a paradigm that had quickly become obsolete, and they had no acceptable replacement. To complicate matters, ridicule remained a concern as did witness veracity. After thirty years of reports UFO proponents had made little headway. They were still searching for an intellectual framework that would allow them suc-

cessfully to confront the increasingly mysterious phenomenon, and they
seemed as far away as ever from finding it. Placing UFOs in the realm of
the occult, where rational explanations and methodology were less necessary, seemed to some proponents the only reasonable way out of what
had become a maze of frustration. Yet the occult was precisely the area
that had damaged the UFO researchers' chances of obtaining scientific
legitimacy for the phenomenon.

By the 1980s UFO proponents were divided and confused. Older
theories had failed to explain the totality of UFOs, no newer theories
had evolved to solve the enigma, and the subject had taken on occult
qualities that helped prevent scientific explanation. Thus UFOs seemed
as shrouded in mystery as ever, and the solution to their mystery was
still remote.

NOTES

1. Ted Bloecher, *Report on the UFO Wave of 1947* (By the author, 1967).

2. For a description of Air Force involvement in UFOs, see David M. Jacobs, *The UFO Controversy in America* (Bloomington: Indiana University Press, 1975).

3. Many of the occult emanation stories can be found in the pages of *Flying Saucer Magazine,* edited by Ray Palmer. See, for instance, Flammonde, *The Age of Flying Saucers* (New York: Hawthorne, 1971), pp. 135–45.

4. Flammonde, *Age of Flying Saucers.*

5. Jacobs, *UFO Controversy,* pp. 108–31.

6. *U.F.O. Investigator,* Aug.-Sept., 1957, pp. 4–5; "Statement of Purposes," *Civilian Saucer Intelligence of New York,* Oct., 1955, p. 1.

7. See, for example, Donald E. Keyhoe, *Flying Saucers Are Real* (New York: Fawcett Publications, 1950) and *Flying Saucers from Outer Space* (New York: Holt, 1953), and Frank Scully, *Behind the Flying Saucers* (New York: Holt, 1950).

8. Edward J. Ruppelt, *Report on Unidentified Flying Objects* (Garden City, N.Y.: Doubleday, 1956).

9. For a discussion of the 1957 wave, see Charles Maney and Richard Hall, *The Challenge of Unidentified Flying Objects* (Washington, D.C.: By the authors, 1961), pp. 70–76.

10. Donald Menzel, *Flying Saucers* (Cambridge, Mass.: Harvard University Press, 1953). See also J. Allen Hynek, "Special Report on Conferences with Astronomers on Unidentified Flying Objects," report to the Air Technical Intelligence Center, Wright Patterson Air Force Base, Aug. 6, 1952, p. 18.

11. Coral Lorenzen, *The Great Flying Saucer Hoax* (New York: New American Library, 1962).

12. Richard Hall, ed., *The UFO Evidence* (Washington, D.C.: National Investigations Committee on Aerial Phenomena, 1964).

13. For discussion of the 1965–67 wave, see Coral and Jim Lorenzen, *UFOs: The Whole Story* (New York: Signet, 1969). Reports are also contained in issues of *Flying Saucer Review* magazine for the 1960s.

14. For UFO occupants reports, see Coral and Jim Lorenzen, *UFO Occupants* (New York: Signet, 1967) and *Encounters with UFO Occupants* (New York: Berkeley Books, 1976), and Charles Bowen, ed., *Encounter Cases from Flying Saucer Review* (New York: Signet, 1977).

15. Edward U. Condon, *Scientific Study of Unidentified Flying Objects* (New York: Bantam, 1969).

16. See, for instance, J. Allen Hynek, "The Condon Report and UFOs," *Bulletin of the Atomic Scientists,* Apr., 1969, pp. 39–47, and Robert M. L. Baker, "The UFO Report: Condon Study Falls Short," *Scientific Research,* Apr. 14, 1969, p. 41.

17. Papers presented at the AAAS symposium were published as Carl Sagan and Thornton Page, eds., *UFOs: A Scientific Debate* (Ithaca, N.Y.: Cornell University Press, 1973).

18. John Fuller, *The Interrupted Journey* (New York: Dial Press, 1966).

19. Lorenzen, *UFO Occupants*, pp. 42–72.

20. Aime Michel, "The Strange Case of Dr. X.," *Flying Saucer Review* special edition, "UFO Percipients" (1972), pp. 11–32.

21. Jacques Vallee, *Passport to Magonia* (Chicago: Henry Regnery, 1969); John Keel, *Operation Trojan Horse* (New York: Putnam, 1970).

22. "The McKay Questionnaire," *Proceedings of the 1976 CUFOS Conference* (Evanston, Ill.: Center for UFO Studies, 1976), p. 319.

23. Alvin Lawson, "What Can We Learn from Hypnosis of Imaginary Abductees?" *1977 MUFON UFO Symposium Proceedings* (1977), pp. 107–36.

24. R. Laurence Moore, *In Search of White Crows: Spiritualism, Parapsychology, and American Culture* (New York: Oxford University Press, 1977), p. 19.

The Contributors

HOWARD KERR is associate professor of English at the University of Illinois, Chicago. He is the author of *Mediums, and Spirit-Rappers, and Roaring Radicals: Spiritualism in American Literature, 1850–1900* (1972).

CHARLES L. CROW is associate professor of English at Bowling Green State University. He is the author of *Janet Lewis* (1981), a study of the twentieth-century poet and novelist, and with Howard Kerr and John W. Crowley has co-edited *The Haunted Dusk: American Supernatural Fiction, 1820–1920* (1983).

ROBERT GALBREATH, coordinator of the honors program at the University of Wisconsin-Milwaukee, has edited *The Occult: Studies and Evaluations* (1972) and written the chapter on "The Occult and the Supernatural" for the *Handbook of American Popular Culture*, vol. 2 (1980). His articles have appeared in such journals as *History of Religions, Journal of Religion, Bulletin of Bibliography, Journal of Popular Culture*, and *Science-Fiction Studies*.

CHADWICK HANSEN is professor of English at the University of Illinois, Chicago. He is the author of *Witchcraft at Salem* (1969) and co-editor, with Art Hodes, of *Selections from the Gutter: Portraits from the Jazz Record* (1977). He has published articles on witchcraft, jazz, Mark Twain, and various other subjects in such journals as *American Quarterly, Massachusetts Review, New England Quarterly*, and *Nineteenth-Century Fiction*.

JON BUTLER is associate professor of history at the University of Illinois, Chicago. He is the author of *Power, Authority, and the Origins of American Denominational Order* (1978), "Magic, Astrology, and the Early American Religious Heritage, 1600–1760," *American Historical Review* (1979), and *The Huguenots in America: A Refugee People in New World Society* (forthcoming).

Ernest Isaacs is professor of history at California State University, Sacramento. He has been a Carnegie research fellow and was visiting professor of American studies at the University of Nottingham, 1981–82. He is currently completing a comparative history of the First and Second Reconstructions.

Robert S. Ellwood, Jr., is Bashford Professor of Oriental Studies at the School of Religion, University of Southern California. His many books include *Religious and Spiritual Groups in Modern America* (1973) and *Alternative Altars: Unconventional and Eastern Spirituality in America* (1979).

R. Laurence Moore, professor of history and department chair at Cornell University, is the author of *European Socialists and the American Promised Land* (1970) and *In Search of White Crows: Spiritualism, Parapsychology, and American Culture* (1977). He has held research grants from the Rockefeller Foundation, the National Endowment for the Humanities, and the American Philosophical Society. His essay in the present volume is part of a larger project on "outsider" groups in American religious history.

Steven F. Walker is associate professor of comparative literature at Rutgers University. His *Theocritus* (1980) is the first book-length critical introduction in English to the works of the ancient Greek poet; his articles on various topics have appeared in such journals as *PMLA*, *Studies in Philology*, and *Literature East and West*.

Mary Farrell Bednarowski is director of the master of arts in religious studies program at United Theological Seminary of the Twin Cities. Her articles on women in American religion have appeared in the *Wisconsin Magazine of History* and the *Journal of the American Academy of Religion*. She is currently writing a text on American religion from a cultural perspective.

Larry Danielson is associate professor of English at the University of Illinois, Urbana. He has edited *Studies in Folklore and Ethnicity* (1978) and has published essays on ethnic folklore, demonic folklore in literature, the urban legend, and the supernatural experience narrative in such journals as *Western Folklore*, *Journal of the Folklore Institute*, *Indiana Folklore*, and the *Swedish Pioneer Historical Quarterly*.

David M. Jacobs is associate professor of history and director of the American studies program at Temple University. He is the author of *The UFO Controversy in America* (1975) and numerous articles on the same subject. He is currently writing about anticommunism in America from 1945 to 1950.

Index

Abbot, Benjamin, 42–43
Adams, Judge James, 141–42
Adamski, George, 220
Adepts, 119
Adler, Margot, 187–88, 190
Adorno, Theodore, 24
AE. *See* Russell, George William
Aether, 118
Aetherius Society, 17
African religious practices, imported,
   61–67. *See also* Slaves
Agassiz, Louis, 96
Age of Aquarius, 5
Akasha, 118
Albanese, Catherine L., 10n12, 126
Alchemy: in colonial period, 59;
   decline of, 67, 71; Stiles's interest
   in, 70–71; De Brahm's interest in,
   71; and Theosophy, 119; in
   Neoplatonic tradition, 121
Allport, Gordon W., 203–4
American Association for the
   Advancement of Science, 225
American Humanist Association, 28
Amish Mennonites, 25
Ancient astronauts, 12
Ancient wisdom, 112, 117, 119.
   See also Theosophy
Andover, Mass.: contrasted with
   Salem, 40

Animal magnetism, 118, 121–22.
   See also Malicious animal
   magnetism; Mesmerism
Anthroposophy: classified, 17, 25;
   and secrecy, 18; defined by R.
   Steiner, 19; as metaphysical move-
   ment, 34n14; Theosophy and, 111.
   See also Steiner, Rudolf
Apocalypticism, 19, 24, 26
Apparitions, studies of, 201–4.
   See also Ghosts; Ghost stories
Arnold, Kenneth, 218
Asian religions, 21, 32n21, 137.
   See also Eastern thought
Astral body, 119
Astrology: and early colonists, 2;
   and present occult movements, 3;
   in American culture, 5; classified,
   12; in 1930s, 21; in eighteenth and
   nineteenth centuries, 23, 68–69;
   counterculture attracted to, 24; and
   science, 29; and medicine, 70; and
   Theosophy, 111, 120; and new
   nineteenth-century religions, 135;
   and feminist witchcraft, 189;
   mentioned, 11
Avard, Sampson, 139

Baba, Pavhari, 175n10
Bailey, Alice A., 30

Bainbridge, William Simms, 10n4
Ball, Charles, 65
Ballard, John, 46
Banner of Light, 153, 180, 188
Barker, William, Sr., 51
Barrett, Linda K., 29
Barron, Henry D., 85
Bartlett, Frederic C., 203
Baughman, Ernest W., 205
Bayard, Dr. Edward, 101
Beecher, Charles, 4–5
Bellah, Robert N., 24
Bennett, John C., 158n20
Berlin, Ira, 62
Besant, Annie, 30, 132–33n6, 164
Bethurum, Truman, 220
Beyond, 25
Bhagavad-Gita, 127, 149
Bigsby, Hannah, 48
Bishop, Bridget, 39
Bissell, Josiah, 84–85
Black Death, 26
Black magic, 42, 48, 49, 147, 151.
  See also Magic
Blake, William, 123–24; "The Tyger,"
  124
Blassingame, John, 60, 61, 67
Blavatsky, Helena Petrovna: and
  spiritualism, 3–4, 115, 116, 127,
  150; journey to India, 4, 7, 116,
  128; *Isis Unveiled,* 6, 112, 116–30
  passim, 134n22; on conflict of
  science and religion, 6, 30, 117,
  118, 119, 128, 130–31; early career
  of, 112–15, 131n2; and Olcott,
  115–16; and Theosophical Society,
  116, 136, 143; basic teaching of,
  117–20; on Judaism, 117, 132–33n6;
  and Gnosticism, 117, 124–25; and
  adepts, 119; on Mesmer and mesmerism, 127; *The Secret Doctrine,*
  127; books consulted by, 129; and
  Cabala, 132–33n6; accused of
  plagiarism, 133–34n22; on Christian Science, 143; on Mother Goddess, 185; mentioned, 163, 183.
  See also Olcott, Henry S.; Theosophy
Block, Marguerite, 125

Boehme, Jacob, 72–74
Book of Jeu, 123
Book of Mormon, 138, 139.
  See also Mormonism
Booth, Ezra, 142–43
Boston Courier, 96
Boyer, Paul, 38, 39, 50
Bradstreet, Dudley, 41
Brahmavidya, 115
Bridges, Hal, 19
Bridges, Mary, Sr., 46
Brittan, Samuel Byron, 151
Britten, Emma Hardinge, 150
Brodie, Fawn, 138, 142
Brotherhood of Luxor, 118
Brown, Antoinette, 191
Brown, Lucretia L. S., 147
Budapest, Z.: on patriarchal society,
  179; on neopagan witchcraft, 188;
  *The Holy Book of Women's
  Mysteries,* 188; feminist views of,
  189, 190, 194n40. *See also*
  Feminist witchcraft
Buddhism, 119, 125
Buddhism, Zen, 21, 112
Buffalo, N.Y., physicians, 93–95
Bull, Mrs. Ole, 169
Bullock, John, 47
Burke, Marie Louise, 163
Burke, Peter, 22
Burkhardt, Jacob, 30
Burr, Charles Chauncey, 93, 95
Burr, Heman, 93, 95
Butler, Jon, 10n4, 59
Byrd, William, II, 64

Cabalism: in early American occultism, 59; Stiles's interest in, 70–71;
  and Theosophy, 117, 119; and
  Neoplatonism, 121; and Gnosticism,
  124; Blavatsky and, 132n6; and new
  nineteenth-century religions, 135;
  and Freemasonry, 142; repudiated
  by spiritualists, 151
Cagliostro, 121
Calef, Robert, 50, 52
Campbell, Bruce F., 10n4, 134n22
Campbell, Joseph, 117

Caporeal, Linnda R., 38
Capron, Eliab Wilkinson, 84–85, 86–90, 92, 95, 100
Cardano, Girolamo, 151
Carrier, Martha, 41–46, 50, 51
Carrier, Richard, 43, 45
Carter, Landon, 64
Carter, Paul A., 175n8
Carter, Robert, 71
Cayce, Edgar, 12, 21
Census of Hallucinations, 201, 202, 204
Chaldean mysteries, 119, 121
Chandler, Phoebe, 45–46
Charismatic religion, 24
Chase, Warren, 74
Chatterji, Rakhahari, 163
Chiropractic, 6
Christ, Carol, 189, 192n3, 195n60
Christian Science: and occult-metaphysical tradition, 6; classified, 17, 25; magical and esoteric in, 135, 146; contrasted with occultism, 136–37; occult features of, 137, 143–49; and Vedanta, 143; and Theosophy, 143, 145, 149; intellectual origins of, 145, 159n29; biblical interpretation in, 145; secrecy in, 146–47, 148, 154–55, 159n39; hierarchical wisdom in, 147; and malicious animal magnetism, 147–48; mentioned, 150, 151. See also Eddy, Mary Baker
Christian Science Publishing House, 149
Church of Jesus Christ of Latter-day Saints. See Mormonism
Clairvoyance, 92, 122
Coleman, William Emmette, 133–34n22
Coleridge, Samuel Taylor, 122
Colville, W. J., 178–79
Committee for the Scientific Investigation of Claims of the Paranormal, 20, 28
Condon, Edward U., 225
Conjurers, 60–61, 67, 69. See also Magic

Corey, Arthur, 159n39
Corey, Martha, 39
Corpus Hermeticum, 123
Cott, Nancy, 191
Cowing, Cedric B., 38
Crowley, Aleister, 30
Culver, Mrs. Norman, 95
Cunningham, Raymond J., 75–76n2

Daly, Mary, 190, 195n51
Dane, Rev. Francis, 51, 52–53
Danites, 139–40
Darwinism, 119–20
Davenport, Reuben Briggs, 104
Davis, Andrew Jackson: occult treatises of, 30, 81; contrasted with Fox sisters, 80–81, 82, 98, 105; Harmonial Philosophy of, 81–82, 145, 152; Divine Revelations, 81; Great Harmonia, 81; later career of, 105; influence on Quimby, 145; and occult tradition, 151–52; as magus, 152; The Magic Staff, 152; and science, 152; mentioned, 92, 128. See also Spiritualism
Day, Horace H., 100
De Brahm, John William Gerar, 71
De Körös, Csoma, 125
Demonology, 149
Demos, John, 38
Despard, Charlotte, 183–84, 185
Dewey, Dellon M., 85
Dewey, J. H., 149
Dianetics, 6
Dickey, Adam H., 148–49
Divination, 3, 11, 12, 21, 30
Dixon, William H., 182
Dodds, E. R., 32
Dorson, Richard, 68
Doten, Lizzie, 181, 182–83
Doubleday, Abner, 116
Doukhobors, 25
Dowsers and dowsing, 1, 29–30, 69
Drake, Frederick C., 54, 55
Dresher, George, 70
DuBois, W. E. B., 60, 61
Dunlop, S. F., 129
Durkheim, Émile, 136

Dutch, Martha, 47

Eastern thought: in esoteric systems,
  1; and occult in America, 4, 21, 59;
  and Theosophy, 5, 112; and spiritualism, 154; mentioned, 119.
  See also Asian religions
Eddas, 119
Eddy brothers: seances of, 115
Eddy, Mary Baker: treatises of, 30;
  accused of occultism, 135, 143, 147;
  and Freemasons, 143; philosophical
  idealism of, 143, 145; *Science and
  Health,* 143, 145, 146, 147; on
  Theosophy, 143, 146; intellectual
  debts of, 145, 159n29; on ordinary
  language and biblical interpretation,
  145–46; compared with Ouspensky,
  146; and secrecy, 146–47; and
  power to heal, 147; and malicious
  animal magnetism, 147–48, 160n45;
  on occult methods, 149; on science,
  149; mentioned, 155, 159n39,
  160n45, 160n50. *See also* Christian
  Science
Egyptian mysteries, 121
Elder Brothers, 119
Eliade, Mircea, 5, 34n17, 127, 147
Eliot, George, 102
Elite culture: occult in, 22, 31
Elkins, Stanley M., 77n14
Ellwood, Robert S., Jr., 10n4, 58, 59
Ephrata settlement, 70
Ergotism, 38
Esotericism: in occult, 1; in colonial
  period, 2; in nineteenth century, 4;
  characterized, 16, 17–18, 136–37;
  in new nineteenth-century religions,
  135; in Christian Science, 146
ESP, 1, 3, 16
Est, 6
Evans, Frederick, 192n3
Evans, Warren Felt, 149
Existentialism, 123
Eyres, Bess, 208–9

Farmer, Sarah, 173
Fate, 25, 198, 200

Feminist witchcraft: and occult as
  social criticism, 5; and spiritualism,
  178–79, 187, 188, 190; and
  Theosophy, 178–79, 187, 190;
  distinguished from neopagan witch-
  craft, 187; and Dianic tradition,
  187; rituals of, 189–90; beliefs of,
  190–92; mentioned, 177. *See also*
  Budapest, Z.; Witchcraft
Ferris, Benjamin, 139
Festinger, Leon, 29
Fichte, J. G., 122
Florentine symposium, the, 121
Fludd, Robert, 124, 151
Flying saucer cults, 1, 29.
  See also UFOs
Folk medicine, occult, 60, 69–70
Fortune telling, 50
Foster, Ann, 46
Fourier, Charles, 80
Fourierist socialism, 81
Fowler, Orson Squire, 93
Fox family, 3, 82, 90
Fox, George, 74
Fox, John, 82–83
Fox, Kate: and rise of spiritualism,
  80, 82–84, 90, 91; seances of, 97,
  101–3; in 1850s, 100; in 1860s,
  100–102; alcoholism of, 101, 102–4;
  personality of, 103; trance writing
  of, 102–3, 106; in England, 103–4;
  last years, 104, 105; mentioned, 80,
  95, 96. *See also* Fox sisters;
  Spiritualism
Fox, Leah: and rise of spiritualism,
  83, 84, 90; accused of exploiting
  sisters, 92, 104; investigated, 94–96;
  seances of, 97, 98; later life of, 98,
  105; *Missing Link in Modern
  Spiritualism,* 98; mentioned, 80, 90.
  See also Fox sisters; Spiritualism
Fox, Margaret (mother), 82, 86
Fox, Margaret: and rise of spiritualism, 82–84, 90; investigated, 94, 99–
  100; and Kane, 98–99; denounces
  spiritualism, 104; confesses fraud,
  104–5; last years of, 105; mentioned, 80, 90, 101. *See also* Fox

sisters; Spiritualism

Fox sisters: as founders of new religion, 80, 82, 98, 106; contrasted with Davis, 80–82; and Hydesville rappings, 80, 82–83; and Rochester rappings, 83–84, 86; in New York City, 90–92; accused of fraud, 91–95; investigated, 93–96, 99–100; Owen and, 97; paradoxical careers of, 98, 105–6; mentioned, 2, 3, 59, 72, 126, 135. *See also* Fox, Kate; Fox, Leah; Fox, Margaret; Spiritualism

Franklin, Benjamin, spirit of, 101, 103, 105

Frazer, Sir James, 136

Freemasonry: and occult tradition, 6, 71; Neoplatonism and, 121; and Theosophy, 128–29; and Mormonism, 141–43, 158n20

Freud, Sigmund, 220

Fry, Daniel, 220

Furness, Horace Howard, 105

Galbreath, Robert, 10n4

Geertz, Hildred, 29

Genovese, Eugene, 61, 62, 65, 76n4

German idealism, 122

Ghosts, 1, 3, 4, 6, 11, 79. *See also* Apparitions; Ghost stories; Paranormal memorates

Ghost stories, 196–217. *See also* Ghosts; Paranormal memorates

Gibbon, Edward, 117

Gildrie, Richard P., 40

Gnosticism: and Theosophy, 4, 111, 117, 123–25; of Valentinus and Basilides, 26; classified, 34n14; modern, 111, 123; Judaeo-Christian, 123; pagan, 123; Blavatsky and, 124–25

Goldenberg, Naomi, 189

Gooch, Stan, 33n11

Good, Sarah, 39

Gordon, Joshua, 69

Greek mysteries, 121

Greeley, Horace, 85, 91, 93, 95, 100, 105

Greenacre conference, 173

Greven, Philip J., Jr., 40

Grimes, James Stanley, 92–93

Grimstad, Kirsten, 177–78

Guénon, René, 34n17

Gurdjieff, G. L., 21

Hale, John, 50, 51

Hallucinations. *See* Apparitions

Hammond, Rev. Charles, 86

Hansen, Chadwick, 10n4, 65

Harmonial Philosophy, 80, 145, 152. *See also* Davis, Andrew Jackson

Harrison, J. F. C., 23

Hart, Hornell, 200, 202–3, 204

Harvard committee, 96

Hathorne, John, 41, 55

Hawthorne, Nathaniel, 175n8

Healing movements, 19

Hegel, G. W. F., 122

Hermes, books of, 3

Hermes-Fire, 118

Hermes Trismegistus, 124

Hermeticism: in occult tradition, 1, 4; and Gnosticism, 123; Blavatsky and, 124; criticized by Brittan, 151; mentioned, 15

Hermetic societies, 117

Herskovits, Melville, 66, 77n16

Heese, Herman, 21

Heym, Paul, 70

Heyting, W. K., 185

Higginson, Thomas Wentworth, 74, 96, 162

Hill, Barney, 225–26

Hill, Betty, 225–26

Holmes, Mr. and Mrs. Nelson, 97–98

Holmes, Oliver Wendell, 5

Home, Daniel Dunglas, 128

Homeopathy, 72

Hooker, Isabella Beecher, 104

Horsmanden, Daniel, 62–63

Howe, Eber, 138–39

Humanist, 28

Hutterians, 25

Huxley, T. H., 129

Hydesville rappings, 82–83. *See also* Fox sisters

Hymes, Dell, 207

I Am, 111
Iamblichus, 121
I Ching, 1
Illuminism, 2
Illuminati, 121
India, in Theosophical thought, 111, 125, 127–28
Initiation, 120, 123, 128, 129, 137, 138
Institute of Psychophysical Research, 201

Jacolliot, L., 129
Jaffe, Aniela, 207–8
Jahoda, Gustav, 24, 27, 36n32
James, Henry, 179–80
James, William, 30–31, 163, 169
Jarvis, Asahel H., 86
Jehovah's Witnesses, 25
Jencken, Henry D., 103–4
Jennings, Hargrave, 129
Jernegan, Marcus W., 64
Joslyn, Hezekiah, 95
Judah, J. Stillson, 10n4, 16–17, 34n14
Judge, William Q., 116
Jungian thought, 6, 24, 123

Kane, Elisha Kent, 98–99
Kelpius, Johannes, 70
Kennedy, Richard, 159n37
Kerr, Howard, 10n4, 58
Kidder, Daniel, 139
Kimball, Heber, 158n20
King, C. W., 124–25, 129, 133n22
King, Katie, scandal, 97–98
Knoche, Grace, 187
Knothe, Helen, 179, 185
Koehler, Lyle, 38
Konig, David Thomas, 38, 48
Krishnamurti, 21
Kulikoff, Allan, 62
Kurtz, Paul, 28

Lacey, Mary, Jr., 46, 50–51
Lacey, Mary, Sr., 46
Landsberg, Leon, 165

Larry, Anthony, 70
Lawson, Alvin, 228
Leadbeater, Charles, 30
Lee, Dr. Charles, 94–95
Lee, Mother Ann, 127
Lee, Rev. Luther, 191
LeJau, Francis, 62
Lemuria, 12
Leventhal, Herbert, 10n4, 70–71
Lévi, Éliphas, 30, 128, 151, 160n52
Levine, Lawrence, 67, 76n4
Lévi-Strauss, Claude, 12
Liberal Catholic Church, 119
Livermore, Charles F., 101, 103
Lorenzen, Coral, 223
Lukes, Steven, 37n44
Lytton, Edward Bulwer, 128

McFarland, Morgan, 194n40
McGinn, Bernard, 26
McLoughlin, William G., 35–36n28
McVaugh, Michael, 10n4
Magic: definitions of, 16, 33n10; Geertz debates Thomas on, 29; Thomas on, 32n2; and Neoplatonism, 121; ideas of, in new nineteenth-century religions, 135; secrecy in, 137; and spiritualism, 153; mentioned, 5, 15, 50, 117, 142, 152. See also Black magic; Conjurers; Magical healing; Malefic magic; Ritual magic; White magic
Magical healing, 2, 11, 25, 69. See also Folk medicine; Magic; Occult
Maharishi, 21
Malefic magic, 48, 49. See also Black magic; Magic
Malicious animal magnetism, 147–48. See also Animal magnetism; Black magic; Mesmerism
Malinowski, Bronislaw, 136
Mansel, Henry, 125
Marginal groups and marginality, 19, 24, 27, 31, 32
Marty, Martin, 25
Marx, Karl, 12
Masons. See Freemasonry

Materialization, 80, 92, 97–98, 101
Mather, Cotton, 4, 50–51, 55
Mather, Increase, 51
Matter, M. Jacques, 124, 125
Maule, Robert, 62
Mauskopf, Seymour, 10n4
Mayavic power, 120
Mead, G. R. S., 21
Mede, Joseph, 22
Mediums and mediumship, 3, 4, 19,
    86, 98, 153, 181, 182
Melton, J. Gordon, 20, 34n14, 34n21
Menger, Howard, 220
Mesmer, Franz Anton: and spiritual-
    ism, 80, 126; and Theosophy, 118;
    Blavatsky on, 121–22. See also
    Animal magnetism; Mesmerism
Mesmerism: and spiritualism, 3, 126;
    and nineteenth-century occultism, 2,
    4, 6, 72; popularity of, 21, 71–72;
    Blavatsky on, 122; as malicious
    animal magnetism, 147. See also
    Animal magnetism; Malicious ani-
    mal magnetism; Mesmer
Metaphysical movements, 16–17,
    34n14, 34–35n21
Metrovich, Agardi, 131n2
Meyer, Donald H., 162
Millennialism, 19, 24, 25–26
Monter, E. William, 70
Moor, E., 129
Moore, R. Laurence, 10n4, 19, 33n8,
    58, 179, 180, 228
Mormons, 25–26
Mormonism: magical and esoteric
    ideas in, 135; contrasted to occult-
    ism, 136–37; occult features of,
    137–43; attacked as occult, 137–39,
    141, 142–43; initiatory rites in, 138–
    41; secrecy in, 138–41, 154–55,
    157–58n13; persecuted, 139–40;
    ascending order of spirituality in,
    140–41; Freemasonry and, 141–43,
    158n20; mentioned, 150, 152
Mother Goddess, the, 185
Muller, Max, 129
Mullin, Michael, 65
Murphy, Gardner, 215n15

Mystery schools, 18

National Investigations Committee on
    Aerial Phenomena (NICAP), 221,
    223
National Enquirer, 6, 196
Neau, Elie, 62
Necromancy, 138
Nelson, G. K., 24, 26
Neoplatonism: and Theosophy, 118–
    19, 120–22, 137; and transcen-
    dentalism, 126; and Freemasonry,
    129; mentioned, 15
New Thought, 6, 16–17, 20, 34n14,
    34–35n21
Newton, Isaac, 22
Nissenbaum, Stephen, 38, 39, 50
Nostradamus, 151
Noyes, John Humphrey, 126
Numerology, 5

"Objections to Astrology," 28
Occult: problems in defining, 1, 15–
    20, 136; definitions of, 1, 15–20;
    in popular culture, 1, 23, 30–31;
    warnings against, 1; history of, in
    America, 2–4; scholars and, 2,
    10n4, 11–15, 58–59, 136; and
    American culture, 4, 6, 25, 32, 136,
    156; and religion, 4–5, 6, 17, 20,
    24–26, 136; and counterculture, 5,
    6, 24; and science, 5–6, 17, 19, 23–
    24, 28–31, 32n2, 135, 137, 152, 154;
    and conflict of science and religion,
    6, 30, 122, 130–31, 149, 152; prob-
    lems in explaining, 14–15; and
    related terms, 16–18; explained in
    terms of revivals, 20–23, 156; popu-
    larity of, 21, 135; explained as sign
    of historical crisis, 23–26; cultural
    stratification and, 23, 27, 31; ex-
    plained as irrationalism, 26–31;
    from 1760 to 1848, 58–77; as sub-
    jective label, 136; characteristics of,
    136–37; in new nineteenth-century
    religions, 137–56; Vivekananda on,
    162–73. See also entries for indi-
    vidual sects and movements

Occult-metaphysical tradition, 6
Occult revivals, 1, 20–23, 156
Occult science, 135, 143, 160n50
Odd Fellows, 6
Odic force, 118
Olcott, Henry S.: on Theosophical
   Society, 3; on spiritualism, 3–4;
   journey to India, 4, 128; back-
   ground of, 115; and Blavatsky,
   115–16; *Old Diary Leaves,* 116,
   117; studies occult, 118; and adepts,
   119; mentioned, 112, 125, 127, 150.
   See also Blavatsky, Helena Petrovna;
   Theosophy
Orientalism, 127–28
Osburn, Sarah, 39
Osofsky, Gilbert, 60
Owen, Robert Dale, 96–98, 103
Ouspensky, P. D., 146

Palmistry, 2
Papus, 30
Paracelsus, 121, 124, 138, 151
Paranormal, 6, 16, 28, 33n11
Paranormal memorates: defined, 197;
   conventions in, 198–200, 201, 211,
   213; as performances, 207, 209,
   213; and cases from psychical re-
   search, 197, 201, 202–4, 207, 208;
   folk motifs in, 205–9; Gardner
   Murphy on, 215n15. *See also*
   Ghosts; Ghost stories
Parapsychology. *See* Psychical
   research
Parker, Mary, 46–48, 50
Partridge, Charles, 91, 92
Peel, Robert, 159n29
Peirce, Benjamin, 96
Phelps, Sarah, 48
Phalanstery, 72
Philadelphia Social History Project,
   68–69, 70
Phrenology: popularity of, 21; and
   reform, 25; in Harlem, 60; in
   nineteenth-century Philadelphia, 70;
   mesmerism and, 72; used to describe
   Fox sisters, 92
Pistis Sophia, 123, 124

Plato, 121
Platonism, 119, 122, 125
Plotinus, 121
Post, Isaac, 83, 84
Postman, Leo, 203–4
Practical occultism, 137, 152–53
Pratt, J. G., 33n8
Preston, Samuel, 42
Priestley, Joseph, 123
Pritchard, Jack, 67
Pritchard, Linda K., 35n28
*Proceedings of the Society for
   Psychical Research,* 205
Process, the, 17
Proclus, 121
Prophecies, 11, 18, 22, 23
Prosser, Gabriel, 65
Psi phenomena, 1, 3, 12, 16
Psychedelics, 21
Psychic, definition of, 16
Psychical phenomena, 18, 20, 196
Psychical research: and occult tradi-
   tion, 3, 4; popularity of, 21; William
   James on, 31; denies occultism, 154;
   studies paranormal memorates, 197,
   201, 202–4, 207–8
Psychokinesis, 16, 122

Quimby, Phineas Parkhurst, 145,
   159n29
Quinn, William, 184

Raboteau, Albert J., 64, 67, 76n4
Ramakrishna mission, 112, 163
Rappites, 25
Religion: and occult. *See* Occult
Rennie, Susan, 177–78
Reorganized Church of Jesus Christ of
   Latter Day Saints, 158n17
Riddle, Dorothy, 189
Riegel, Robert, 180
Rigdon, Sidney, 139
Righter, Carroll, 24
Ritual magic, 1, 21, 22, 25. *See also*
   Magic; White magic
Roberts, B. H., 140
Robinson, Henry Crabb, 124
Rochester rappings, 83–86

Roger, John, 42
Rosemary's Baby, 21
Rosicrucian enlightenment, 121, 129
Rosicrucianism: and secrecy, 18; classified, 34n14; in early American occultism, 59; declines in America, 67, 71; at Kelpius's settlement, 70; and Gnosticism, 117; linked by critics with Christian Science, 143; repudiated by spiritualists, 151
Rosswurm, Stephen, 68
Roszak, Theodore, 12–13
Russell, George William (pseud. AE), 132n6

Saint-Germain, 121
Salem witchcraft trials: scholarly explanations of, 38–39; hostility theories on, 38–39, 53, 54; towns of accused in, 39–40; Andover cases, 40–53; Court of Oyer and Terminer, 48, 55; causes of, 53–55; and other colonial witchcraft trials, 54–55; spectral evidence in, 54–55; confessions in, 54–55; mentioned, 3, 4, 147. *See also* Witchcraft
Satanism, 1
Schelling, F. W. J. von, 122
Schopenhauer, 118, 122
Science: and occult. *See* Occult
Science and religion, conflict between. *See* Occult
Scientology, 17
Scott, Cora L. V. *See* Tappan, Cora L. V.
Search for Bridey Murphy, The, 21

Secrecy in new nineteenth-century religions, 137, 138–41, 146–47, 154–55, 158n17
Secret societies, 21, 117–18, 139, 141, 154
Seventh Day Adventists, 25
Seybert Commission, 99, 100, 105
Seybert, Henry, 99, 100
Shakers, 127, 192
Shamanism: Native American, 23, 126; and Neoplatonism, 121; initiation in, 128; and Christian Science, 147
Shattuck, Samuel, 47–48
Shekinah, 72, 101, 152
Shipton, mother, 23
Simmel, Georg, 154–55
Simpson, Jacqueline, 23
Sims, Victor, 207–8
Sinnett, A. P., 157n3, 160n50
Slaves: occult religion among, 59–67; Christianization of, 61, 64, 65, 66–67; rebellions of, 62–67; anomie among, 65–66; occultism of, and occultism among whites, 67, 69
Sleeping Prophet, The, 21
Slotkin, Richard, 38
Smith, Francie, 208–9
Smith, Hyrum, 158n20
Smith, Joseph: and occult, 135, 138, 143, 157n8; on persecution, 139; and Danites, 140; and ascending order of spirituality, 140–41; and temple ceremonies, 141–42; and Freemasonry, 141–42, 158n20; mentioned, 152, 155, 158n17. *See also* Mormonism
Society for Psychical Research, 201
Sotheran, Charles, 116
Spectral evidence, 41, 43, 46, 48, 50, 51, 54–55
Spencer, Herbert, 129
Spirit rapping, 80–101 *passim,* 104
Spiritualism: popularity of, 2, 21, 92, 95; and occult tradition, 3–4, 59, 80, 83, 122; and Theosophy, 3–4, 126–27, 150–51, 153; attacked, 3, 92–93, 104–5, 135, 150, 153; classified, 16–17, 25; shamanism and, 23, 126; and Protestantism, 72–73; rise of, 72–74, 79–92; two levels of, 80–82; Fox sisters and, 80–106; Davis and, 80–82, 105, 151–52; investigated, 93–100; Blavatsky and, 115, 116; defined, 126; contrasted with occultism, 136–37; occult features of, 137, 149–54; and science, 149–50, 154; occultism repudiated by leaders of, 150–51; feminism in, 177, 178,

179–83; and suffrage, 180–81; and birth control, 180; and marriage, 181–82; mediums of, and stereotypes of womanhood, 182–83; compared with interest in UFOs, 228, 229. *See also* Davis, Andrew Jackson; Fox, Kate; Fox, Leah; Fox, Margaret; Fox sisters

Spiritualist, 180–81

Spiritual Telegraph, 72, 74

Spirit writing, 82, 86, 99–103

Spofford, Daniel, 147

Sprague, Martha, 48, 50

Starhawk, 189

Steiner, George, 11–13, 20

Steiner, Rudolf, 19, 21, 30. *See also* Anthroposophy

Stoughton, William, 55

Stowe, Harriet Beecher, 102, 103

Strauss, Gerald, 70

Strong, George Templeton, 79

Subud, 17

Sufi societies, 117

Supernatural, 16, 22–23

Superstition, 12, 23, 24, 27, 36n32, 136

Survival phenomena, 3, 16

Swan, Timothy, 46

Swedenborg, Emanuel: and spiritualism, 74, 80, 126; and Neoplatonism, 121; and transcendentalism, 127; and M. B. Eddy, 145; *Dictionary of Correspondences,* 145, 149; imitated by Davis, 152; mentioned, 128. *See also* Swedenborgian thought

Swedenborgian thought: in eighteenth-century, 2, 71–72; and nineteenth-century occultism, 3–4, 59, 71–72; popular interest in, 21; influences Davis, 81, 151; and Theosophy, 125–26; and nineteenth-century philosophical idealism, 145; and Christian Science, 145. *See also* Swedenborg, Emanuel

Table tipping, 82, 86, 94

Tappan, Cora L. V., 153, 180

Tarot, 1, 189

Taylor, Dr. George H., 101

Taylor, Sarah Longworthy, 101, 102

Telepathy, 122

Theosophical Society: Olcott on, 3; in 1900, 111–12; founding of, 116; early members, 116; as occult group, 136–37. *See also* Blavatsky, Helena Petrovna; Olcott, Henry S.; Theosophy

Theosophic Messenger, 111–12

Theosophist, 184

Theosophy: and esoteric tradition, 2–3, 4, 5; today, 3, 112; and spiritualism, 3–4, 19, 125, 126–27, 150–51, 153; and conflict of religion and science, 6, 118, 130–31; classified, 16–17, 25; popularity of, 21; role of, in modern occultism, 111, 112; early years of, 111–16; basic teaching of, 117–20; and Cabalism, 117, 119; and Neoplatonism, 117, 118–19, 120–22; and Gnosticism, 123–25; and Christianity, 123; India and Tibet in, 124–25, 127–28; and transcendentalism, 125–26, 127; and Swedenborgian thought, 125–26, 127; and Orientalism, 127–28; and Bulwer-Lytton, 128; and Freemasonry, 128–29; concerns of, 129–30; program of, 130–31; and anti-Semitism, 132–33n6; occult features of, 136; and Christian Science, 149; Vivekananda on, 163–64; feminism in, 177, 178, 183–87; importance of Mother Goddess in, 185. *See also* Blavatsky, Helena Petrovna; Olcott, Henry S.; Theosophical Society

Tibet, in Theosophical thought, 111, 125, 127–28

Tyler, Martha, 51–52

Thomas, Keith, 11–13, 15, 22, 23, 29, 32n2, 33n10

Thompson, E. P., 23

Thompson, Stith, 205

Thoreau, Henry David, 127

Thorndike, Lynn, 33n10

Tibetan masters, 119

Tingley, Katherine, 185–87, 194n36

Tiryakian, Edward A., 10n4, 16–18, 146
Tituba, 65
Toothaker, Allen, 43
Transcendental meditation, 17, 112
Transcendentalism: and occult-metaphysical tradition, 6; classified, 17; and social reform, 25–26; and Neoplatonism, 122; and Theosophy, 125–26, 127; and Christian Science, 145; and Davis, 152
Truzzi, Marcello, 15
Tully, Raymond, 151
Turner, Nat, 65
2001: A Space Odyssey, 21
Tyler, Alice Felt, 25–26

UFOs: first sighted, 218; investigated by Air Force, 219; organizations' studies of, 219; extraterrestrial hypothesis about, 219–20; difficulties in proving, 220; "contactees" on, 220–21; reports on, change in 1957, 222; extraterrestrial hypothesis in doubt, 223–24; investigated by House Committee on Armed Services, 224–25; investigated by Condon committee, 225; abduction cases, 225–28; and occult, 226–30; questioned by Lawson, 228; failure to gain scientific acceptance of, 225, 229–30; ultraterrestrial theories about, 227–28; belief in, compared with spiritualism, 228, 229. *See also* Flying saucer cults
Univercoelum, 152
Universal Mystic Brotherhood, 118
Upanishads, 163, 174
Utopianism, 24, 25–26

Vajrayana systems, 125
Van Pelt, Gertrude, 187
Vedanta, 17, 21, 112, 143, 163, 164–73 *passim. See also* Vivekananda, Swami
Vedanta Society of Northern California, 163

Vedas, the, 3
Vesey, Denmark, 65, 67
Vivekananda, Swami: in United States, 162–76; William James on, 163; criticizes Theosophy, 163–65; on occult phenomena, 165–73; on hypnosis, 168; treated by magnetic healer, 168–69; on afterlife, 169; on spiritualism, 169–70; and psychical research, 170–71; at Harvard, 172; on reincarnation, 172–73; on Greenacre conference, 173; on Western occultism, 173. *See also* Vedanta
Vogt, Evon Z., 29
Von Mosheim, Johan Lorenz, 123
Von Reichenbach, Karl, 118
Vril, 118

Wardwell, Samuel, 48–49
Webb, James, 15, 24, 26–27
Weber, Eugen, 23
West, D. J., 201–5
Westgate, John, 46–47
White magic, 42, 50, 147, 151. *See also* Magic
White witchcraft, 3, 5, 54. *See also* Witchcraft
Whitman, Walt, 127–28
Wilder, Alexander, 116, 118
Willets, George, 84, 85
Willis, Frederick, 96
Willis, N. P., 91
Wilson, Bryan, 17, 25
Wilson, Sarah, Sr., 51
Wisdom religions, 3
Wisewomoon, Carol, 190
Witchcraft: neopagan, 1, 5; in colonial period, 2, 23, 38–55, 68; at Salem, 3, 38–40; and spiritualism, 4; mentioned, 11, 22, 135, 142
—at Andover: number of persons accused, 40, 50; applicability of community studies to, 40; and witchcraft at Salem, 41; accusations of, 41–54 *passim*; confessions of, 41, 46, 50–52; spectral evidence of, 41, 43, 46, 48, 50, 51; motives for

confession of, 50–52; family and community bonds broken in, 52–53. *See also* Feminist witchcraft; Salem witchcraft trials
Witt, Christopher, 70
Witte, Count S. Y., 131n2
Woodhull, Victoria, 98
World Parliament of Religions, 21, 143, 162
Wright, Henry C., 180

Wright, John Henry, 162
Wuthnow, Robert, 24, 29

Yates, Frances, 15, 58, 71, 121
Yoga groups, 112, 119
Young, Brigham, 152, 158n20
Young, Rev. Thomas W., 157–58n13

Zend-Avesta, the, 125